Silver Burdett Ginn
Mathematics

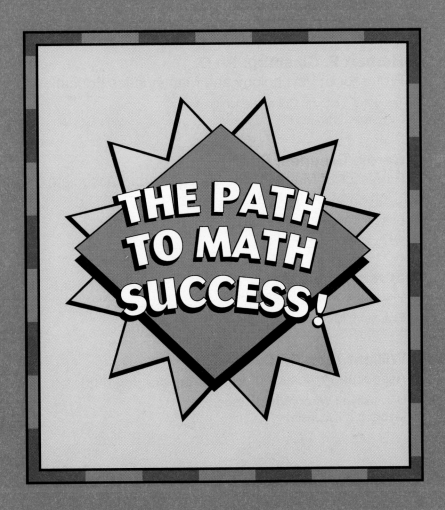

THE PATH TO MATH SUCCESS!

Silver Burdett Ginn
Parsippany, NJ • Needham, MA
Atlanta, GA • Deerfield, IL • Irving, TX • Santa Clara, CA

Program Authors

Francis (Skip) Fennell, Ph.D.
Professor of Education and Chair, Education Department

Western Maryland College
Westminster, Maryland

Joan Ferrini-Mundy, Ph.D.
Professor of Mathematics

University of New Hampshire
Durham, New Hampshire

Herbert P. Ginsburg, Ph.D.
Professor of Psychology and Mathematics Education

Teachers College, Columbia University
New York, New York

Carole Greenes, Ed.D.
Professor of Mathematics Education and Associate Dean,
 School of Education

Boston University
Boston, Massachusetts

Stuart J. Murphy
Visual Learning Specialist

Evanston, Illinois

William Tate, Ph.D.
Associate Professor of Mathematics Education

University of Wisconsin-Madison
Madison, Wisconsin

ISBN 0-382-37002-3

17 18 19 20 BAM 07 06 05 04 03

Senior Author

Mary Cavanagh, M.S.
Principal Investigator, Math,
Science, and Beyond

Solana Beach School District
Solana Beach, California

Grade Level Authors

Mary Behr Altieri, M.S.
Mathematics Teacher
1993 Presidential Awardee

Lakeland Central School District
Shrub Oak, New York

Jennie Bennett, Ed.D.
Instructional Mathematics Supervisor

Houston Independent School District
Houston, Texas

Charles Calhoun, Ph.D.
Associate Professor of Elementary
 Education Mathematics

University of Alabama at Birmingham
Birmingham, Alabama

Lucille Croom, Ph.D.
Professor of Mathematics

Hunter College of the City University
 of New York
New York, New York

Robert A. Laing, Ph.D.
Professor of Mathematics Education

Western Michigan University
Kalamazoo, Michigan

Kay B. Sammons, M.S.
Supervisor of Elementary Mathematics

Howard County Public Schools
Ellicott City, Maryland

Marian Small, Ed.D.
Professor of Mathematics Education

University of New Brunswick
Fredericton, New Brunswick, Canada

Contributing Authors

Stephen Krulik, Ed.D.
Professor of Mathematics Education

Temple University
Philadelphia, Pennsylvania

Donna J. Long
Mathematics/Title 1 Coordinator

Metropolitan School District of
 Wayne Township
Indianapolis, Indiana

Jesse A. Rudnick, Ed.D.
Professor Emeritus of Mathematics
 Education

Temple University
Philadelphia, Pennsylvania

Clementine Sherman
Director, USI Math and Science

Dade County Public Schools
Miami, Florida

Bruce R. Vogeli, Ph.D.
Clifford Brewster Upton Professor of
 Mathematics

Teachers College, Columbia University
New York, New York

Silver Burdett Ginn
299 Jefferson Road, P.O. Box 480
Parsippany, NJ 07054-0480

Contents

Chapter 1

Exploring Numbers and Patterns

Chapter Theme: Counting Carnival

Math Storybook: *Fun at the Fair*

Chapter 2

Understanding Addition

Chapter Theme: Creepy-Crawly Critters

Math Storybook: *The Bug Book*

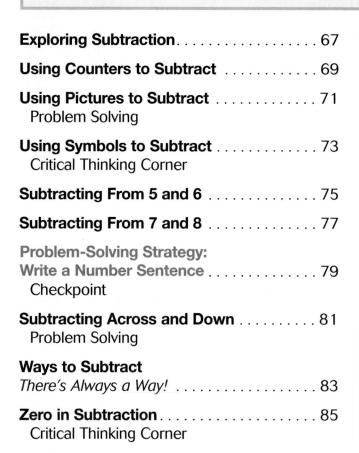

Geometry and Fractions

Chapter Theme: Art Action

Math Storybook: *Stitching Stories*

Chapter 6

Patterns and Numbers to 100

Chapter Theme: Home Zone

Math Storybook: *Too Many Birds!*

Money

Chapter Theme: What a Deal!

Math Storybook: *Silly Sam*

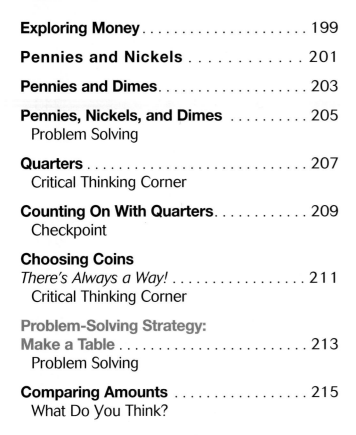

Relating Addition and Subtraction

Chapter Theme: Munch a Bunch

Math Storybook: *Behind the Door*

Chapter 9

Time and Probability

Chapter Theme: All in a Day

Math Storybook: *A Rainy Day*

Hooray for you, Big Bert!

Chapter 11

Addition and Subtraction to 18

Chapter Theme: The Desert

Math Storybook: *Look Who's Here!*

Subtracting tens is like subtracting ones.

Chapter 12

Exploring Two-Digit Addition and Subtraction

Chapter Theme: In My Pocket

Math Storybook: *Po Lan's Pocket*

Fun at the Fair

written *by* Shereen Gertel Rutman

illustrated by Patrick Girouard

This Math Storybook

belongs to

_____

A

The Gladstone Geese are at the fair.
How many geese are there?
Count the geese.
Count each one.

13

The geese see horses at the fair.
How many horses are there?
Count the horses.
Count each one.

4 TICKETS

The geese see fish at the fair.
How many fish are there?
Count the fish.
Count each one.

Count the things you see at the fair.
Groups of 1 to 12 will be there.

G

A Note to the Family

Here are some learning ideas you can share with your child.

Enjoy *Fun at the Fair* Together

- Read each page with your child. Then count some of the items on the page together.

- Help your child find all the groups on the last page of the story. Some possible groups in the picture are 1 ticket booth, 2 drinks with straws, 3 flowers, 4 carousel horses, 5 candy apples, 6 silly hats, 7 geese, 8 tickets for rides, 9 balloons, 10 blue balls, 11 bees, and 12 ice-cream cones.

At-Home Activity

- Use mealtime or cleanup time at home as a fun way to practice counting. Have your child help set the table. As she or he places each napkin down, count out loud. Encourage your child to count, too. Repeat this activity with the cutlery, glasses, and plates.

- Pick an item in the house that needs to be put away. For example, ask your child to put away 6 blocks. Then ask your child to put away 4 books. Repeat this activity, changing the number each time. You can take turns asking each other to clean up a certain number of objects. The room will be clean in a short time, and your child will have a great time playing the game!

Read More About It!

To read more about counting, look for these books in your local library.
- *Have You Seen My Duckling?* by Nancy Tafuri (Greenwillow, 1985)
- *One, Two, Three, Count With Me* by Catherine and Laurence Anholt (Viking, 1993)
- *Ten Black Dots* by Donald Crews (Greenwillow, 1986)

Visit Our Web Site!

www.sbgmath.com

Name_____

Use . Then draw.

I. Draw a group with the **same** number.

2. Draw a group with **more**.

3. Draw a group with **fewer**.

Home Connection Show your child a group of household objects. Ask him or her to show you either the same number, more, or fewer objects.

one   **1**

Look at each group.
Draw a group to show 1 fewer.
Draw a group to show 1 more.

1.

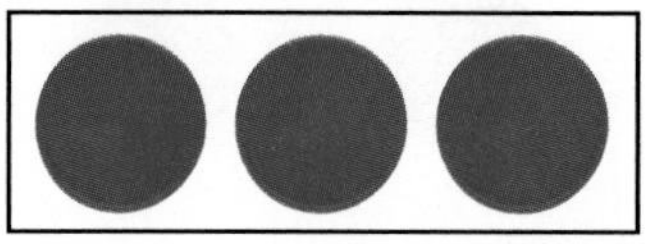

1 fewer	1 more

2.

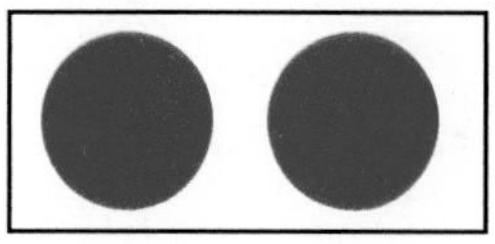

1 fewer	1 more

3.

1 fewer	1 more

Make
Your
Own

2   two

1 one

2 two

3 three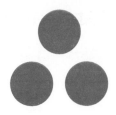

4 four

5 five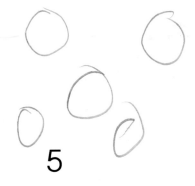

Use  to show each number.

Draw to show how many.

1.

3

2.

5

3.

1

4.

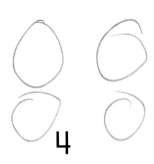

4

5.

2

6.

3

Home Connection Children need many opportunities to show numbers. Ask your child to say a number and hold up that many fingers.

Circle the groups that show each number.

1.

3
three

2.

1
one

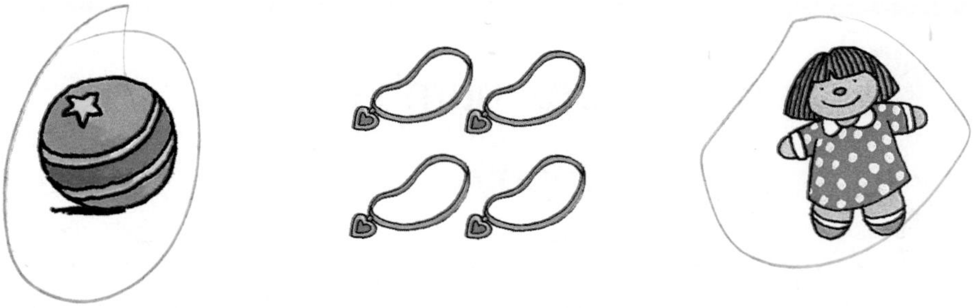

3.

4
four

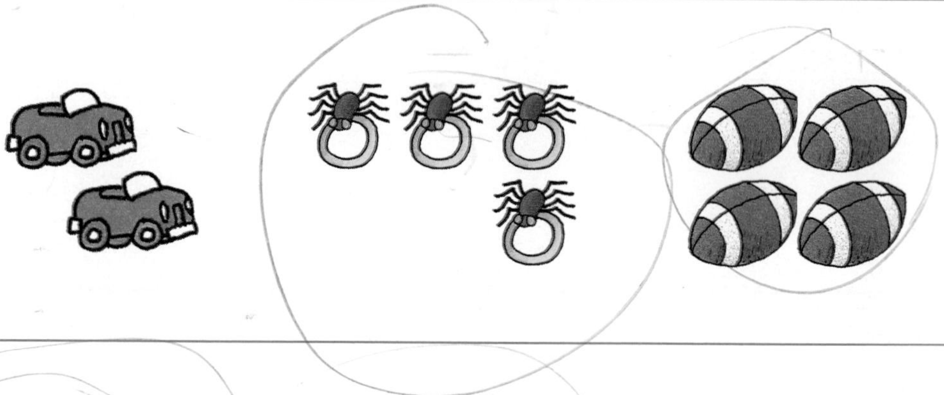

4.

2
two

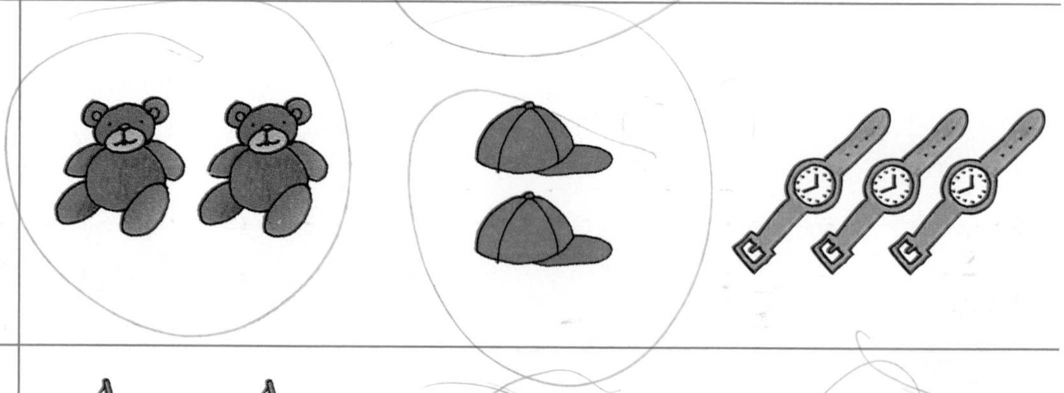

5.

5
five

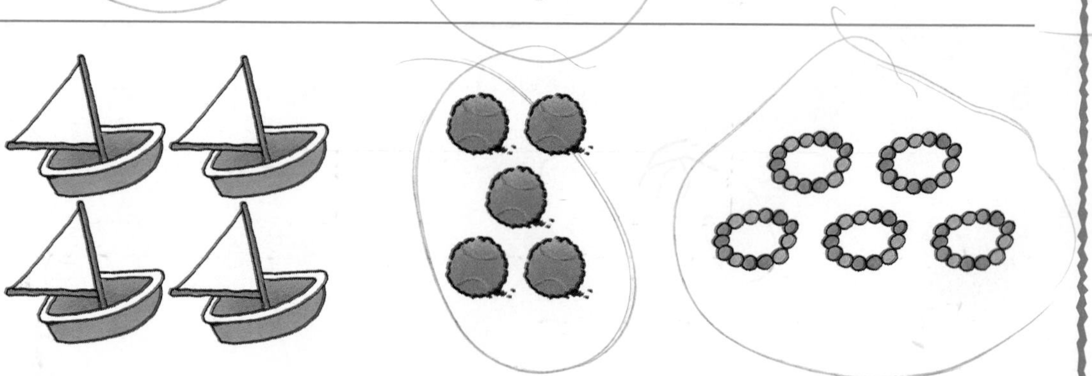

Count.
Write the numbers.

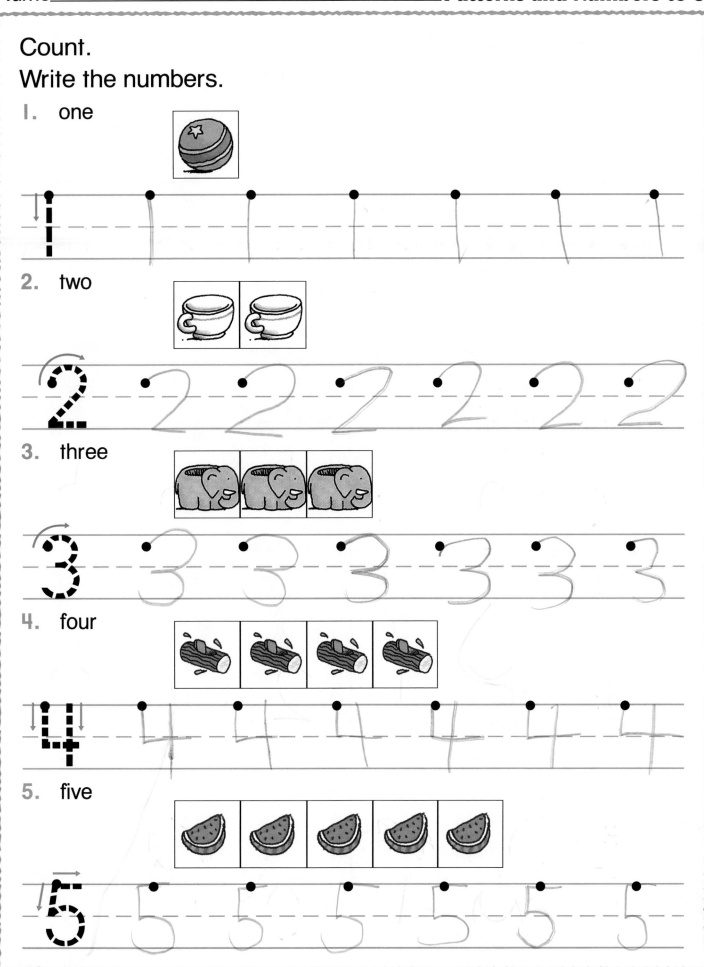

1. one

2. two

3. three

4. four

5. five

Count. Write how many.

Look for a pattern.

1.

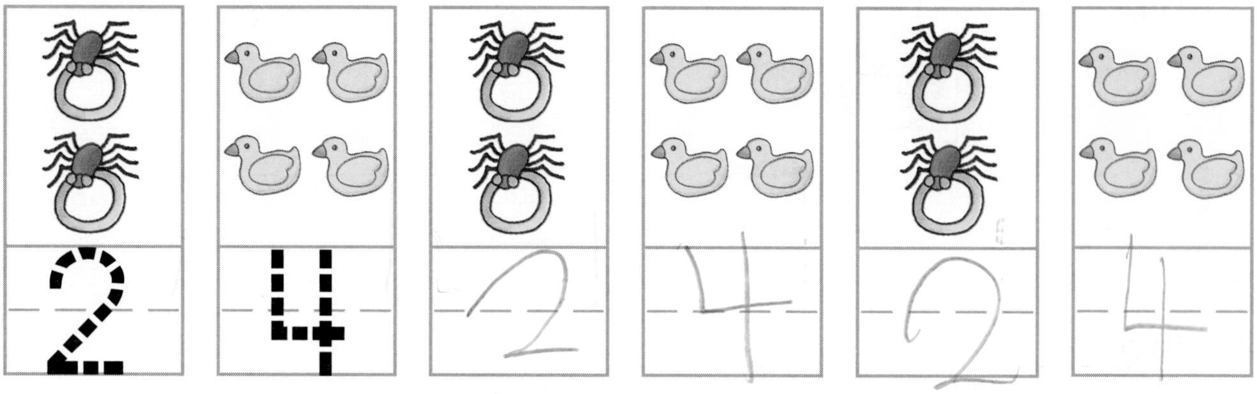

| 2 | 4 | 2 | 4 | 2 | 4 |

2.

| 3 | 5 | 3 | 5 | 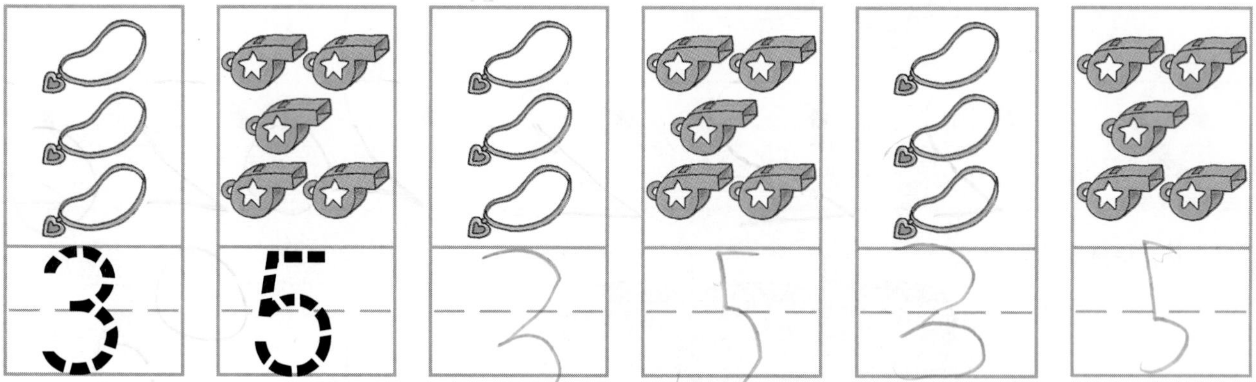 3 | 5 |

3.

|  1 | 2 | 1 | 2 | 1 | 2 |

4.

| 1 | 0 | 1 | 0 | 1 | 0 |

Make Your Own

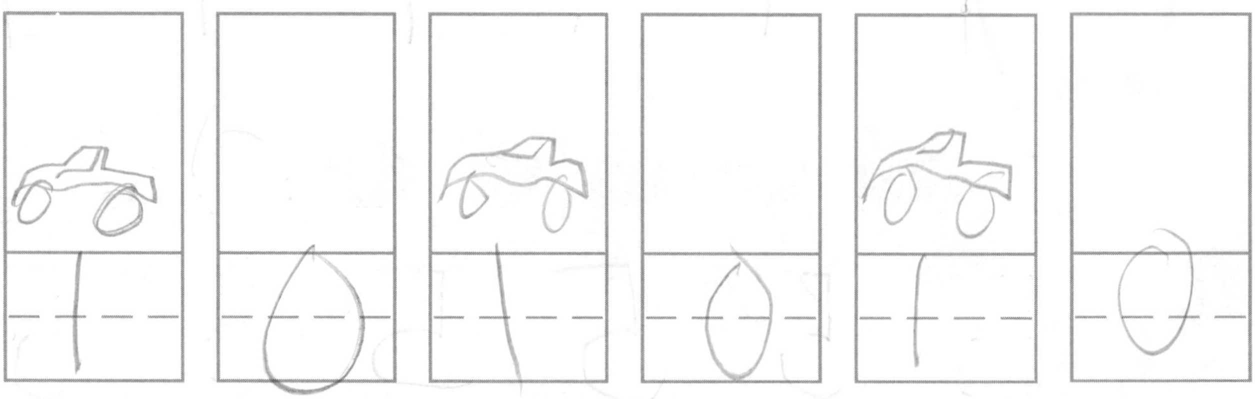

6   six

There are zero children.

1. Write the number.

zero

2. Write how many children.

Home Connection Have your child show you which teacups show zero children. Then have your child think of items of which there are zero in your home: for example, live elephants.

Write how many.

1.

4

2.

3.

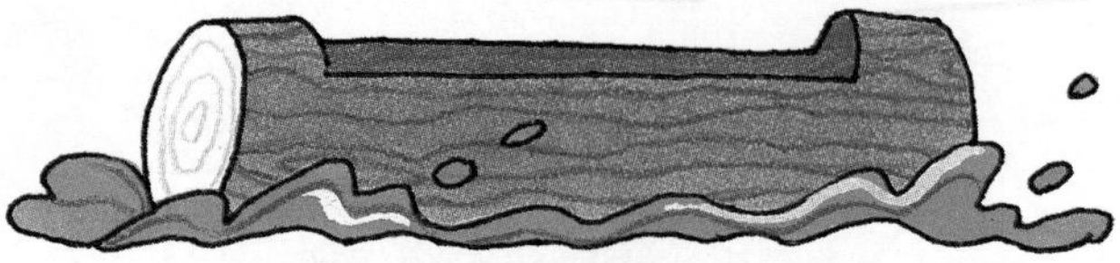

4.

5.

Name_____

Graphs can let you see how many.

Rides

	1	2	3	4	5

Use the picture to make a graph.
Color the balloons to show how many.

Word Bank

graph

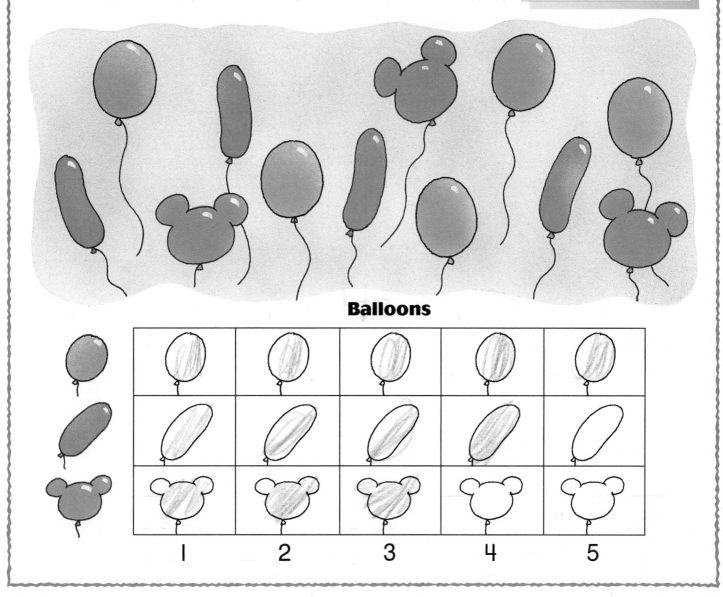

Balloons

	1	2	3	4	5

Home Connection Pictographs can help children count objects. Pick some simple objects in your house and help your child make a pictograph to show how many.

nine **9**

1. Use the picture to make a graph.
Color to show how many of each.

Prizes

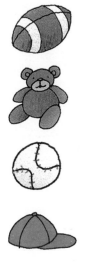

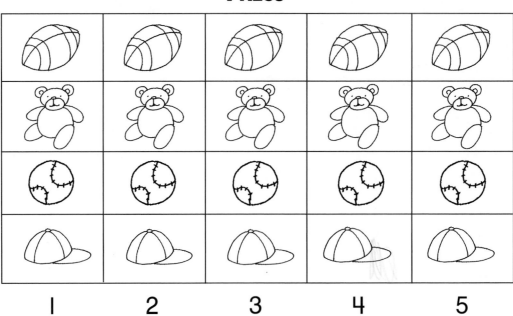

| | 1 | 2 | 3 | 4 | 5 |

2. How many of each are there?

 _____   _____   _____

Name_____ **Ways to Show Numbers**

Show each number with .
Draw a picture. Write the number.

1.

2.

3.

 Home Connection Encourage your child to talk about the different ways to show numbers. Have your child show numbers 1 to 12 in different ways.

nineteen **19**

Draw and write.

	Word	Picture	Number
1.	ten	○ ○ ○ ○ ○ ○ ○ ○ ○ ○	10
2.	four		
3.	six		
4.	eleven		
5.			

Make Your Own

20 twenty

5

7 is greater than 5.
5 is less than 7.

7

Word Bank

greater
less

Write how many.
Circle the greater number.

1.

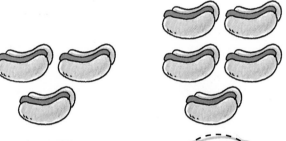

  3   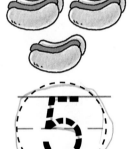 (5)

2.

12   8

3.

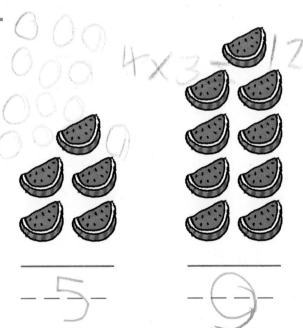

5   9

4.

4   8

Write each number.
Circle the number that is less.

1.

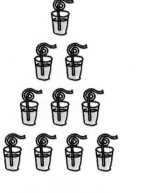 

10 7

2.

 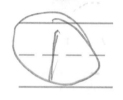 

1 4

3.

3 4

4.

5 2

What Do You Think?

8 is greater than 5. What is another number that is greater than 5?

Journal Idea

2 comes before 3.
3 comes after 2.
3 comes between 2 and 4.

Word Bank

before
after
between

Write each missing number.

	Before	After	Between
1.	**2** , 3	5, 6	6, 7 , 8
2.	7 , 8	11, 12	0, 1 , 2
3.	0 , 1	9, 10	10, 11 ,12
4.	5 , 6	4, 5	5, 6 ,7

Home Connection Play a guessing game with your child. For example, "I am thinking of the number that comes before 6. What number is this?"

twenty-three   **23**

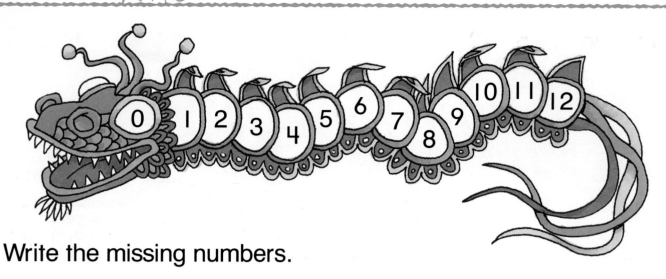

Write the missing numbers.

1.

1, **2** , 3, 4 , 5, 6 , 7, 8

2.

6 , 7, 8 , 9, 10 , 11 , 12

3.

4, 5 , 6, 7 , 8, 9 , 10, 11

4.

0, 1 , 2 , 3 , 4, 5 , 6,

5.

3 , 4, 5 , 6, 7 , 8 , 9

Name_____

What comes next?
Color to show the pattern.

Word Bank

pattern

1.

2.

3.

4.

5.

 Home Connection Ask your child to tell you about each pattern. Then have your child make a pattern with household objects such as forks and spoons.

Draw and color to show a pattern.

1. 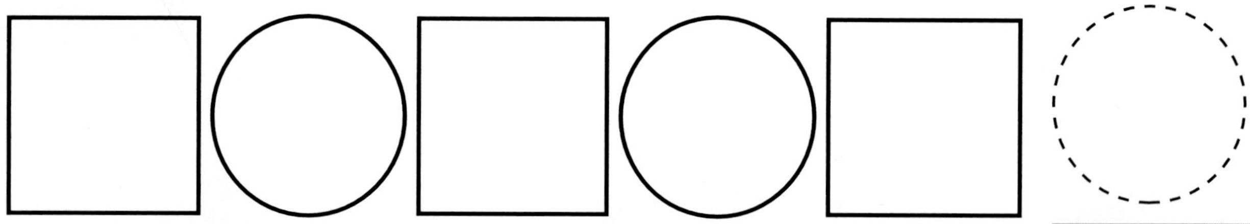 ☐ ◯ ☐ ◯ ☐ ◯

2. 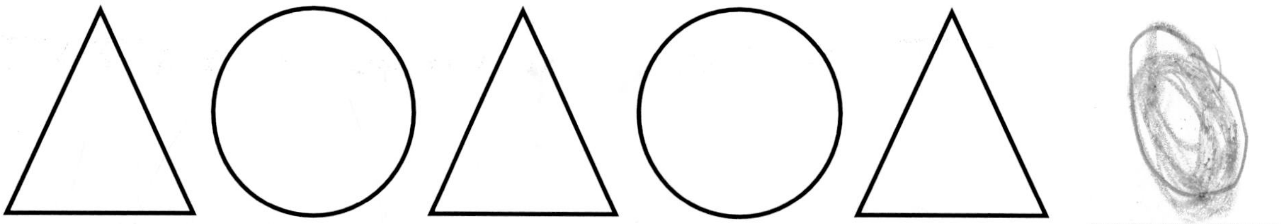 △ ◯ △ ◯ △

3. 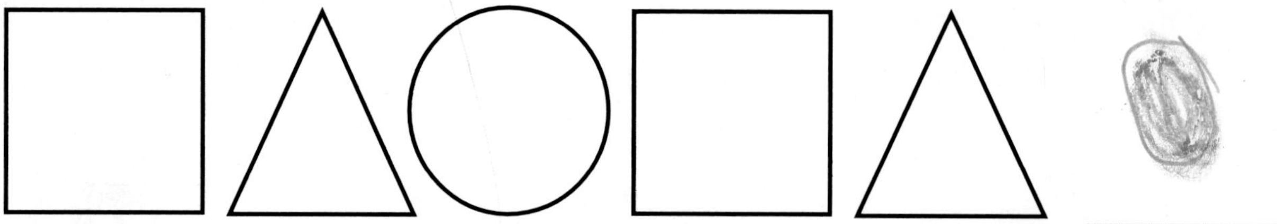 ☐ △ ◯ ☐ △

4.  ◯ ◯ △ ◯ ◯

5. 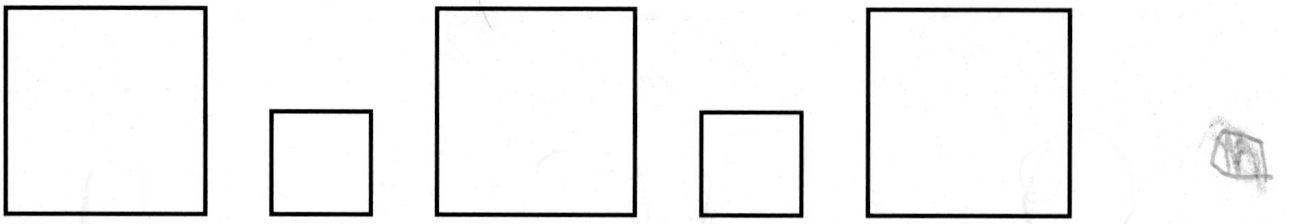 ☐ ▫ ☐ ▫ ☐

6. Draw and color to make a pattern.

Make Your Own

first   second   third   fourth   fifth   sixth   seventh   eighth   ninth   tenth

Circle the correct place.

1.

second

(third)

fourth

2.

third

fourth

(fifth)

3.

(first)

fifth

seventh

4.

(ninth)

seventh

sixth

5.

tenth

first

(fourth)

6.

(eighth)

sixth

fourth

7.

(sixth)

ninth

third

8.

second

tenth

(seventh)

9.

eighth

third

(second)

Home Connection Discuss with your child the order in which the steps of a task are done. For example, when putting on socks and shoes, "First, I put on my socks. Second, I put on my shoes. Third, I tie my laces."

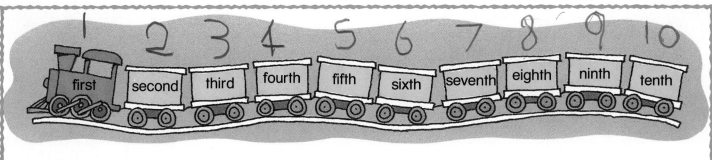

1 2 3 4 5 6 7 8 9 10

first second third fourth fifth sixth seventh eighth ninth tenth

Color.

1. third [blue]

seventh [green]

2. fifth [orange]

tenth [red]

3. sixth [yellow]

eighth [green]

Problem Solving

4. Bob says he is first in line.
Tina says she is first in line.
Who is right?

bath

Bob   Jane   Brian   Carlos   Tina

Favorite Prizes

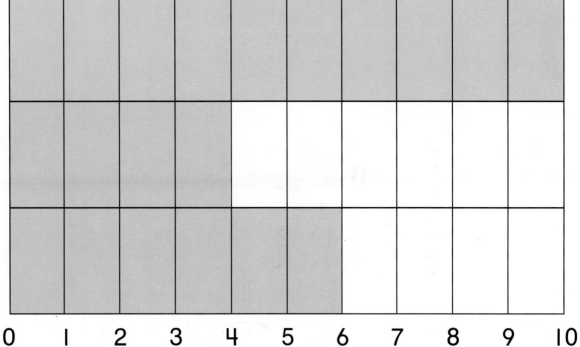

0 1 2 3 4 5 6 7 8 9 10

Use the graph.

1. Write how many.

 10   _4_   _6_

2. Circle the favorite.

  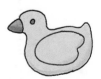

3. Circle the least favorite.

Home Connection Talk to your child about the graph. Discuss how he or she knew how many of each there were. Ask other questions about the graph.

twenty-nine **29**

Silly Hats

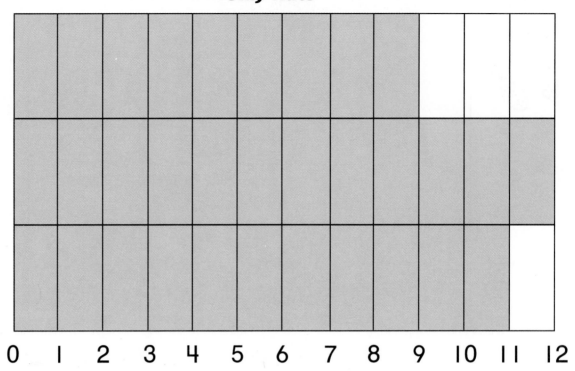

0 1 2 3 4 5 6 7 8 9 10 11 12

Use the graph.

1. Write how many.

 9    12    11

2. Circle the hat that has 1 more than 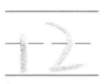.

3. Circle the hat that has 2 fewer than 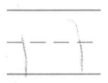.

30   thirty

1. Write the missing numbers.

1, 2 , 3, 4 , 5, 6 , 7, 8

2. Write each number. Circle the greater number.

3   ⑤

3. Color to show the pattern.

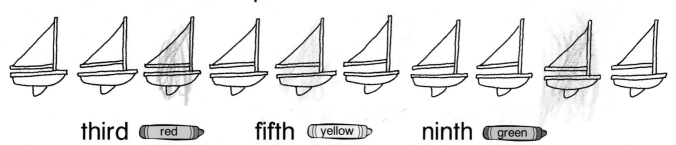

4. Color to show each place.

third (red)   fifth (yellow)   ninth (green)

5. Use the graph. Write how many.

Favorite Food

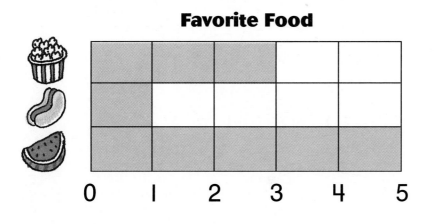

| | 0 | 1 | 2 | 3 | 4 | 5 |

6

1

5

I. Color each group.

3  red

6 blue

2 green

---

2. Start at 0.
    Connect the dots in order.

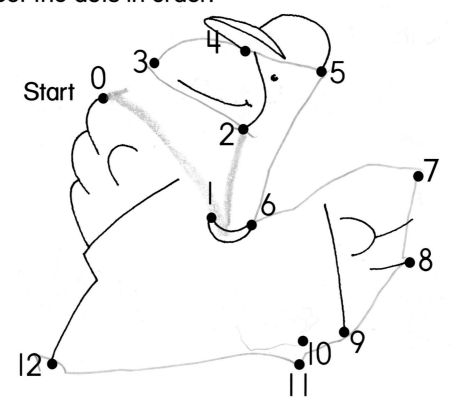

1. Draw a group to show 1 fewer.
   Draw a group to show 1 more.

1 fewer	1 more

2. Circle the groups that show 9.

  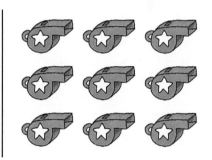

3. Color the third 🖍 yellow and the eighth 🖍 orange .

4. Color to show the pattern.

What You Need

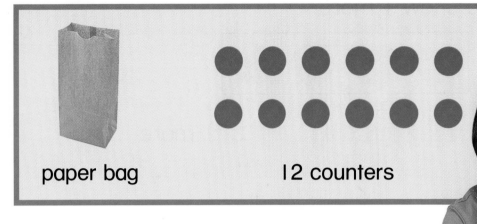

paper bag   12 counters

① Put all the ⬤ in the 🛍 .

② Take some out.
Draw and write how many.

③ Draw and write to show 1 more.

How many	1 more
1.	
2.	
3.	

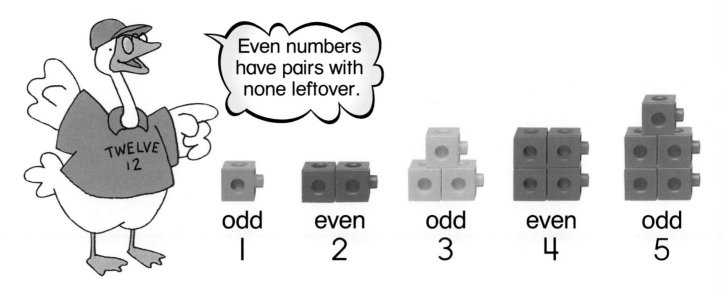

Even numbers have pairs with none leftover.

odd 1   even 2   odd 3   even 4   odd 5

Use 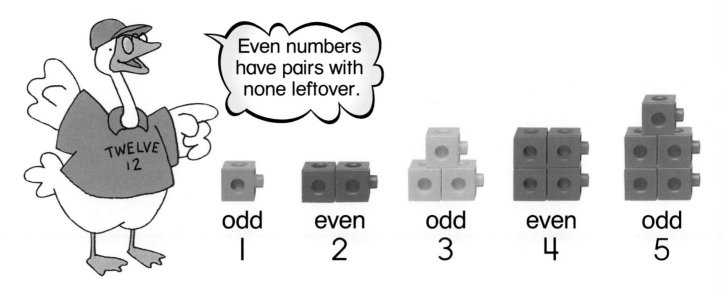 to build each number.

Circle **even** or **odd**.

1. **3** even (odd)	2. **5** even odd
3. **6** even odd	4. **1** even odd
5. **2** even odd	6. **10** even odd
7. **9** even odd	8. **11** even odd

Name_____

Look at a .

Write the missing numbers.

The Bug Book

written by Leslie Barna

illustrated by Liisa Guida

This Math Storybook

belongs to

_____

One big ladybug
sits in a tree.

Two more join her.
Now there are three.

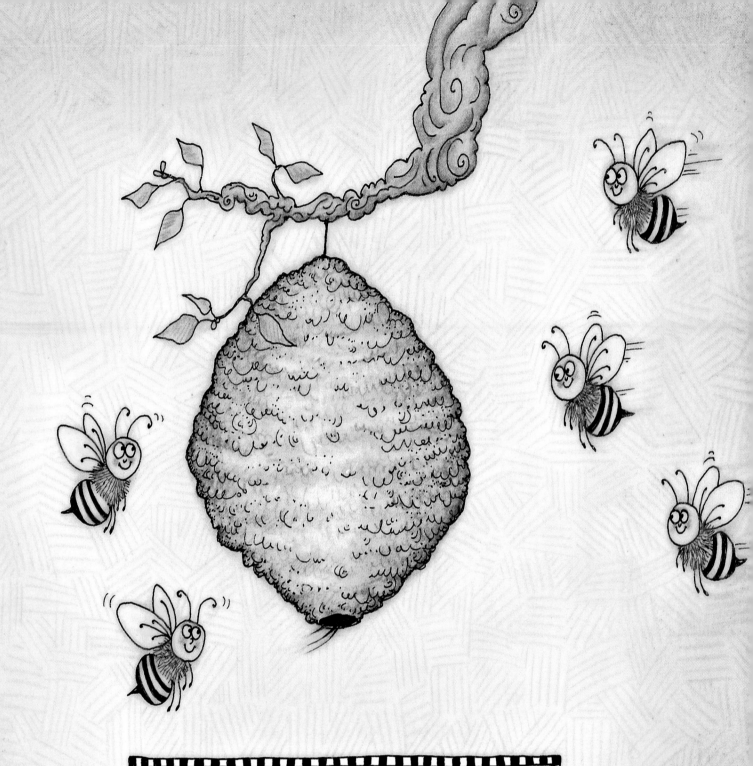

Two little bumblebees
fly near a hive.

Three more join them.
Now there are five.

One bug is all alone.
What will she do?

One more joins her.
Now there are two.

D

Three happy butterflies
smile as they wait.

Five more join them.
Now there are eight.

Three spiders spin
and get in a fix.

Three more join them.
Now there are six.

F

www.sbgmath.com

Draw some bugs
for all to see.

If two more join them,
how many will there be?

G

A Note to the Family

Here are some learning ideas you can share with your child.

 Enjoy The Bug Book Together

- Read each page with your child. Ask your child to count the number of bugs in each group on the page. Then talk about how to find how many there are in all. Show your child how to write an addition sentence.

  For example: 1 big ladybug and 2 little ladybugs are 3 in all
  $$1 + 2 = 3$$

- Encourage your child to show you what she or he drew on the last page of *The Bug Book*. Ask your child how many bugs there would be if three more flew into the picture.

 At-Home Activity

- Make "Edible Ants on a Log" to help your child practice addition. You will need pieces of celery filled with peanut butter for the logs and raisins for the ants. Say a number between 0 and 6 and tell your child to place that many "ants" on the log. Then name a second number of ants to put on the log. Ask "How many ants are there in all?" Make several logs so that the activity can be repeated. The logs make good treats for the entire family!

 Read More About It!

To read more stories about addition with your child, look for the following books in your local library.

- *Anno's Counting House* by Mitsumasa Anno (Putnam, 1982)
- *One Gorilla* by Atsuko Morozumi (Farrar, Straus & Giroux, 1990)
- *So Many Cats!* by Beatrice Schenk de Regniers (Clarion Books, 1985)

Visit Our Web Site!

www.sbgmath.com

Use counters to tell addition stories.
Then draw or write one story.

Home Connection Using counters to show number stories gives children a chance to show what they know about adding. Help your child make up addition stories and solve them together.

Solve.
Use counters if you like.

1. 3 🐝 are on the 🌸 .
   What if 2 more 🐝 come?
   How many 🐝 will there be?

   _____

2. 4 🦋 are on the 🌸 .
   What if 1 more 🦋 comes?
   How many 🦋 will there be?

   _____

3 and **2** _5_ in all

Word Bank

in all
altogether

Use counters.
Write how many.

1. I and 3 _____ in all

2. 4 and I _____ in all

3. 2 and 2 _____ altogether

4. 4 and 2 _____ altogether

Write how many.

		●	●	
1. 	●●● ●●	3	2	5 altogether
2. 	●● ●●	___	___	___ in all
3. 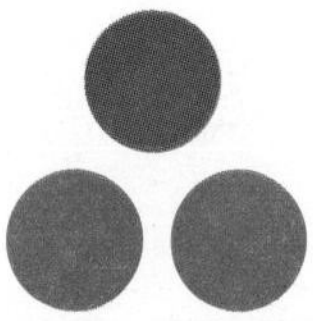	● ●●	___	___	___ in all
4. 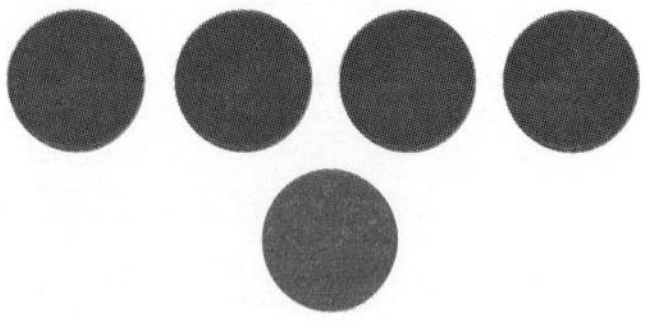	●●●● ●	___	___	___ altogether
5. 	●● ●●●	___	___	___ in all
6. 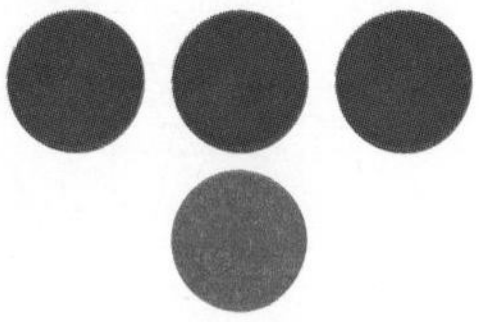	●●● ●	___	___	___ altogether
7.	●●●	___	___	___ in all

40   forty

Write the numbers.

1.

   2 and **2** are **4** in all

2.

   _____ and _____ are _____ in all

3.

   _____ and _____ are _____ in all

4.

   _____ and _____ are _____ in all

5.

   _____ and _____ are _____ in all

6.

   _____ and _____ are _____ in all

7.

   _____ and _____ are _____ in all

Home Connection Pictures can help children add. Ask your child to draw simple pictures to make up addition stories.

forty-one **41**

Draw to show each number.
Write how many.

1.

2 and 3 are _____ in all

_____

2.

4 and 1 are _____ altogether

_____

3. Draw 2 groups. Write how many.

_____ and _____ are _____ in all

Make Your Own

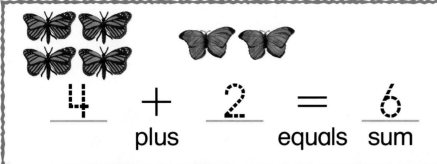

4 + 2 = 6
plus   equals sum

Write the numbers. Add.

1.

_____ + _____ = _____

2.

_____ + _____ = _____

3.

_____ + _____ = _____

4.

_____ + _____ = _____

5.

_____ + _____ = _____

6.

_____ + _____ = _____

7.

_____ + _____ = _____

8.

_____ + _____ = _____

Home Connection Give your child some pennies to add. Ask your child to write the problems using the symbols + and =.

forty-three **43**

Find each sum.
Use counters if you like.

1. $3 + 1 =$ _4_ $4 + 2 =$ _6_ $3 + 3 =$ _6_

2. $2 + 3 =$ _5_ $1 + 1 =$ _5_ $4 + 1 =$ _5_

3. $2 + 2 =$ _4_ $5 + 1 =$ _6_ $1 + 3 =$ _4_

4. $2 + 4 =$ _6_ $3 + 2 =$ _5_ $1 + 4 =$ _5_

5. $1 + 2 =$ _3_ $1 + 5 =$ _6_ $2 + 3 =$ _5_

Problem Solving

Solve.

6. Takara has 4 butterflies.
   Circle the groups that could be hers.

I can make sums for 3 in many ways.

0 + 3 = 3

1 + 2 = 3

2 + 1 = 3

3 + 0 = 3

How many ways can you make 5?
Use counters. Color.
Write each addition sentence.
Look for a pattern.

Word Bank

addition sentence

1. ○○○○○ 0 + 5 = 5

2. ○○○○○ 1 + 4 = 5

3. ○○○○○ 2 + 3 = 5

4. ○○○○○ 3 + 2 = 5

5. ○○○○○ 4 + 1 = 5

6. ○○○○○ 5 + 0 = 5

Home Connection Review the different ways to show sums for 5 and 6. Encourage your child to write sums for other numbers.

forty-five **45**

How many ways can you make 6?
Use counters. Color.
Write each addition sentence.

1. ◯ ◯ ◯ ◯ ◯ ◯   ____ + ____ = ____

2. ◯ ◯ ◯ ◯ ◯ ◯   ____ + ____ = ____

3. ◯ ◯ ◯ ◯ ◯ ◯   ____ + ____ = ____

4. ◯ ◯ ◯ ◯ ◯ ◯   ____ + ____ = ____

5. ◯ ◯ ◯ ◯ ◯ ◯   ____ + ____ = ____

6. ◯ ◯ ◯ ◯ ◯ ◯   ____ + ____ = ____

7. ◯ ◯ ◯ ◯ ◯ ◯   ____ + ____ = ____

Critical Thinking Corner

Number Sense

8. Are there more ways to make 4 or to make 6? Tell why. Then try it.

Name_____

Solve.

Draw a picture or write a number sentence.

1. 2  crawl.

    3 more come.

    How many are there in all? _____

2. 3 fly.

    4 more join them.

    How many are there altogether? _____

3. 2 buzz.

    2 more join them.

    How many are there in all? _____

Home Connection Encourage your child to talk about the different ways to solve addition problems. Make up some problems for your child to solve.

fifty-one **51**

1. Ask 5 friends how they like to add.
   Color a box to show each friend's way.

How We Like to Add

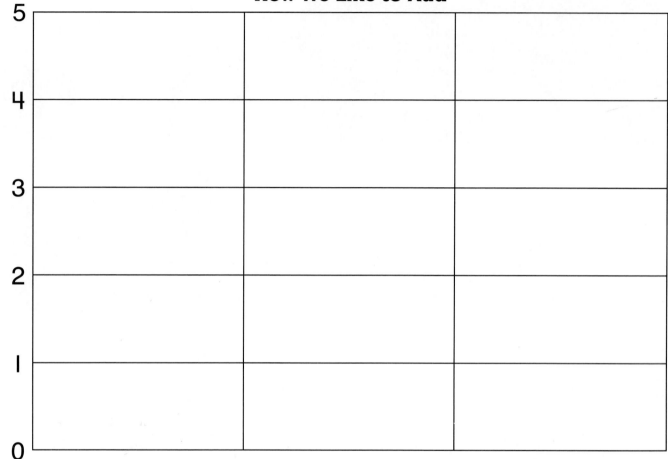

5		
4		
3		
2		
1		
0		

Use counters	**Use pictures**	**Use numbers**
		$2 + 5 = 7$

 Critical Thinking Corner

Number Sense

2. Share your graph with a friend.
   Tell how your graphs are the same.
   Tell how they are different.

Use counters to solve.

1. 3 🐸 are in the pond.
   In hop 3 more.
   How many are there
   in all? 6

2. 1 🦆 flies.
   2 🦆 swim.
   How many are there
   in all? _____

3. On a rock are 2 🦋 .
   2 more join them.
   How many are there
   in all? _____

4. 1 🐢 is on a log.
   3 more join it.
   How many are there
   now? _____

5. There are 2 🪰 .
   On a log are 3 🪰 .
   How many are there
   now? _____

6. 4 🐸 swim.
   2 🐸 hop in.
   How many are there
   in all? _____

Home Connection Children can use counters or common household objects to act out a problem. Make up some problems for your child to act out.

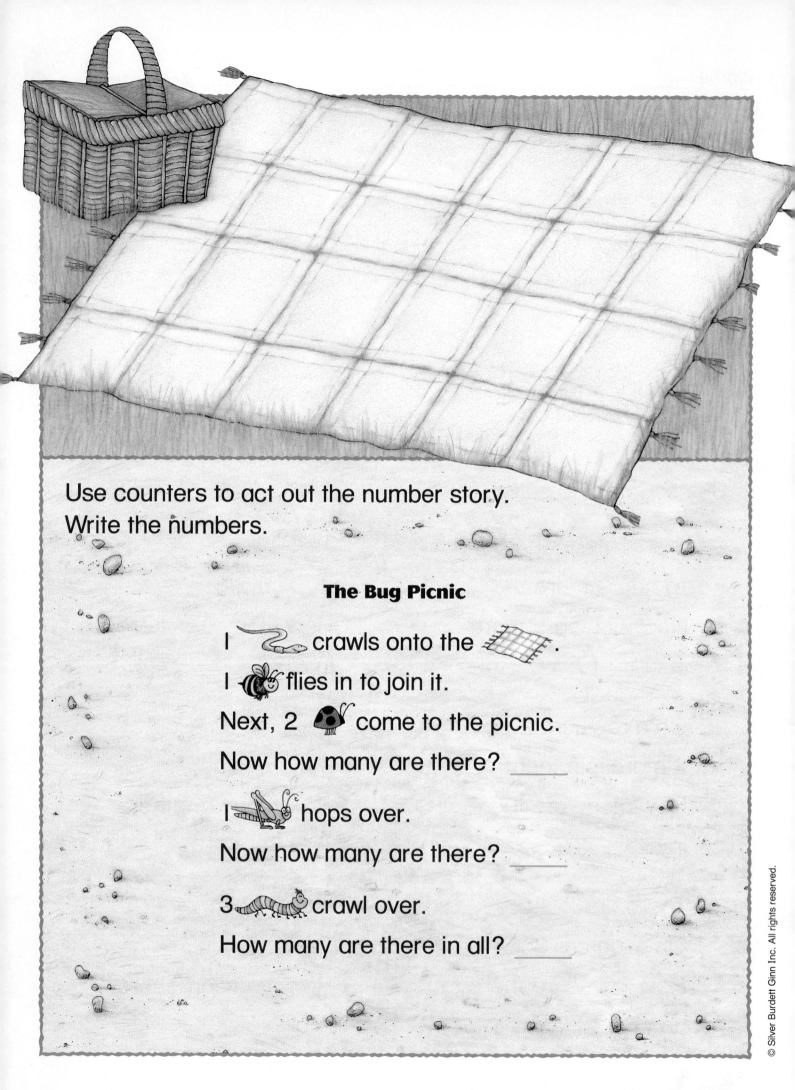

Use counters to act out the number story.
Write the numbers.

The Bug Picnic

1 🐛 crawls onto the ▦ .

1 🐝 flies in to join it.

Next, 2 🐞 come to the picnic.

Now how many are there? _____

1 🦗 hops over.

Now how many are there? _____

3 🐛 crawl over.

How many are there in all? _____

54 fifty-four

Name_____

What happens when you add zero?

Use counters and the [   ].
Solve.

1. Put in 2 ●.
   Put in 0.
   How many are there altogether? _2_

2. Put in 8 ●.
   Put in 0.
   How many are there altogether? _____

3. Put in 7 ●.
   Put in 0.
   How many are there in all? _____

4. Put in 5 ●.
   Put in 0.
   How many are there now? _____

5. Put in 1 ●.
   Put in 0.
   How many are there now? _____

6. Put in 6 ●.
   Put in 0.
   How many are there in all? _____

Home Connection When 0 is added to any number, the sum is the same as that number. Ask your child, "How much is one million and one plus zero?" and similar questions with very large numbers.

Add. Use counters if you like.
Look for facts with zero.

1.
$$\begin{array}{r} 0 \\ + 2 \\ \hline 2 \end{array}$$
$$\begin{array}{r} 1 \\ + 3 \\ \hline \end{array}$$
$$\begin{array}{r} 5 \\ + 2 \\ \hline \end{array}$$
$$\begin{array}{r} 3 \\ + 0 \\ \hline \end{array}$$
$$\begin{array}{r} 0 \\ + 4 \\ \hline \end{array}$$
$$\begin{array}{r} 3 \\ + 3 \\ \hline \end{array}$$

2.
$$\begin{array}{r} 2 \\ + 2 \\ \hline \end{array}$$
$$\begin{array}{r} 0 \\ + 0 \\ \hline \end{array}$$
$$\begin{array}{r} 1 \\ + 4 \\ \hline \end{array}$$
$$\begin{array}{r} 4 \\ + 0 \\ \hline \end{array}$$
$$\begin{array}{r} 0 \\ + 1 \\ \hline \end{array}$$
$$\begin{array}{r} 0 \\ + 7 \\ \hline \end{array}$$

3.
$$\begin{array}{r} 0 \\ + 4 \\ \hline \end{array}$$
$$\begin{array}{r} 4 \\ + 2 \\ \hline \end{array}$$
$$\begin{array}{r} 7 \\ + 0 \\ \hline \end{array}$$
$$\begin{array}{r} 3 \\ + 2 \\ \hline \end{array}$$
$$\begin{array}{r} 6 \\ + 0 \\ \hline \end{array}$$
$$\begin{array}{r} 0 \\ + 3 \\ \hline \end{array}$$

4. $0 + 6 = \underline{}$ $7 + 1 = \underline{}$ $0 + 7 = \underline{}$

5. $4 + 3 = \underline{}$ $0 + 5 = \underline{}$ $8 + 0 = \underline{}$

What Do You Think?

I think that 0 is the easiest number in the world to add. Do you? Why or why not?

$4 + 1 = \underline{5}$

I can add in any order.

$1 + 4 = \underline{5}$

Use counters.
Write each sum.

1. $4 + 3 = \underline{}$

   $3 + 4 = \underline{}$

2. $5 + 1 = \underline{}$

   $1 + 5 = \underline{}$

3. $1 + 3 = \underline{}$

   $3 + 1 = \underline{}$

4. $6 + 1 = \underline{}$

   $1 + 6 = \underline{}$

5. $5 + 2 = \underline{}$

   $2 + 5 = \underline{}$

6. $3 + 2 = \underline{}$

   $2 + 3 = \underline{}$

7. $5 + 3 = \underline{}$

   $3 + 5 = \underline{}$

8. $7 + 1 = \underline{}$

   $1 + 7 = \underline{}$

Home Connection The order in which two numbers are added does not change the sum. Give your child some addition examples. Have him or her change the order of the numbers and find each answer.

fifty-seven **57**

Add. Then change the order.
Use counters if you like.

1. 1
   + 2
   —
    3

    2
   + 1
   —
    3

2. 3
   + 2
   —

   [ ]
  +[ ]
   —

3. 0
   + 4
   —

   [ ]
  +[ ]
   —

4. 6
   + 2
   —

   [ ]
  +[ ]
   —

5. 2
   + 4
   —

   [ ]
  +[ ]
   —

6. 1
   + 6
   —

   [ ]
  +[ ]
   —

Problem Solving

7. Look at the picture.
   How many are there in all?
   Write two addition sentences.

_____ + _____ = _____

_____ + _____ = _____

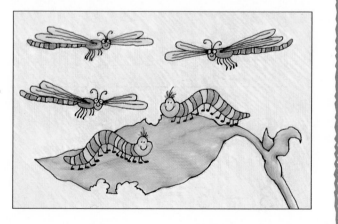

Name_____

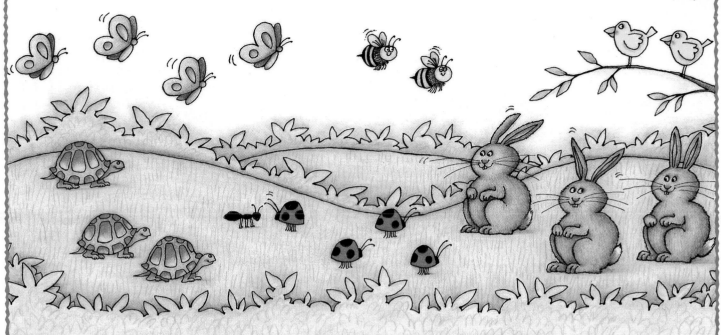

Use the picture to solve each problem.

1. There are __2__ 🐝 .

   There are __4__ 🦋 .

   How many are there
   in all? __6__

2. There are ____ 🐞 .

   There is ____ 🐜 .

   How many are there
   altogether? ____

3. There are ____ 🐢 .

   There are ____ 🐰 .

   How many are there
   in all? ____

4. There are ____ 🐦 .

   There are ____ 🐢 .

   How many are there
   in all? ____

5. There are ____ 🦋 .

   There are ____ 🐞 .

   How many are there
   in all? ____

6. There is ____ 🐜 .

   There are ____ 🐝 .

   How many are there
   altogether? ____

Home Connection Children can get information from a picture
and use it to solve addition problems. Show your child a magazine
picture. Help her or him make up and solve addition problems.

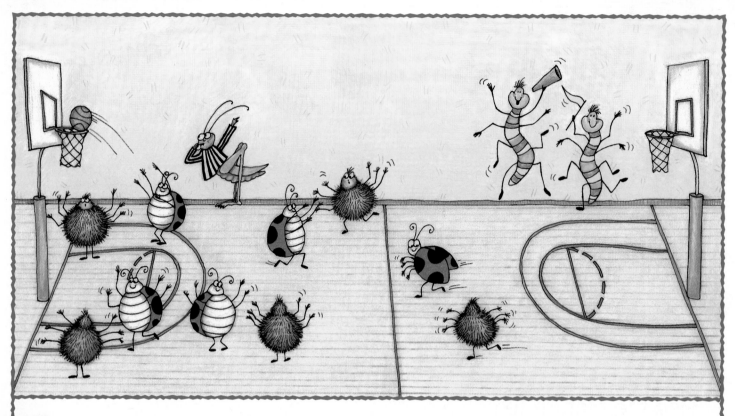

 Look at the picture.
What number stories can you tell?
Draw or write two stories below.

1.

_____

2.

1. Write the numbers. Add.

$4 + 1 = 5$

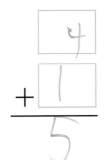

$\begin{array}{r} 4 \\ +\ 1 \\ \hline 5 \end{array}$

Add. Use counters if you like.

2.
$\begin{array}{r} 1 \\ +\ 5 \\ \hline 6 \end{array}$
$\begin{array}{r} 5 \\ +\ 1 \\ \hline 6 \end{array}$
$\begin{array}{r} 4 \\ +\ 3 \\ \hline 7 \end{array}$
$\begin{array}{r} 3 \\ +\ 4 \\ \hline 7 \end{array}$
$\begin{array}{r} 2 \\ +\ 6 \\ \hline 8 \end{array}$
$\begin{array}{r} 6 \\ +\ 2 \\ \hline 8 \end{array}$

3. $6 + 0 = 6$ $\qquad$ $7 + 1 = 8$ $\qquad$ $0 + 7 = 7$

Use the picture to solve.

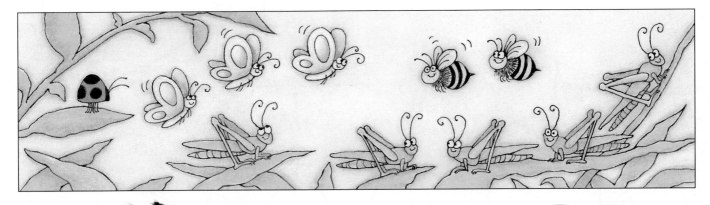

4. There is ___ 🐞.
   There are _5_ 🦗.
   How many are there
   in all? _6_

5. There are _2_ 🐝.
   There are _3_ 🦋.
   How many are there
   in all? _5_

Find each sum. Color.

4 red   5 (yellow)   6 (green)   7 (orange)   8 (blue)

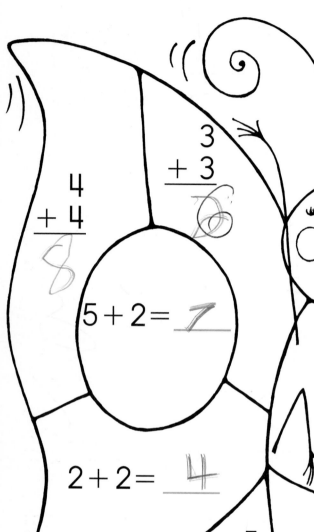

$$\begin{array}{r} 4 \\ + 4 \\ \hline 8 \end{array}$$

$$\begin{array}{r} 3 \\ + 3 \\ \hline 6 \end{array}$$

$$5 + 2 = 7$$

$$2 + 2 = 4$$

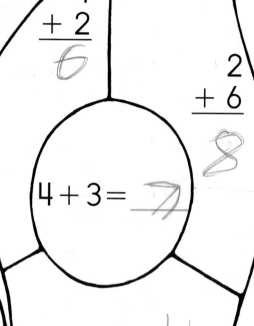

$$\begin{array}{r} 4 \\ + 2 \\ \hline 6 \end{array}$$

$$\begin{array}{r} 2 \\ + 6 \\ \hline 8 \end{array}$$

$$4 + 3 = 7$$

$$3 + 1 = 4$$

$$\begin{array}{r} 1 \\ + 4 \\ \hline 5 \end{array}$$

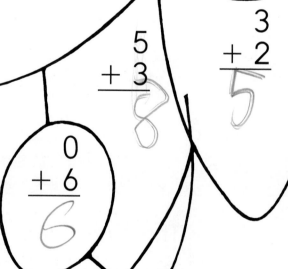

$$\begin{array}{r} 5 \\ + 3 \\ \hline 8 \end{array}$$

$$\begin{array}{r} 3 \\ + 2 \\ \hline 5 \end{array}$$

$$\begin{array}{r} 0 \\ + 6 \\ \hline 6 \end{array}$$

$$\begin{array}{r} 6 \\ + 1 \\ \hline 7 \end{array}$$

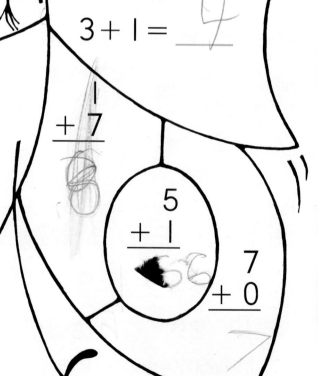

$$\begin{array}{r} 1 \\ + 7 \\ \hline 8 \end{array}$$

$$\begin{array}{r} 5 \\ + 1 \\ \hline 6 \end{array}$$

$$\begin{array}{r} 7 \\ + 0 \\ \hline 7 \end{array}$$

Write each addition sentence.

1.

   2 + 6 = 8

2.

   2 + 4 = 6

3. Use 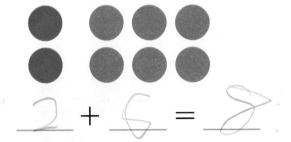 red and 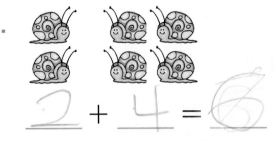 yellow . Color to make 6.
   Write the addition sentence.

   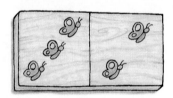 4 + 2 = 6

4. Write the numbers. Add.

   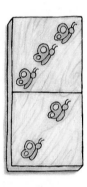

   3 + 2 = 5

   $\begin{array}{r} 3 \\ + 2 \\ \hline 5 \end{array}$

5. Add.

   $\begin{array}{r} 5 \\ + 2 \\ \hline 7 \end{array}$
   $\begin{array}{r} 2 \\ + 5 \\ \hline 7 \end{array}$
   $\begin{array}{r} 3 \\ + 0 \\ \hline 3 \end{array}$
   $\begin{array}{r} 0 \\ + 3 \\ \hline 3 \end{array}$
   $\begin{array}{r} 2 \\ + 4 \\ \hline 6 \end{array}$
   $\begin{array}{r} 4 \\ + 2 \\ \hline 6 \end{array}$

6. Use the picture to solve.

   There are ___ 4 .
   There are ___ 2  .
   How many are there in all?

   6

Name_____

What You Need

| paper bag | red and yellow counters | Workmat 4 |

① Put the counters in the . Shake.

② Take some counters out.

③ Sort the counters on .

④ Write an addition sentence below.

⑤ Repeat steps 1 – 4.

1.

_____ + _____ = _____

2.

_____ + _____ = _____

3.

_____ + _____ = _____

4.

_____ + _____ = _____

5.

_____ + _____ = _____

6.

_____ + _____ = _____

Draw ● to make each sum.
Complete the addition sentence.

1.

5 = 2 + 3

2.

7 = 4 + 3

3.

6 = 5 + 1

4.

4 = 1 + 2

5.

8 = 2 + 6

6.

3 = 1 + 2

7.

5 = 4 + 1

8.

7 = 3 + 4

9.
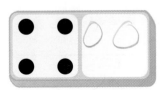

6 = 4 + 2

10.

8 = 5 + 3

Name _____ 7/16/05

Use a . Press the keys.

Write the number you see.

1. Press   **5**

2. Press

3. Press

4. Press

5. Press

6. Press

Miss Terry's Toy Store

written by Roxane Fox

illustrated by Kathi Ember

This Math Storybook

belongs to

_____

A

In Miss Terry's toy store there are boats.
She has big boats, small boats, short boats, and tall boats.
The children buy 2 boats.
How many are left?

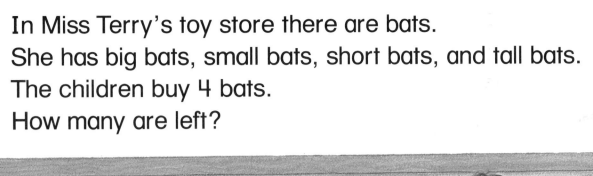

In Miss Terry's toy store there are bats.
She has big bats, small bats, short bats, and tall bats.
The children buy 4 bats.
How many are left?

In Miss Terry's toy store there are hats.
She has big hats, small hats, short hats, and tall hats.
The children buy 3 hats.
How many are left?

D

In Miss Terry's toy store there are bears.
She has big bears, small bears, short bears, and tall bears.
The boy buys 4 bears.
How many are left?

In Miss Terry's toy store there are kites.
There are big kites, small kites, short kites, and tall kites.
The children buy all of Miss Terry's kites.
Miss Terry closes the door and goes home.

Draw some balls on the shelf.
What if 2 balls were sold?
Tell how many balls would be left.

G

A Note to the Family

Here are some learning ideas you can share with your child.

Enjoy *Miss Terry's Toy Store* Together

- Read the story with your child. Ask your child to count the number of items on each page. Then talk about how to find how many are left after the children buy some. Show your child how to write a subtraction sentence.

    For example: 6 boats take away 2 boats are 4 boats
    $$6 - 2 = 4$$

- Encourage your child to show you what she or he drew on the last page of the story. Ask your child how many balls would be left if 2 were sold. What if 3 were sold?

At-Home Activity

- Cut out eight items or shapes from construction paper or use a picture from a magazine or newspaper that has eight separate items. Cross out or take away some of the items and ask your child to tell or write the matching subtraction sentence. Ask your child to point out the numbers that show how many there were altogether, how many were taken away, and how many are left.

Read More About It!

To read more about subtraction with your child, look for these books in your local library.

- *Seven Little Hippos* by Mike Thaler (Simon & Schuster, 1991)
- *Take Away Monsters* by Colin Hawkins (Putnam, 1984)
- *The Great Take-Away* by Louise Matthews (Dodd, Mead, 1980)

Visit Our Web Site!

www.sbgmath.com

H

Use counters to tell subtraction stories
about children in the park.
Draw or write one story.

Solve. Use counters if you like.

1. 2 children are on the  .

   What if one goes away?

   How many will there be? _____

2. 4 children are on the .

   What if 2 go away?

   How many will there be? _____

Use ● and the ▢ to subtract.

Write how many are left.

1. 2 ● take away 1 ● ___|___ left

2. 5 ● take away 3 ● __2__ left

3. 4 ● take away 2 ● __2__ left

4. 3 ● take away 2 ● __1__ left

Home Connection Counters can help children understand subtraction. Use household items such as buttons or beans to help your child show numbers and subtract.

Use counters to subtract.
Write how many are left.

	Show	Take away	Left
1.	4	3	_____
2.	2	1	_____
3.	5	2	_____
4.	3	2	_____
5.	5	1	_____
6.	4	1	_____

5   take away   4   __1__ left

Write how many are left.

1.

3   take away   1   __2__ left

2.

6   take away   2   __4__ left

3.

5   take away   3   __2__ left

4.

6   take away   1   __5__ left

Home Connection Have your child use the pictures on this page to tell subtraction stories. Encourage him or her to say how many toys are in each picture, how many are leaving, and how many will be left.

Write the numbers.

1.

<u> 4 </u> take away <u> 1 </u> <u> 3 </u> left

2.

<u>   </u> take away <u>   </u> <u>   </u> left

3.

<u>   </u> take away <u>   </u> <u>   </u> left

Problem Solving

Solve. Use counters if you like.

4. You had 5 🚗.

2 🚗 drive away.

How many 🚗 are left? <u>   </u>

Tell how you know.

Name _____ 7/16/05 _____

$$4 - 2 = \underline{2}$$

minus   difference

Cross out to subtract.

1.

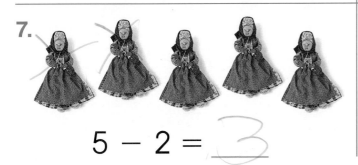

$$6 - 2 = \underline{4}$$

2.

$$4 - 1 = \underline{3}$$

3.

$$8 - 2 = \underline{6}$$

4.

$$6 - 1 = \underline{5}$$

5.

$$6 - 3 = \underline{3}$$

6.

$$5 - 1 = \underline{4}$$

7.

$$5 - 2 = \underline{3}$$

8.

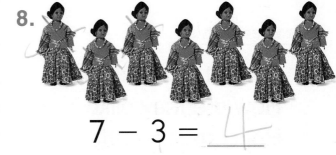

$$7 - 3 = \underline{4}$$

Home Connection Crossing out pictures can help your child understand subtraction. Have your child draw and cross out simple shapes to show subtraction.

Cross out to subtract.

1.

$3 - 2 = \underline{1}$

2.

$6 - 2 = \underline{}$

3.

$5 - 4 = \underline{}$

4.

$2 - 1 = \underline{}$

5.

$4 - 3 = \underline{}$

6.

$4 - 2 = \underline{}$

7.

$8 - 5 = \underline{}$

8.

$8 - 3 = \underline{}$

 Critical Thinking Corner

Number Sense

9. Look at 7 and 8 above.
   How are they alike?
   How are they different?

Look at the cube train.
Write how many of each color.
Complete each subtraction sentence.

1.

2 and 3

$5 - 3 = 2$

$5 - 2 = 3$

2.

_____ and _____

$5 - 4 = $ _____

$5 - 1 = $ _____

3.

_____ and _____

$5 - 0 = $ _____

$5 - 5 = $ _____

Home Connection To help your child practice subtracting, put
5 or 6 pennies or other household items in your hand. Take some out.
Ask your child how many are still in your hand. Then count them together.

seventy-five   **75**

Look at the cube train.
Write how many of each color.
Complete each subtraction sentence.

1.

   __4__ and __2__

   $6 - \underline{2} = \underline{4}$

   $6 - \underline{4} = \underline{2}$

2.

   _____ and _____

   $6 - \underline{} = \underline{}$

   $6 - \underline{} = \underline{}$

3.

   _____ and _____

   $6 - \underline{} = \underline{}$

4.

   _____ and _____

   $6 - \underline{} = \underline{}$

   $6 - \underline{} = \underline{}$

Use two colors of  to show ways
to make 7. Color.
Write the subtraction sentences.

1.
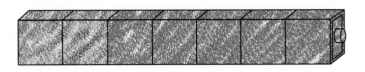

_2_ and _5_

$7 - 5 = 2$

$7 - 2 = 5$

2.
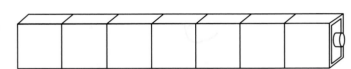

____ and ____

____ − ____ = ____

____ − ____ = ____

3.
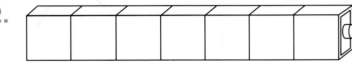

____ and ____

____ − ____ = ____

____ − ____ = ____

4.
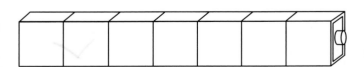

____ and ____

____ − ____ = ____

____ − ____ = ____

Home Connection Challenge your child to name a combination for 7.
Ask your child to write two subtraction sentences to show the combination.

seventy-seven   **77**

Use two colors of 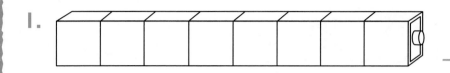 to show ways
to make 8. Color.
Write the subtraction sentences.

1.

_____ — _____ = _____

_____ and _____   _____ — _____ = _____

2.

_____ — _____ = _____

_____ and _____   _____ — _____ = _____

3.

_____ — _____ = _____

_____ and _____   _____ — _____ = _____

4.

_____ — _____ = _____

_____ and _____   _____ — _____ = _____

5.

_____ — _____ = _____

_____ and _____   _____ — _____ = _____

Name_____

There are 4 children.
Then 1 goes home.
4 − 1 = 3

4 − 1 = 3

Write each number sentence.

1.

____ − ____ = ____

2.

____ − ____ = ____

3.

____ − ____ = ____

4.

____ − ____ = ____

Home Connection Act out simple math stories using common household items. Ask your child to write number sentences to go with each story.

seventy-nine **79**

Write each number sentence.

1.

$$\underset{\cdots}{3} - \underset{\cdots}{1} = \underset{\cdots}{2}$$

2.

___ – ___ = ___

3.

___ – ___ = ___

4.

___ – ___ = ___

Subtract.

1. 5   take away   3   _____ left

Cross out to subtract.

2.

4 – 2 = ___

3.

6 – 3 = ___

Write each number sentence.

4.

___ – ___ = ___

5.
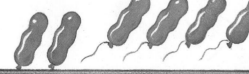

___ – ___ = ___

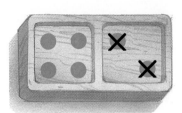 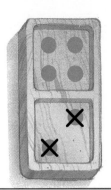

$6 - 2 = 4$

$$\begin{array}{r} 6 \\ -\ 2 \\ \hline 4 \end{array}$$

Write the numbers. Subtract.

1.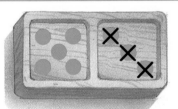

_____ — _____ = _____

$$\begin{array}{r} \\ -\ \\ \hline \end{array}$$

2.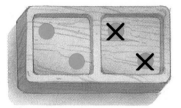

_____ — _____ = _____

$$\begin{array}{r} \\ -\ \\ \hline \end{array}$$

3.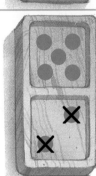

_____ — _____ = _____

$$\begin{array}{r} \\ -\ \\ \hline \end{array}$$

4.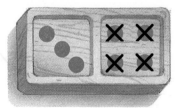

_____ — _____ = _____

$$\begin{array}{r} \\ -\ \\ \hline \end{array}$$

Home Connection Ask your child to place some small items such as beans or pennies across or down, make up a subtraction problem, and write it horizontally and vertically.

Find each difference.

Write the matching subtraction sentence.

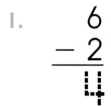

1.
$$\begin{array}{r} 6 \\ -\ 2 \\ \hline 4 \end{array}$$

$6 - 2 = 4$

2.
$$\begin{array}{r} 5 \\ -\ 2 \\ \hline \end{array}$$

___ − ___ = ___

3.
$$\begin{array}{r} 4 \\ -\ 2 \\ \hline \end{array}$$

___ − ___ = ___

4.
$$\begin{array}{r} 6 \\ -\ 5 \\ \hline \end{array}$$

___ − ___ = ___

Problem Solving

Solve.

5. There are 8 .

   2 sail away.

   How many  are

   there now? _____

6. There are 3 .

   2 drive away.

   How many are

   there now? _____

Solve. Draw or write to show how.

1. There are 5 .

   2 roll away.

   How many are left? _____

2. There are 8 .

   Leon takes 4.

   How many are left? _____

3. There are 6 .

   Linda takes 5.

   How many are left? _____

Home Connection Make up a subtraction problem.
Encourage your child to show you different ways to solve it.

Solve.

Draw or write to show how.

1. 7  are sailing.

   2 sail away.

   How many are left?

   _____

2. There are 4 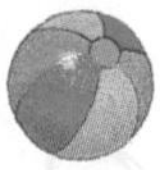 .

   3 roll away.

   How many 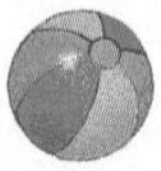 are left?

   _____

3. There are 6 .

   4 blow away.

   How many 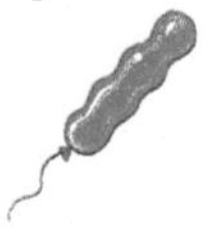 are left?

   _____

4. 8  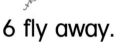 are flying.

   6 fly away.

   How many are left?

   _____

Use counters and the . Solve.

1. Show 3.
   Take away 3.
   How many are left?

   _____

2. Show 5.
   Take away 5.
   How many are
   there now?

   _____

3. Show 6.
   Take away 0.
   How many are left?

   _____

4. Show 4.
   Take away 0.
   How many are
   there now?

   _____

5. Show 8.
   Take away 8.
   How many are
   there now?

   _____

6. Show 7.
   Take away 0.
   How many are left?

Home Connection Give your child buttons or other household
items to practice subtraction. Have him or her solve problems involving
taking away zero or taking away all; for example, 5−5 and 5−0.

Subtract.
Use counters if you like.

1.

$$\begin{array}{r} 5 \\ -\ 0 \\ \hline \end{array}$$ 5

$$\begin{array}{r} 2 \\ -\ 2 \\ \hline \end{array}$$ 0

$$\begin{array}{r} 7 \\ -\ 2 \\ \hline \end{array}$$ 5

$$\begin{array}{r} 4 \\ -\ 0 \\ \hline \end{array}$$ 4

$$\begin{array}{r} 5 \\ -\ 4 \\ \hline \end{array}$$ 1

$$\begin{array}{r} 6 \\ -\ 6 \\ \hline \end{array}$$ 0

2.

$$\begin{array}{r} 8 \\ -\ 8 \\ \hline \end{array}$$ 0

$$\begin{array}{r} 6 \\ -\ 0 \\ \hline \end{array}$$ 6

$$\begin{array}{r} 4 \\ -\ 4 \\ \hline \end{array}$$ 0

$$\begin{array}{r} 2 \\ -\ 0 \\ \hline \end{array}$$ 2

$$\begin{array}{r} 7 \\ -\ 3 \\ \hline \end{array}$$ 4

$$\begin{array}{r} 1 \\ -\ 1 \\ \hline \end{array}$$ 0

3.

$$\begin{array}{r} 7 \\ -\ 0 \\ \hline \end{array}$$ 7

$$\begin{array}{r} 8 \\ -\ 3 \\ \hline \end{array}$$ 5

$$\begin{array}{r} 5 \\ -\ 5 \\ \hline \end{array}$$ 0

$$\begin{array}{r} 7 \\ -\ 4 \\ \hline \end{array}$$ 3

$$\begin{array}{r} 3 \\ -\ 0 \\ \hline \end{array}$$ 3

$$\begin{array}{r} 7 \\ -\ 7 \\ \hline \end{array}$$ 0

4.

$$\begin{array}{r} 3 \\ -\ 3 \\ \hline \end{array}$$ 0

$$\begin{array}{r} 8 \\ -\ 0 \\ \hline \end{array}$$ 8

$$\begin{array}{r} 6 \\ -\ 5 \\ \hline \end{array}$$ 1

$$\begin{array}{r} 1 \\ -\ 0 \\ \hline \end{array}$$ 1

$$\begin{array}{r} 0 \\ -\ 0 \\ \hline \end{array}$$ 0

$$\begin{array}{r} 8 \\ -\ 7 \\ \hline \end{array}$$ 1

 Critical Thinking Corner

Number Sense

5. How is subtracting 0 like adding 0?

Name_____

Would you add or subtract?
Write the number sentence.

1. 2 seahorses leave.

add   (subtract)

4 ..... 2 = 2

2. 2 fish join the others.

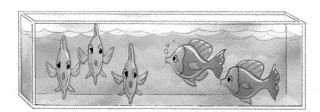

add   subtract

___ ◯ ___ = ___

3. 3 fish come to play.

add   subtract

___ ◯ ___ = ___

4. 2 fish leave.

add   subtract

___ ◯ ___ = ___

5. 2 fish go away.

add   subtract

___ ◯ ___ = ___

6. 4 fish join the others.

add   subtract

___ ◯ ___ = ___

 Home Connection Use favorite toys to make up addition
and subtraction problems. Ask your child if he or she would
add or subtract to solve the problem. Then find the solution.

Would you add or subtract?
Write each number sentence.

1. 2 elephants walk in.

add   subtract

____ ◯ ____ = ____

2. 3 lions come to play.

add   subtract

____ ◯ ____ = ____

3. 1 giraffe goes home.

add   subtract

____ ◯ ____ = ____

4. 4 hippos leave.

add   subtract

____ ◯ ____ = ____

What Do You Think?

Sometimes I add and subtract when I play a game. Think of a game in which you add or subtract.

Journal Idea

Write the numbers.
Then subtract.

1.

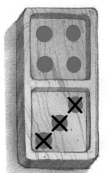

_____ − _____ = _____

2.

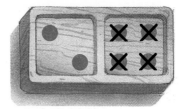

_____ − _____ = _____

3. Subtract.

$$
\begin{array}{cccccc}
4 & 8 & 8 & 7 & 7 & 6 \\
-1 & -0 & -6 & -7 & -6 & -3 \\
\hline
\end{array}
$$

Add or subtract.
Write the number sentence.

4. 5 toys walk away.

add   subtract

____ ◯ ____ = ____

5. 2 trucks come back.

add   subtract

____ ◯ ____ = ____

Name_____ **Extra Practice**

Subtract. Use counters if you like.

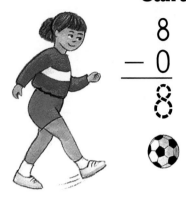

Start

$$8 - 0 = 8$$

$$8 - 1 = \underline{7}$$

$$
\begin{array}{r}
8 \\
- 3 \\
\hline
\end{array}
$$

$$7 - 1 = \underline{}$$

$$
\begin{array}{r}
7 \\
- 4 \\
\hline
\end{array}
$$

$$6 - 2 = \underline{}$$

$$
\begin{array}{r}
4 \\
- 2 \\
\hline
\end{array}
$$

$$7 - 6 = \underline{}$$

$$4 - 4 = \underline{}$$

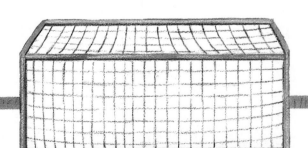

Write how many are left.

1. 5 take away 3 _____ left

2. 4 take away 3 _____ left

Cross out to subtract.

3.

8 − 5 = _____

4.

4 − 4 = _____

Subtract.

5. 5 − 3 = _____   7 − 6 = _____   3 − 0 = _____

6.
$$\begin{array}{cc} 5 \\ -\ 0 \\ \hline \end{array} \quad \begin{array}{cc} 6 \\ -\ 6 \\ \hline \end{array} \quad \begin{array}{cc} 8 \\ -\ 4 \\ \hline \end{array} \quad \begin{array}{cc} 7 \\ -\ 3 \\ \hline \end{array} \quad \begin{array}{cc} 5 \\ -\ 4 \\ \hline \end{array} \quad \begin{array}{cc} 4 \\ -\ 2 \\ \hline \end{array}$$

Add or subtract.
Write the number sentence.

7. 4 fish join the others.

add   subtract

_____ ◯ _____ = _____

8. 1 car leaves.

add   subtract

_____ ◯ _____ = _____

Name_____

What You Need

Workmat 1

8 counters

1. Put some counters on the workmat.

2. Then take some away.

3. Write the number sentence below.

1.	2.
____ − ____ = ____	____ − ____ = ____
3.	4.
____ − ____ = ____	____ − ____ = ____
5.	6.
____ − ____ = ____	____ − ____ = ____

How many toys are in the ?
Use counters.

1. 7 toys in all

_____ toys in the box

2. 3 toys in all

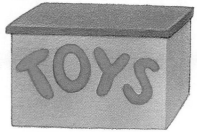

_____ toys in the box

3. 5 toys in all

_____ toys in the box

4. 6 toys in all

_____ toy in the box

5. 5 toys in all

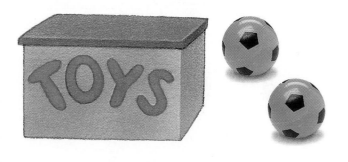

_____ toys in the box

6. 8 toys in all

_____ toys in the box

Use a . Press the keys.

Write the number you see.

1. Press

_____

2. Press

_____

3. Press

_____

4. Press

_____

5. Press

_____

6. Press

Name_____

Fill in the ⬭ for the correct answer.

1. Which is more?

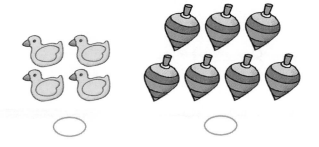

⬭   ⬭

2. Which is fewer?

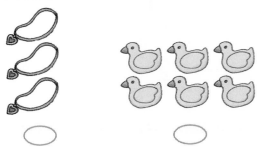

⬭   ⬭

3. How many are there?

⬭   ⬭   ⬭   ⬭

4   5   6   7

4. Which number comes before?

____, 4, 5

⬭   ⬭   ⬭   ⬭

2   3   6   1

5. What comes next?

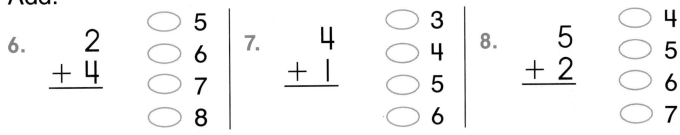

⬭
⬭
⬭

Add.

6. $\begin{array}{r} 2 \\ + 4 \\ \hline \end{array}$
⬭ 5
⬭ 6
⬭ 7
⬭ 8

7. $\begin{array}{r} 4 \\ + 1 \\ \hline \end{array}$
⬭ 3
⬭ 4
⬭ 5
⬭ 6

8. $\begin{array}{r} 5 \\ + 2 \\ \hline \end{array}$
⬭ 4
⬭ 5
⬭ 6
⬭ 7

9. $2 + 3 = $ ____

⬭   ⬭   ⬭   ⬭

4   3   5   6

10. $8 + 0 = $ ____

⬭   ⬭   ⬭   ⬭

8   5   6   0

Subtract.

11. 2 − 2 = _____

○   ○   ○   ○

1   4   0   8

12. 5 − 2 = _____

○   ○   ○   ○

7   1   3   6

13. 7 − 2 = _____

○   ○   ○   ○

4   6   2   5

14. 8 − 1 = _____

○   ○   ○   ○

7   5   8   6

15.
```
   6
 − 2
```
○ 3
○ 4
○ 5
○ 6

16.
```
   8
 − 5
```
○ 1
○ 2
○ 3
○ 4

17.
```
   7
 − 0
```
○ 0
○ 6
○ 7
○ 8

18. Choose the correct number sentence.

○ 5 + 1 = 6
○ 2 + 5 = 7
○ 7 − 1 = 6
○ 5 − 3 = 2

Use the graph. Solve each problem.

Silly Hats

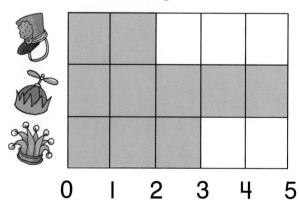

0   1   2   3   4   5

19. How many 🎩 are there?

○   ○   ○   ○

4   5   2   3

20. How many 🎩 are there?

○   ○   ○   ○

4   5   3   2

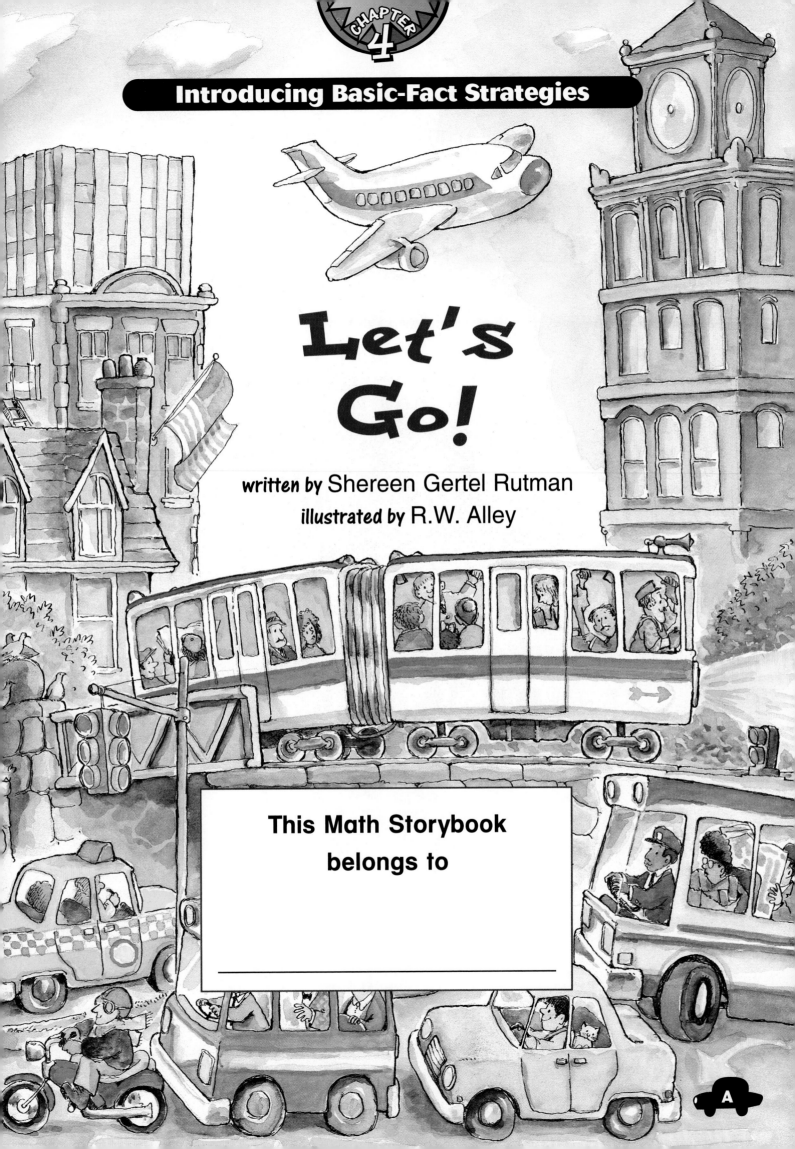

Let's Go!

written **by** Shereen Gertel Rutman

illustrated **by** R.W. Alley

This Math Storybook

belongs to

_____

A

The Travel Club is on the way.
They plan to visit Mandalay.

We have 3 who are inside.
We have 2 who cannot ride.

Oh, no! Oh, no!

Maybe 5 can fit in a van!

Here come 4 more who we know.
5 + 4 makes 9 to go.

How can 9 fit in the van?
8 will fit. That leaves 1 man.

Oh, no! Oh, no!

The 12 of us wait for the bus.
We line up but start to fuss.

We see that 8 have room to sit.
We see that 4 may not fit.

Oh, no! Oh, no!

We find 4 seats in the back row.
That means all of us can go.
8 + 4 makes 12, you know!

Let's go! Let's go!

Draw some friends who sit inside.
Draw some friends who wait outside.
Count your friends who go today
on this trip to Mandalay.

A Note to the Family

Here are some learning ideas you can share with your child.

 ### Enjoy *Let's Go!* Together

• Read each page of *Let's Go!* with your child. Ask your child to count the number of people on each page. Have your child tell addition and subtraction stories for each picture.

 ### At-Home Activities

• The theme of this story is transportation. Make cookies or sandwiches using boat and car cookie cutters. Encourage your child to make up math problems using the shapes.

• Invite your child to cut out pictures of vehicles from magazines. Help your child glue several pictures on a large sheet of paper. Work together to think of addition and subtraction stories for the picture. Write each problem on the page.

 ### Read More About It!

To read more math or theme-related stories with your child, look for the following books in your local library.

• *Freight Train* by Donald Crews (Morrow, 1992)

• *Red Fox and His Canoe* by Nathaniel Benchley (Harper, 1985)

• *Trucks You Can Count On* by Doug Magee (Putnam, 1986)

• *One, Two, Three, and Four. No More?* by Catherine Gray (Houghton Mifflin, 1988)

 ### Visit Our Web Site!

www.sbgmath.com

H

You can count on from any number.

Start at 5.
Count on 6, 7, 8.

5   6, 7, 8

Use counters if you like.
Count on.
Write the numbers.

1. 4 _____ , _____

2. 3 _____ , _____ , _____

3. 6 _____

4. 7 _____ , _____

5. 8 _____ , _____ , _____

6. 5 _____

Home Connection Counting on from a number is a strategy children can use to add. Use pennies or other household items to help your child practice counting on from different numbers.

ninety-seven   **97**

Use counters if you like.
Count on.
Write the numbers.

1.

2
_3_ , _4_

2.

9
_____ , _____ , _____

3.

3
8
_____

4.

6
_____ , _____

5.

3
_____ , _____

6.

7
_____ , _____ , _____

7.

5
_____ , _____

8.

4
_____

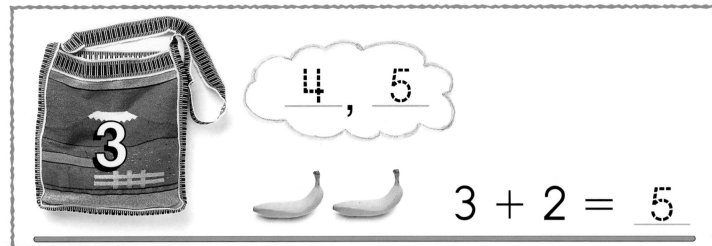

4, 5

3 + 2 = 5

Count on to find each sum.

1.

4 + 1 = ___

2.

6 + 2 = ___

3.

7 + 1 = ___

4.

9 + 2 = ___

 Home Connection Your child has been counting on 1 and 2
to find sums. Use pennies or buttons to practice counting on. Help
your child see that counting on can be quicker than counting all.

Count on to find each sum.

1.

$$\begin{array}{r} 8 \\ + 2 \\ \hline \end{array}$$

2.
$$\begin{array}{r} 7 \\ + 2 \\ \hline \end{array}$$
$$\begin{array}{r} 6 \\ + 1 \\ \hline \end{array}$$
$$\begin{array}{r} 9 \\ + 2 \\ \hline \end{array}$$
$$\begin{array}{r} 3 \\ + 2 \\ \hline \end{array}$$
$$\begin{array}{r} 8 \\ + 2 \\ \hline \end{array}$$
$$\begin{array}{r} 7 \\ + 1 \\ \hline \end{array}$$

3.
$$\begin{array}{r} 4 \\ + 1 \\ \hline \end{array}$$
$$\begin{array}{r} 7 \\ + 2 \\ \hline \end{array}$$
$$\begin{array}{r} 7 \\ + 1 \\ \hline \end{array}$$
$$\begin{array}{r} 4 \\ + 2 \\ \hline \end{array}$$
$$\begin{array}{r} 3 \\ + 1 \\ \hline \end{array}$$
$$\begin{array}{r} 9 \\ + 1 \\ \hline \end{array}$$

4.
$$\begin{array}{r} 5 \\ + 1 \\ \hline \end{array}$$
$$\begin{array}{r} 5 \\ + 2 \\ \hline \end{array}$$
$$\begin{array}{r} 8 \\ + 1 \\ \hline \end{array}$$
$$\begin{array}{r} 6 \\ + 2 \\ \hline \end{array}$$
$$\begin{array}{r} 2 \\ + 1 \\ \hline \end{array}$$
$$\begin{array}{r} 3 \\ + 1 \\ \hline \end{array}$$

 Problem Solving

Solve.

5. You started at 5.
You ended at 7.
How many did you count on? _____

6, 7, 8

$5 + 3 = 8$

Count on to find each sum.

1. $7 + 3 = \underline{\quad}$

2. $9 + 2 = \underline{\quad}$

3. $6 + 3 = \underline{\quad}$

4. $4 + 3 = \underline{\quad}$

5.

$$\begin{array}{cccccc} 9 & 8 & 8 & 4 & 5 & 5 \\ +3 & +1 & +2 & +1 & +2 & +1 \end{array}$$

6.

$$\begin{array}{cccccc} 7 & 3 & 9 & 6 & 8 & 4 \\ +2 & +2 & +1 & +2 & +3 & +2 \end{array}$$

Home Connection Your child has been practicing counting on 1, 2, and 3 to find sums. You can reinforce this strategy by having your child practice counting on when setting a dinner table or putting clothes away.

Follow each rule.
Look for patterns.

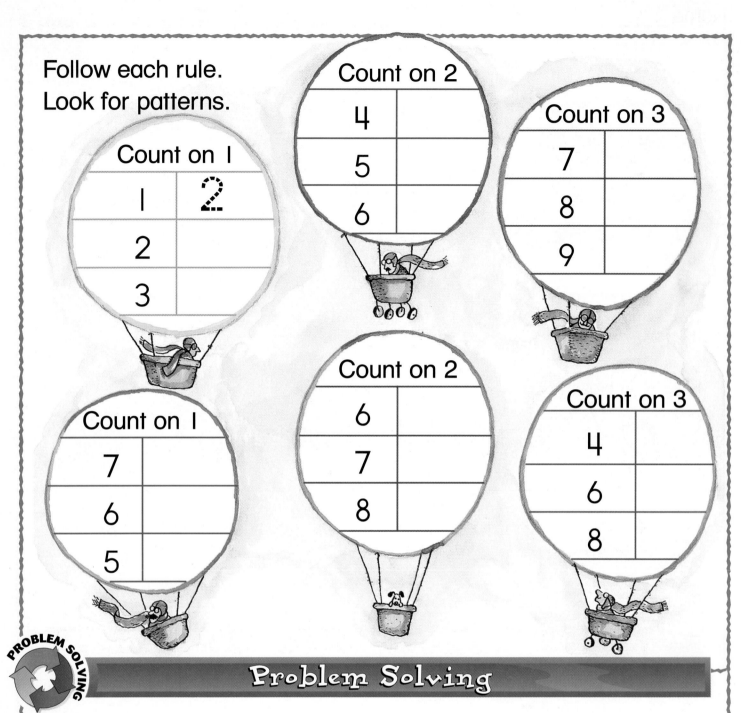

Count on 1

1	2
2	
3	

Count on 2

4	
5	
6	

Count on 3

7	
8	
9	

Count on 1

7	
6	
5	

Count on 2

6	
7	
8	

Count on 3

4	
6	
8	

Problem Solving

Solve.

1. There are 7 🕊️ .

   3 🐦 join them.

   How many birds

   are there in all?

   _____ birds

2. There are 9 🪁 .

   There are 2 🪁 .

   How many kites

   are there altogether?

   _____ kites

$3 + 5 =$ _8_

It's easy to count on when you start with the greater number.

```
0   1   2   3   4   ⑤   6   7   8   9   10   11   12
```

⤵ Start at 5.   ⤵ Count on 3.

Use the number line to count on.
Circle the greater number.
Write each sum.

Word Bank

number line

1.

$2 + 5 =$ _7_

```
0   1   2   3   4   ⑤   6   7   8
```

2.

$7 + 1 =$ ___

```
0   1   2   3   4   5   6   7   8
```

3.

$1 + 5 =$ ___

```
0   1   2   3   4   5   6   7   8
```

4.

$2 + 6 =$ ___

```
0   1   2   3   4   5   6   7   8
```

5.

$4 + 3 =$ ___

```
0   1   2   3   4   5   6   7   8
```

Home Connection Your child is learning to identify the greater of two numbers and then to count on from that number. Have your child tell you how he or she solved each exercise.

Circle the greater number each time.
Count on to add.

1. 2 + ⑦ = 9   3 + 5 = ___   4 + 2 = ___

2. 1 + 8 = ___   6 + 1 = ___   3 + 7 = ___

3. 5 + 3 = ___   2 + 4 = ___   3 + 6 = ___

4. $\begin{array}{r} 7 \\ +\ 1 \\ \hline \end{array}$ $\begin{array}{r} 1 \\ +\ 9 \\ \hline \end{array}$ $\begin{array}{r} 8 \\ +\ 1 \\ \hline \end{array}$ $\begin{array}{r} 2 \\ +\ 5 \\ \hline \end{array}$ $\begin{array}{r} 1 \\ +\ 5 \\ \hline \end{array}$ $\begin{array}{r} 7 \\ +\ 3 \\ \hline \end{array}$

5. $\begin{array}{r} 2 \\ +\ 9 \\ \hline \end{array}$ $\begin{array}{r} 3 \\ +\ 4 \\ \hline \end{array}$ $\begin{array}{r} 2 \\ +\ 8 \\ \hline \end{array}$ $\begin{array}{r} 6 \\ +\ 2 \\ \hline \end{array}$ $\begin{array}{r} 2 \\ +\ 3 \\ \hline \end{array}$ $\begin{array}{r} 1 \\ +\ 7 \\ \hline \end{array}$

6. $\begin{array}{r} 2 \\ +\ 6 \\ \hline \end{array}$ $\begin{array}{r} 3 \\ +\ 2 \\ \hline \end{array}$ $\begin{array}{r} 2 \\ +\ 1 \\ \hline \end{array}$ $\begin{array}{r} 8 \\ +\ 3 \\ \hline \end{array}$ $\begin{array}{r} 9 \\ +\ 3 \\ \hline \end{array}$ $\begin{array}{r} 8 \\ +\ 2 \\ \hline \end{array}$

This is a double.

$$3 + 3 = 6$$

Write each addition sentence.
Use cubes if you like.

1.

___ + ___ = ___

2.

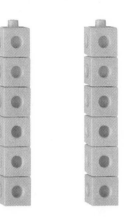

___ + ___ = ___

3.

___ + ___ = ___

4.

___ + ___ = ___

5.

___ + ___ = ___

6.

___ + ___ = ___

Home Connection Your child has been making and adding doubles. Have your child practice making doubles with small objects and then tell you the addition sentence he or she made.

one hundred five   **105**

Add. Circle the double facts.

1.
$$\begin{array}{r} 2 \\ + 2 \\ \hline 4 \end{array}$$
$$\begin{array}{r} 5 \\ + 2 \\ \hline \end{array}$$
$$\begin{array}{r} 3 \\ + 8 \\ \hline \end{array}$$
$$\begin{array}{r} 2 \\ + 4 \\ \hline \end{array}$$
$$\begin{array}{r} 6 \\ + 6 \\ \hline \end{array}$$
$$\begin{array}{r} 2 \\ + 8 \\ \hline \end{array}$$

2.
$$\begin{array}{r} 3 \\ + 1 \\ \hline \end{array}$$
$$\begin{array}{r} 0 \\ + 0 \\ \hline \end{array}$$
$$\begin{array}{r} 6 \\ + 2 \\ \hline \end{array}$$
$$\begin{array}{r} 3 \\ + 9 \\ \hline \end{array}$$
$$\begin{array}{r} 4 \\ + 3 \\ \hline \end{array}$$
$$\begin{array}{r} 1 \\ + 1 \\ \hline \end{array}$$

3.
$$\begin{array}{r} 5 \\ + 3 \\ \hline \end{array}$$
$$\begin{array}{r} 7 \\ + 3 \\ \hline \end{array}$$
$$\begin{array}{r} 0 \\ + 7 \\ \hline \end{array}$$
$$\begin{array}{r} 3 \\ + 3 \\ \hline \end{array}$$
$$\begin{array}{r} 4 \\ + 0 \\ \hline \end{array}$$
$$\begin{array}{r} 1 \\ + 8 \\ \hline \end{array}$$

4.
$$\begin{array}{r} 3 \\ + 2 \\ \hline \end{array}$$
$$\begin{array}{r} 5 \\ + 5 \\ \hline \end{array}$$
$$\begin{array}{r} 6 \\ + 1 \\ \hline \end{array}$$
$$\begin{array}{r} 9 \\ + 2 \\ \hline \end{array}$$
$$\begin{array}{r} 4 \\ + 4 \\ \hline \end{array}$$
$$\begin{array}{r} 0 \\ + 6 \\ \hline \end{array}$$

 Critical Thinking Corner

Visual Thinking

Write the double facts.

5.

_____ + _____ = _____

6.

_____ + _____ = _____

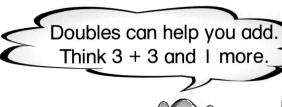

Doubles can help you add.
Think 3 + 3 and 1 more.

$3 + 3 = \underline{6}$ $3 + 4 = \underline{7}$

Use 🔲.

Write each sum.

1.
$2 + 2 = \underline{\hspace{1cm}}$

$2 + 3 = \underline{\hspace{1cm}}$

2.
$5 + 5 = \underline{\hspace{1cm}}$

$5 + 6 = \underline{\hspace{1cm}}$

3.
$4 + 4 = \underline{\hspace{1cm}}$

$4 + 5 = \underline{\hspace{1cm}}$

4.
$3 + 3 = \underline{\hspace{1cm}}$

$3 + 4 = \underline{\hspace{1cm}}$

5.
$1 + 1 = \underline{\hspace{1cm}}$

$1 + 2 = \underline{\hspace{1cm}}$

6.
$2 + 2 = \underline{\hspace{1cm}}$

$2 + 3 = \underline{\hspace{1cm}}$

Home Connection Your child has been using doubles to add.
Give your child some near-double addition problems such as 3 + 4
and have him or her tell you the double that helps solve the problem.

Find each sum. Think of doubles to help you.

1.
$$\begin{array}{r} 0 \\ +\ 0 \\ \hline 0 \end{array}$$
$$\begin{array}{r} 5 \\ +\ 4 \\ \hline \end{array}$$
$$\begin{array}{r} 3 \\ +\ 3 \\ \hline \end{array}$$
$$\begin{array}{r} 4 \\ +\ 3 \\ \hline \end{array}$$
$$\begin{array}{r} 1 \\ +\ 1 \\ \hline \end{array}$$
$$\begin{array}{r} 5 \\ +\ 5 \\ \hline \end{array}$$

2.
$$\begin{array}{r} 2 \\ +\ 2 \\ \hline \end{array}$$
$$\begin{array}{r} 2 \\ +\ 1 \\ \hline \end{array}$$
$$\begin{array}{r} 4 \\ +\ 4 \\ \hline \end{array}$$
$$\begin{array}{r} 0 \\ +\ 1 \\ \hline \end{array}$$
$$\begin{array}{r} 3 \\ +\ 2 \\ \hline \end{array}$$
$$\begin{array}{r} 5 \\ +\ 6 \\ \hline \end{array}$$

3.
$$\begin{array}{r} 3 \\ +\ 4 \\ \hline \end{array}$$
$$\begin{array}{r} 6 \\ +\ 6 \\ \hline \end{array}$$
$$\begin{array}{r} 2 \\ +\ 3 \\ \hline \end{array}$$
$$\begin{array}{r} 6 \\ +\ 5 \\ \hline \end{array}$$
$$\begin{array}{r} 1 \\ +\ 2 \\ \hline \end{array}$$
$$\begin{array}{r} 4 \\ +\ 5 \\ \hline \end{array}$$

Count on.   **Checkpoint**

1.   _____ , _____

2.   _____ , _____ , _____

Find each sum.

3.
$$\begin{array}{r} 1 \\ +\ 4 \\ \hline \end{array}$$
$$\begin{array}{r} 4 \\ +\ 3 \\ \hline \end{array}$$
$$\begin{array}{r} 2 \\ +\ 6 \\ \hline \end{array}$$
$$\begin{array}{r} 8 \\ +\ 2 \\ \hline \end{array}$$
$$\begin{array}{r} 3 \\ +\ 5 \\ \hline \end{array}$$
$$\begin{array}{r} 9 \\ +\ 1 \\ \hline \end{array}$$

4. $4 + 4 =$ _____ $3 + 3 =$ _____ $6 + 6 =$ _____

There are 3  in the yard.
There are 2 on the path.
How many are there?

I can draw a picture
to help me.

$\underline{3} + \underline{2} = \underline{5}$

Draw a picture to solve.
Write the addition sentence.

1. I see 4 .
   I see 3 more.
   How many do I see?

   ____ + ____ = ____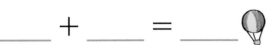

2. 2 are in the water.
   4 others sail in.
   How many are there now?

   ____ + ____ = ____

 Home Connection Drawing pictures can help children solve word problems. Help your child practice this strategy by encouraging him or her to draw pictures to solve problems.

one hundred nine **109**

Draw a picture to solve.
Write the addition sentence.

I. There is 1 big  .

There are 3 little .

How many are there in all?

____ + ____ = ____ kites

2. Mika sees 3 big .

Then she sees 2 little .

How many does she see?

____ + ____ = ____ boats

3. There are 4 .

There are 2 .

How many are there in all?

____ + ____ = ____ wagons

You can count back from any number.

Start at 7.
Count back 6, 5, 4.

7

_6_ , _5_ , _4_

Use counters if you like.
Count back.
Write the numbers.

1. 5   5 +2 = 3
    _4_ , _3_

2. 8   8 – 2 = 6
    _7_ , _6_

3. 9   9 – 1 = 8
    _8_

4. 4
    ___ , ___ , ___

5. 11   11 – 3 = 8
    _10_ , _9_ , _9_

6. 6   6 – 1 = 5
    _5_

Home Connection Counting back from a number is a strategy children can use to subtract. Use buttons or other small items to help your child practice counting back from different numbers.

one hundred eleven **111**

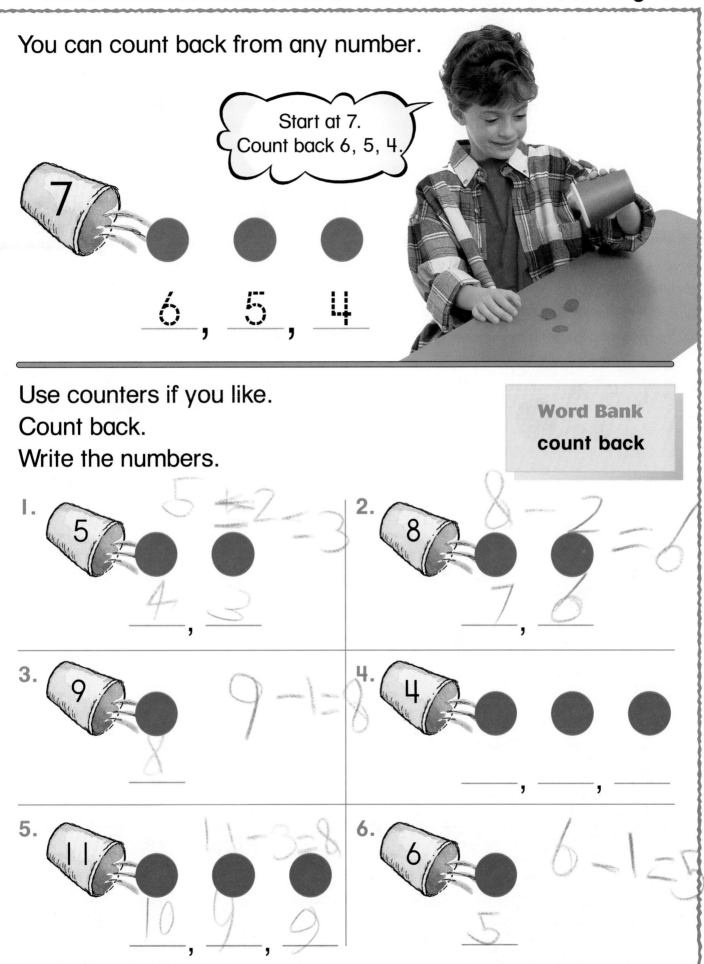

Use counters if you like.
Count back.
Write the numbers.

1.

6 ___

2.

_____ , _____ , _____

3.

_____ , _____ , _____

4.

_____ , _____

5.

_____ , _____

6.

_____

7.

_____ , _____ , _____

8.

_____ , _____

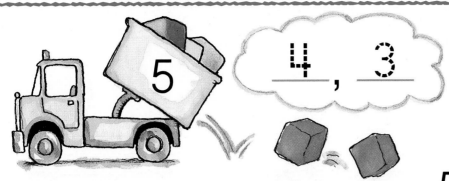

Start with 5. **Count back 2.** $5 - 2 = 3$

Count back to subtract.

1.

$4 - 1 = \underline{}$

2.

$6 - 2 = \underline{}$

3.

$7 - 1 = \underline{}$

4.

$9 - 2 = \underline{}$

 **Home Connection** Your child has been counting back to find differences. Have your child use beans, pebbles, or pennies to review the subtraction problems on this page.

one hundred thirteen **113**

Count back to subtract.

1.

$$\begin{array}{r} 8 \\ -\ 1 \\ \hline \end{array}$$

2.

$$\begin{array}{r} 5 \\ -\ 2 \\ \hline \end{array}$$

3.
$$\begin{array}{r} 6 \\ -\ 1 \\ \hline \end{array}$$
$$\begin{array}{r} 4 \\ -\ 2 \\ \hline \end{array}$$
$$\begin{array}{r} 5 \\ -\ 1 \\ \hline \end{array}$$
$$\begin{array}{r} 9 \\ -\ 2 \\ \hline \end{array}$$
$$\begin{array}{r} 2 \\ -\ 1 \\ \hline \end{array}$$
$$\begin{array}{r} 8 \\ -\ 2 \\ \hline \end{array}$$

4.
$$\begin{array}{r} 9 \\ -\ 1 \\ \hline \end{array}$$
$$\begin{array}{r} 3 \\ -\ 2 \\ \hline \end{array}$$
$$\begin{array}{r} 3 \\ -\ 1 \\ \hline \end{array}$$
$$\begin{array}{r} 4 \\ -\ 1 \\ \hline \end{array}$$
$$\begin{array}{r} 6 \\ -\ 2 \\ \hline \end{array}$$
$$\begin{array}{r} 7 \\ -\ 2 \\ \hline \end{array}$$

 Critical Thinking Corner

Number Sense

5. When would you count on?
When would you count back?
Share your ideas.

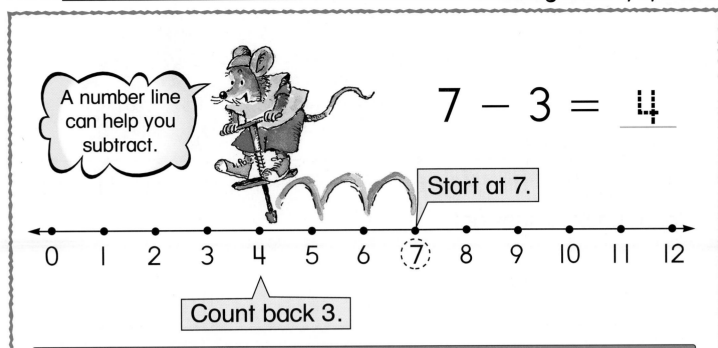

A number line can help you subtract.

$$7 - 3 = 4$$

Start at 7.

Count back 3.

Use the number line to count back.
Circle the number where you start.
Write each difference.

1.

$$8 - 3 = 5$$

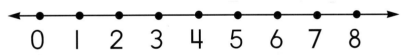

2.

$$5 - 2 = \underline{\hspace{1cm}}$$

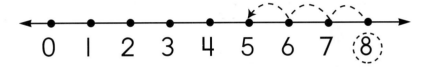

3.

$$4 - 3 = \underline{\hspace{1cm}}$$

4.

$$7 - 2 = \underline{\hspace{1cm}}$$

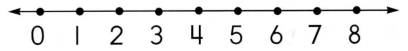

5.

$$6 - 3 = \underline{\hspace{1cm}}$$

Home Connection A number line can be used to count back. Ask your child to show you how he or she used the number line to solve these problems.

one hundred fifteen   **115**

Use the number line to help you.

0 1 2 3 4 5 6 7 8 9 10 11 12

Count back to subtract.

1. $10 - 3 = \underline{7}$ $6 - 2 = \underline{\quad}$ $10 - 1 = \underline{\quad}$

2. $8 - 2 = \underline{\quad}$ $9 - 2 = \underline{\quad}$ $11 - 2 = \underline{\quad}$

3. $4 - 1 = \underline{\quad}$ $12 - 3 = \underline{\quad}$ $5 - 3 = \underline{\quad}$

4.
$$\begin{array}{cccccc} 6 & 7 & 8 & 10 & 4 & 6 \\ -1 & -3 & -1 & -2 & -2 & -3 \end{array}$$

5.
$$\begin{array}{cccccc} 2 & 5 & 9 & 7 & 7 & 3 \\ -1 & -2 & -1 & -2 & -1 & -2 \end{array}$$

6.
$$\begin{array}{cccccc} 3 & 9 & 5 & 4 & 11 & 8 \\ -1 & -3 & -1 & -3 & -3 & -3 \end{array}$$

Name_____ Using Doubles to Subtract

Doubles can help you subtract.

2 + 2 = 4

2 + 2 = **4**

4 − 2 = **2**

Add the double and then subtract.
Use cubes if you like.

1.

3 + 3 = ___

so 6 − 3 = ___

2.

5 + 5 = ___

so 10 − 5 = ___

3.

6 + 6 = ___

so 12 − 6 = ___

4.

4 + 4 = ___

so 8 − 4 = ___

Home Connection Children can use their knowledge of
doubles to make subtraction easier. Have your child add a double
(such as 2 pairs of mittens) and then subtract 1 part (1 pair).

one hundred seventeen **117**

Race down the track.
Add or subtract.

$$\begin{array}{r} 1 \\ -\ 1 \\ \hline 0 \end{array}$$

$$\begin{array}{r} 6 \\ +\ 6 \\ \hline \end{array}$$

$$\begin{array}{r} 10 \\ -\ 6 \\ \hline \end{array}$$

$$\begin{array}{r} 4 \\ +\ 4 \\ \hline \end{array}$$

$$\begin{array}{r} 12 \\ -\ 6 \\ \hline \end{array}$$

$$\begin{array}{r} 4 \\ -\ 2 \\ \hline \end{array}$$

$$\begin{array}{r} 11 \\ -\ 6 \\ \hline \end{array}$$

$$\begin{array}{r} 2 \\ -\ 1 \\ \hline \end{array}$$

$$\begin{array}{r} 3 \\ +\ 3 \\ \hline \end{array}$$

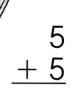

Finish

$$\begin{array}{r} 10 \\ -\ 5 \\ \hline \end{array}$$

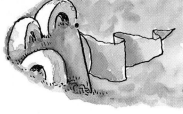

$$\begin{array}{r} 5 \\ +\ 5 \\ \hline \end{array}$$

$$\begin{array}{r} 2 \\ +\ 2 \\ \hline \end{array}$$

$$\begin{array}{r} 8 \\ -\ 4 \\ \hline \end{array}$$

$$\begin{array}{r} 6 \\ -\ 5 \\ \hline \end{array}$$

$$\begin{array}{r} 6 \\ -\ 3 \\ \hline \end{array}$$

$$\begin{array}{r} 1 \\ +\ 1 \\ \hline \end{array}$$

What Do You Think?

When I see 10 − 5, I think of a double.
How do you use doubles to subtract?

Journal Idea

$$5 + 4 = 9 \qquad 9 - 4 = 5$$

$$4 + 5 = 9 \qquad 9 - 5 = 4$$

Write each fact family.
Use cubes if you like.

1.

___ + ___ = ___   ___ − ___ = ___

___ + ___ = ___   ___ − ___ = ___

2.

___ + ___ = ___   ___ − ___ = ___

___ + ___ = ___   ___ − ___ = ___

3.

___ + ___ = ___   ___ − ___ = ___

___ + ___ = ___   ___ − ___ = ___

Home Connection Knowing fact families can help your child add and subtract. Give your child groups of 12 or fewer objects. Have your child divide the group in two and write the fact family.

one hundred nineteen   **119**

Use the pictures.
Write each fact family.

1.

$$6 + 3 = 9$$

___ + ___ = ___

___ − ___ = ___

___ − ___ = ___

2.

___ + ___ = ___

___ + ___ = ___

___ − ___ = ___

___ − ___ = ___

3.

___ + ___ = ___

___ + ___ = ___

___ − ___ = ___

___ − ___ = ___

4.

___ + ___ = ___

___ + ___ = ___

___ − ___ = ___

___ − ___ = ___

Name_____

There are 6 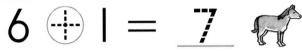.

I more joins them.

How many

are there in all?

6 ⊕ 1 = __7__ 🐴

_____

Do you add or subtract?
Complete each number sentence.

1. Yoshi has 6 ✈.

   He makes 5 more.

   How many ✈ does

   he have now?

   6 ◯ 5 = ____ ✈

2. There are 6 🚗.

   2 leave.

   How many 🚗

   are there now?

   6 ◯ 2 = ____ 🚗

3. Mr. Gomez has 5 🚲.

   He sells 4.

   How many 🚲

   are left?

   5 ◯ 4 = ____ 🚲

4. Kim has 4 toy 🚂.

   She buys 4 more.

   How many 🚂 does

   she have altogether?

   4 ◯ 4 = ____ 🚂

Home Connection Your child has been choosing whether to
add or subtract to solve a word problem. Have your child read these
problems to you and explain when to add or subtract, and why.

one hundred twenty-one   **121**

Complete each number sentence.

1. Greg sees 6 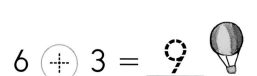.
   Then he sees 3 more.
   How many
   does he see?

   $6 \oplus 3 = \underline{9}$

2. The school has 5 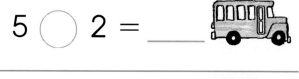.
   They sell 2.
   How many
   are left?

   $5 \bigcirc 2 = \underline{}$

3. There are 9 .
   8 drive away.
   How many
   are left?

   $9 \bigcirc 8 = \underline{}$

4. The team has 8 .
   They buy 4 more.
   How many
   do they have?

   $8 \bigcirc 4 = \underline{}$

5. There are 7 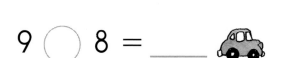 sailing.
   2 more join them.
   How many
   are sailing?

   $7 \bigcirc 2 = \underline{}$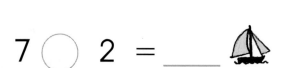

6. 9 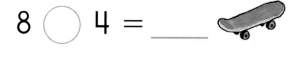 are rolling.
   1 stops.
   How many
   are still rolling?

   $9 \bigcirc 1 = \underline{}$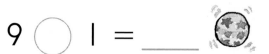

Name_____

Add the double and then subtract.

1.  3 + 3 = _____

   6 − 3 = _____

2. 2 + 2 = _____

   4 − 2 = _____

Count back to subtract.

3.
$$\begin{array}{r} 6 \\ -\ 1 \\ \hline \end{array} \qquad \begin{array}{r} 10 \\ -\ 2 \\ \hline \end{array} \qquad \begin{array}{r} 5 \\ -\ 3 \\ \hline \end{array} \qquad \begin{array}{r} 7 \\ -\ 1 \\ \hline \end{array} \qquad \begin{array}{r} 9 \\ -\ 2 \\ \hline \end{array} \qquad \begin{array}{r} 12 \\ -\ 3 \\ \hline \end{array}$$

Write the fact family.

4. ____ + ____ = ____   ____ − ____ = ____

    ____ + ____ = ____   ____ − ____ = ____

Draw a picture to solve.
Write the addition sentence.

5. There are 2 big .

    There are 5 little .

    How many are there in all?

    ____ + ____ = ____

Name_____

Find each sum and difference.
Color.

4 red   5 blue   6 yellow   7 green

$$\begin{array}{r} 2 \\ + 3 \\ \hline \end{array}$$

$$\begin{array}{r} 11 \\ - 4 \\ \hline \end{array}$$

$$\begin{array}{r} 4 \\ + 2 \\ \hline \end{array}$$

$$\begin{array}{r} 10 \\ - 6 \\ \hline \end{array}$$

$$\begin{array}{r} 3 \\ + 4 \\ \hline \end{array}$$

$$\begin{array}{r} 5 \\ + 0 \\ \hline \end{array}$$

$$\begin{array}{r} 3 \\ + 1 \\ \hline \end{array}$$

$$\begin{array}{r} 11 \\ - 5 \\ \hline \end{array}$$

$$\begin{array}{r} 12 \\ - 8 \\ \hline \end{array}$$

$$\begin{array}{r} 10 \\ - 4 \\ \hline \end{array}$$

$$\begin{array}{r} 1 \\ + 6 \\ \hline \end{array}$$

$$\begin{array}{r} 12 \\ - 7 \\ \hline \end{array}$$

1. Count back to subtract.

_____ , _____

$6 - 2 =$ _____

Add the doubles and then subtract.

2.  $4 + 4 =$ _____

$8 - 4 =$ _____

3. $3 + 3 =$ _____

$6 - 3 =$ _____

Write the fact family.

4. _____ $+$ _____ $=$ _____   _____ $-$ _____ $=$ _____

_____ $+$ _____ $=$ _____   _____ $-$ _____ $=$ _____

Add or subtract.

5.
$$\begin{array}{cccccc} 7 & 6 & 8 & 9 & 3 & 5 \\ -3 & +4 & +3 & -6 & +2 & -3 \end{array}$$

Complete the number sentence.

6. There are 6 .

Joe buys 2 more.

How many are there now?

$6 \bigcirc 2 =$ _____

What You Need

Spinner 1   Spinner 2

1 Spin Spinner 1.
Record the number.

2 Spin Spinner 2.
Record the number.

3 Write a number sentence and solve.

4 Tell how you found each answer.

	Spinner 1	Spinner 2	Number Sentence
1.			___ + ___ = ___
2.			___ + ___ = ___
3.			___ − ___ = ___
4.			___ + ___ = ___
5.			___ − ___ = ___
6.			___ + ___ = ___

You can count up
to subtract 10 − 7.

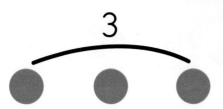

7 , 8 , 9 , 10

$$10 - 7 = 3$$

Start with 7.
Count up to 10.

Count up to subtract.
Use counters if you like.

1. $8 - 5 =$ (?)

Start with 5.
Count up to 8.

5, 6 , 7 , 8

$8 - 5 = 3$

2. $10 - 8 =$ (?)

Start with 8.
Count up to 10.

8, 9 , 10

$10 - 8 = 2$

3. $12 - 9 =$ (?)

Start with 9.
Count up to 12.

9, 10 , 11 , 12

$12 - 9 = 3$

4. $9 - 7 =$ (?)

Start with 7.
Count up to 9.

7, 8 , 9

$9 - 7 = 2$

Name_____

You can use a  to count on.

Press ON/C each time you begin.

Press the keys.

Write the numbers you see.

1. Count on 1.

5 + 1 = 6 = 7 = 8

8 + 1 = ___ = ___ = ___

2. Count on 2.

3 + 2 = ___ = ___ = ___

6 + 2 = ___ = ___ = ___

3. Count on 3.

3 + 3 = ___ = ___ = ___

2 + 3 = ___ = ___ = ___

 4. How could you use a  to count back?

CHAPTER 5

Geometry and Fractions

Stitching Stories

written by Roscoe Murphy

illustrated by Pauline Howard

This Math Storybook

belongs to

_____

A

Today is a special day.
Matt and his mom are making a quilt.
Matt cuts out the squares.
His mom sews them together.

Matt's mom sews pictures on some squares.
Then she tells Matt stories about them.
The stories are about Matt's family.

"This square has 2 equal parts.
One part shows my old teddy bear.
One part shows me as a little girl."

"This square has a circle in it.
The circle is a wedding ring.
One half shows a picture of me.
The other half shows a picture of Dad."

"This square has 3 equal parts.
One part shows a toy.
One part shows a cradle.
The last part shows you as a baby."

Here is one quilt square.
Draw something special.
Tell about the shapes you used.

G

A Note to the Family

**Here are some learning ideas
you can share with your child.**

 ### Enjoy *Stitching Stories* Together

- Read the story together. Talk about how a quilt can tell the story of a person's or a family's life.

- With your child, go through each page of the book to see what shapes you can find. Look for shapes within shapes, such as circles within squares, and triangles within squares. Encourage your child to trace shapes with a finger. Also point out halves, thirds, and fourths in the square designs.

- Look at the last page of the book. Talk with your child about the shapes he or she drew to decorate the quilt square.

 ### At-Home Activities

- Look for shapes around your home or outdoors.
- Make a shape collage out of fabric scraps.
- Explore fractions at snack times and mealtimes.

 ### Read More About It!

To read more stories about quilts, geometry, or fractions with your child, look for the following books in your local library.

- *My Grandmother's Patchwork Quilt* by Janet Bolton (Delacorte Press, 1993)

- *The Patchwork Quilt* by Valerie Flournoy (Dial Books, 1985)

- *The Quilt-Block History of Pioneer Days* by Mary Cobb (Millbrook, 1995)

- *The Shape of Things* by Dayle Ann Dodds (Candlewick Press, 1994)

 ### Visit Our Web Site!

www.sbgmath.com

H

Name_____ **Space Shapes**

 cube

 sphere

 cone

 rectangular prism

cylinder

Circle the objects with the same shape.
Tell how they are the same.

1.

2.

3.

4.

 Home Connection Have your child look for objects that are shaped like cubes, cones, rectangular prisms, spheres, and cylinders. Encourage your child to use the correct vocabulary.

one hundred twenty-nine **129**

Put an X on the object that does not belong.
Tell why it is different.

1.

2.

3.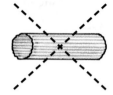

4.

Critical Thinking Corner

Visual Thinking

5. Tell how these shapes are the same.
   Tell how they are different.

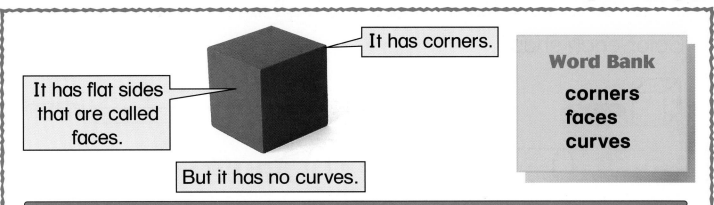

It has corners.

It has flat sides that are called faces.

But it has no curves.

Word Bank

corners
faces
curves

Use shapes if you like.
Does the shape have corners, faces, and curves?
Write **yes** or **no** in each box.

		Corners	Faces	Curves
1.	cube	yes	yes	no
2.	sphere			
3.	rectangular prism			
4.	cylinder			
5.	cone			

Home Connection Give your child different household objects such as a cereal box, a funnel, and a paper-towel roll. Ask whether each shape has corners, faces, and/or curves.

one hundred thirty-one **131**

Color each shape.

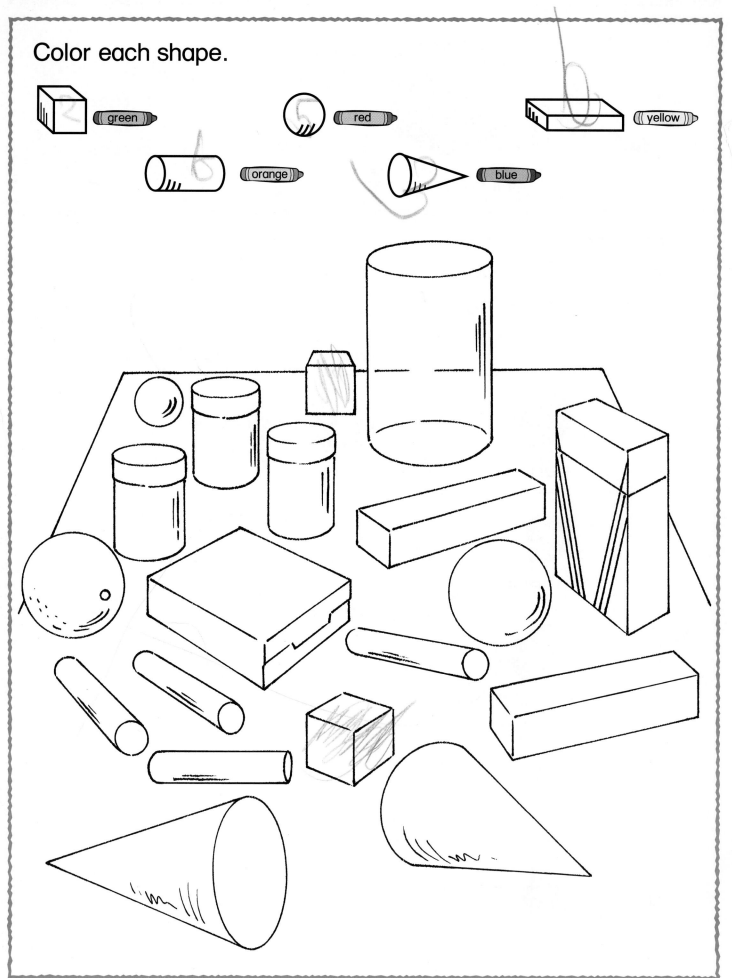

green · red · yellow · orange · blue

Look for a pattern.

Draw and color to show what comes next.

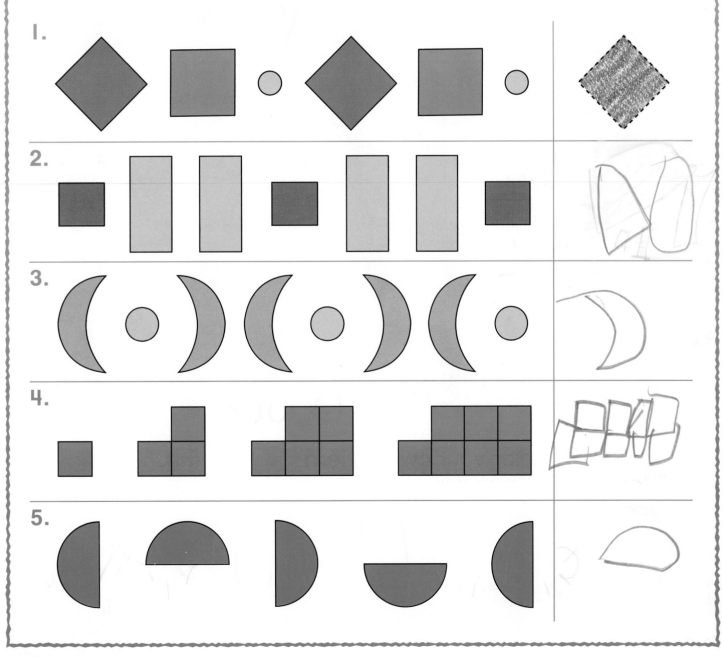

1.

2.

3.

4.

5.

Home Connection With your child, search your home for repeating patterns on floor tiles, wallpaper, and furniture. Encourage your child to describe each pattern.

one hundred thirty-nine **139**

Draw and color to complete the pattern.

1.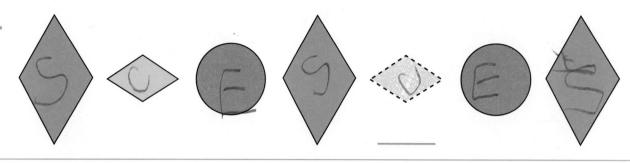

2.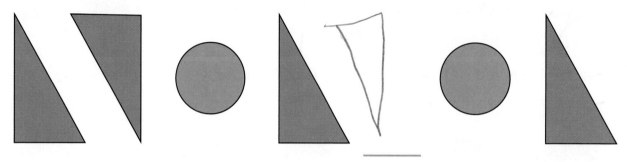

3.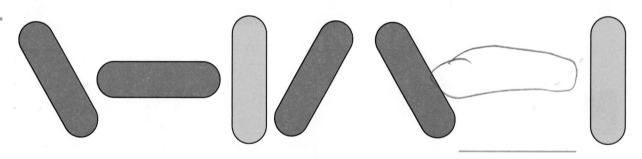

4.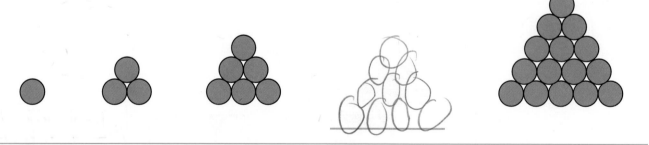

5. Draw and color your own pattern.

RYAN Ryan Ryan

140 one hundred forty

Name_____

7/25/05

These triangles are the same size and the same shape.

Draw a shape that matches.

1.

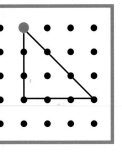

2.

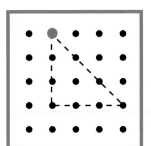 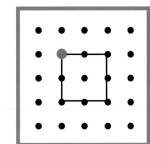 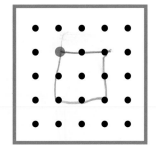

3.

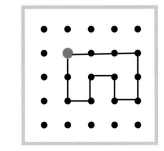 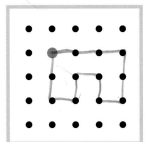 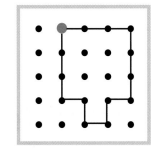 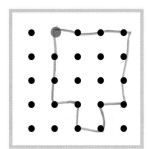

4.

5.

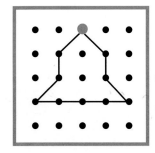 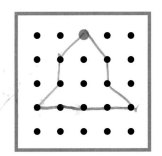 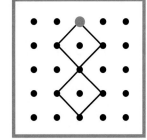 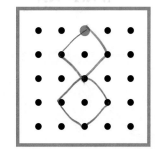

6.

Home Connection Your child is learning to identify shapes that match in size and shape. Help your child find things around the house that are the same size and shape.

Circle the shapes that match.

1.

2.

3.

4.

1. Put an X on the object that does not belong.

2. Color inside the closed figures.

3. Draw and color the missing shape.

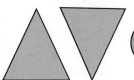   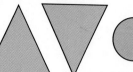 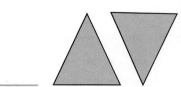

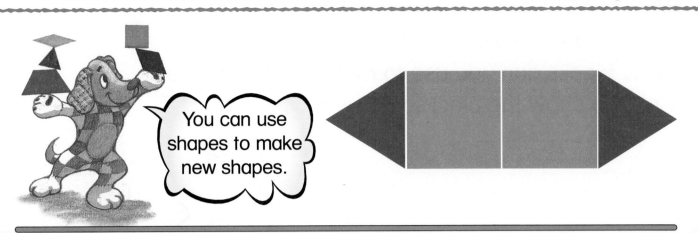

You can use shapes to make new shapes.

Use pattern blocks.

What blocks can you use to make each of these?

Color to show the blocks you use.

1.

2.

3.

4.

5.

6.

 Home Connection Your child has been combining shapes to make new shapes. Look for shapes within shapes around your home and have your child tell you the shapes he or she sees.

Use pattern blocks.
What blocks can you use to make each of these?
Color to show the blocks you use.

1.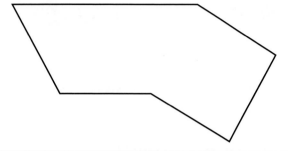

2.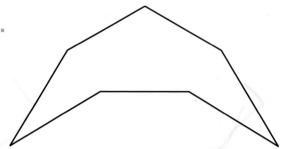

3. Make your own shape with blocks.
Trace around it.
Have a friend find which blocks you used.

Make Your Own

Problem Solving

Use pattern blocks to
make this shape 3 ways.
Color to show each way.

4.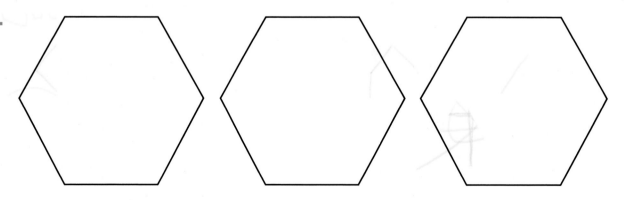

Name_____

Circle the correct shape.

1. I have sides.
   I do not have 4 corners.
   What shape am I?

2. I have 0 sides.
   I have 0 corners.
   What shape am I?

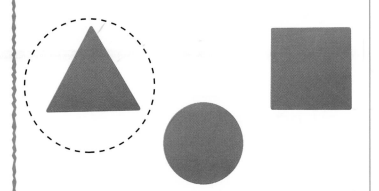
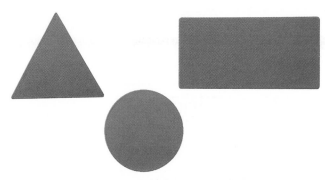

3. I have curves.
   I have faces.
   What shape am I?

4. I have curves.
   I do not have a face.
   What shape am I?

5. I have 4 corners.
   All my sides are the same.
   What shape am I?

6. I have 4 sides.
   I am not a square.
   What shape am I?

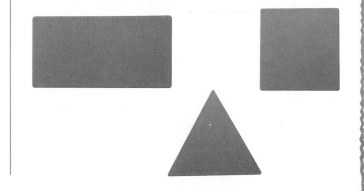

Home Connection Your child has been using logical reasoning to solve shape riddles. Ask your child to create an original shape riddle for you to solve.

one hundred forty-five   **145**

Circle the correct answer.

1. I am a cube.

   I _____ have curves.

   do   (do not)

2. I am a cylinder.

   I _____ have curves.

   do   do not

3. I am a triangle.

   I _____ have 3 corners.

   do   do not

4. I am a rectangle.

   I _____ have 5 sides.

   do   do not

5. I am a circle.

   I _____ have corners.

   do   do not

6. I am a cone.

   I _____ have 2 faces.

   do   do not

7. I am a sphere.
   I _____ have faces.

   do   do not

8. I am a square.
   My sides _____ the same.

   are   are not

Both parts match.

Do both parts match?

Circle the objects with matching parts.

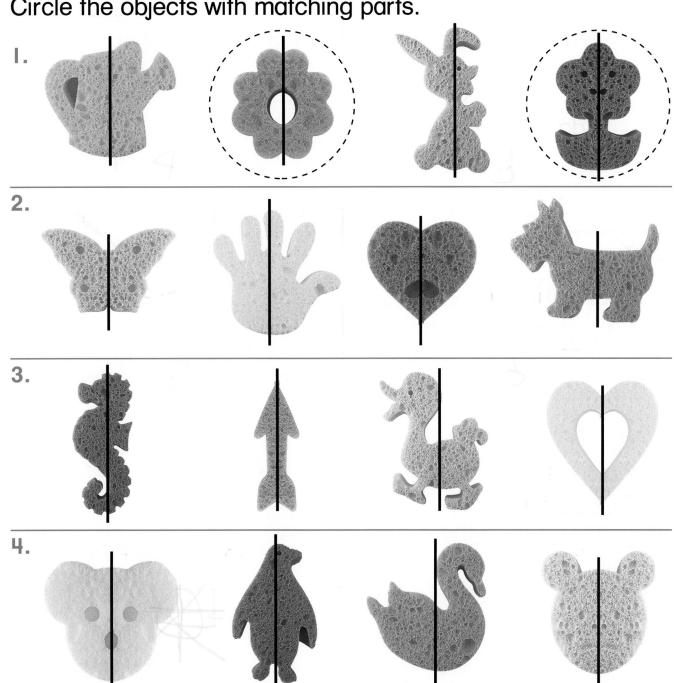

1.

2.

3.

4.

Home Connection Your child is learning to recognize symmetrical objects. Have your child look at home for shapes or objects that are symmetrical.

one hundred forty-seven **147**

Draw a part to match.

1.

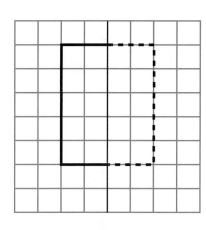

2.

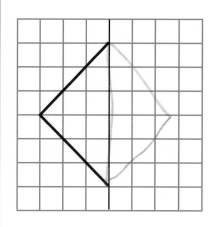

3.

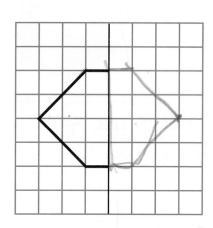

4.

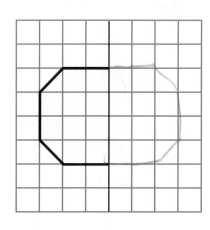

5.

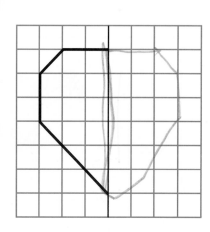

6.

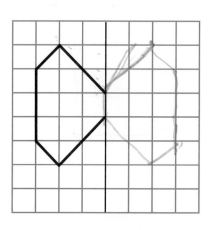

What Do You Think?

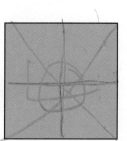

I think there is more than one way to show matching parts of a square. Do you agree? Tell why or why not.

Journal Idea

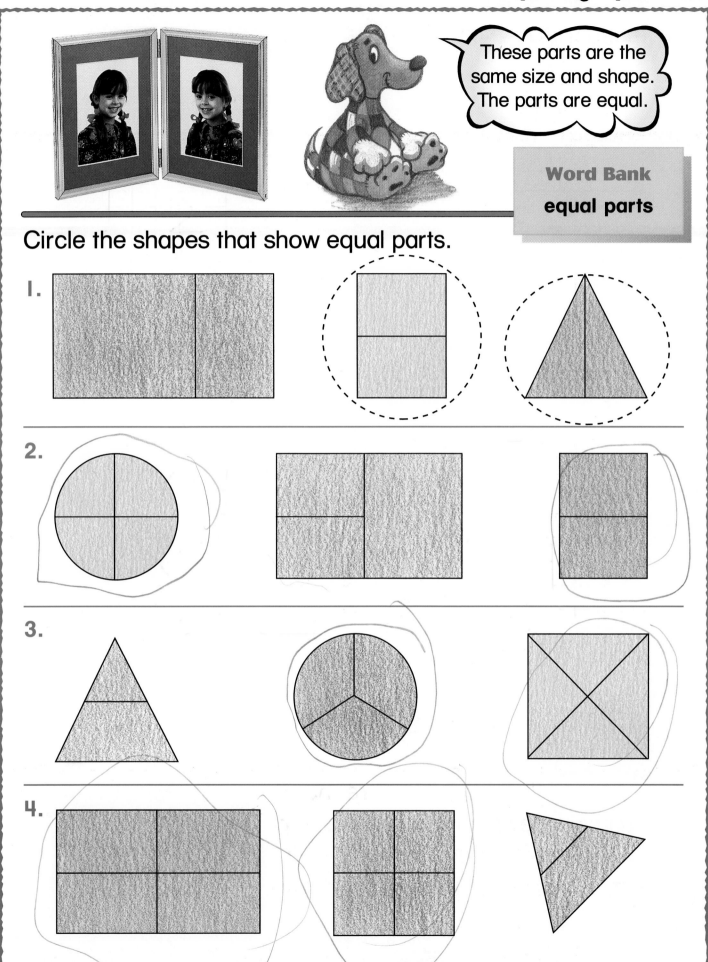

These parts are the same size and shape. The parts are equal.

Word Bank

equal parts

Circle the shapes that show equal parts.

1.

2.

3.

4.

Home Connection Recognizing equal parts helps to understand fractions. Cut out some shapes and fold them in different ways. Ask your child to tell how many equal parts are in each shape.

one hundred forty-nine   **149**

Write the number of equal parts.

1.

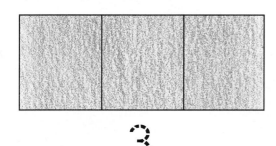

3

2.

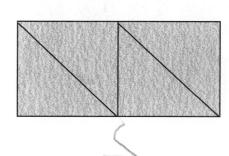

3

3.

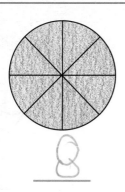

8

4.

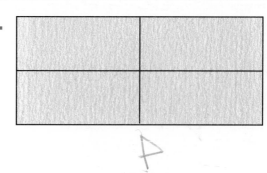

4

5.

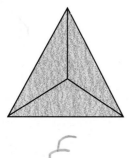

3

6.

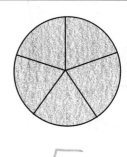

5

 Problem Solving

Solve.

7. Tomás wants to cut this paper into 8 equal parts. Draw lines to show where he could cut.

Name_____ **Exploring Halves**

There are 2 equal parts.
Each part is one half
of the whole.

$\frac{1}{2}$ | $\frac{1}{2}$

Word Bank

one half

Circle each shape that shows halves.

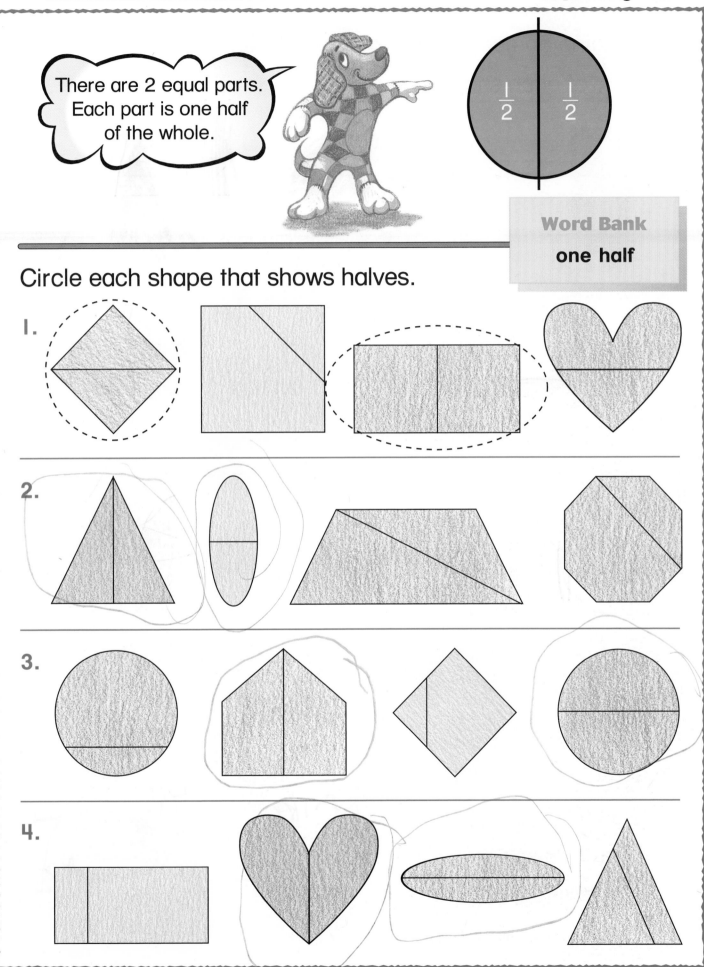

1.

2.

3.

4.

Home Connection Your child is learning to recognize
halves. Help your child cut paper shapes into two parts. Make
some parts equal. Ask your child to tell which shapes show halves.

one hundred fifty-one   151

Draw a line on each shape to show halves.
Color $\frac{1}{2}$ of each shape.

1.

2.

3.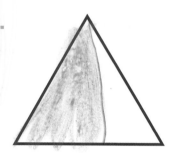

4.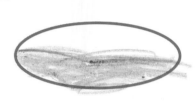

5.

6.

7.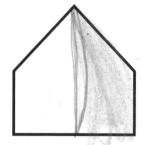

8.

9.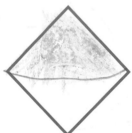

Critical Thinking Corner

Number Sense

10. Andy has $\frac{1}{2}$ of a sandwich.

Eva has $\frac{1}{2}$ of a sandwich.

Eva says she has more than Andy.

Could she be right?

 Tell why or why not.

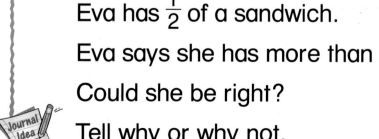

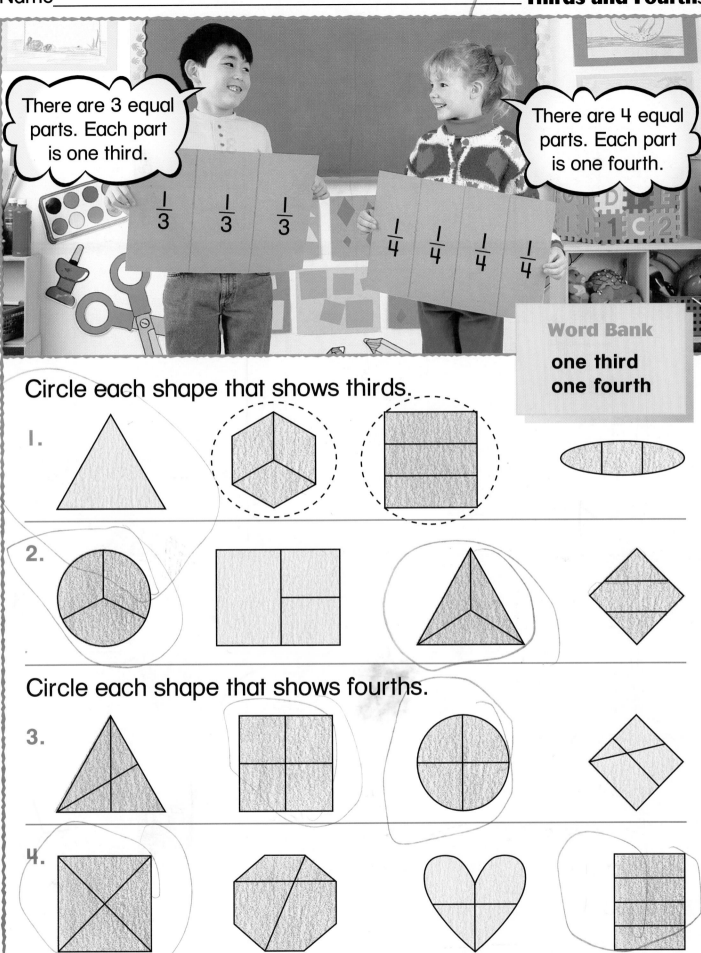

There are 3 equal parts. Each part is one third.

There are 4 equal parts. Each part is one fourth.

$\frac{1}{3}$ $\frac{1}{3}$ $\frac{1}{3}$

$\frac{1}{4}$ $\frac{1}{4}$ $\frac{1}{4}$ $\frac{1}{4}$

Word Bank

one third
one fourth

Circle each shape that shows thirds.

1.

Circle each shape that shows fourths.

3.

4.

Home Connection Help your child make paper shapes and then fold or cut them to show thirds and fourths.

Color $\frac{1}{3}$ of each shape.

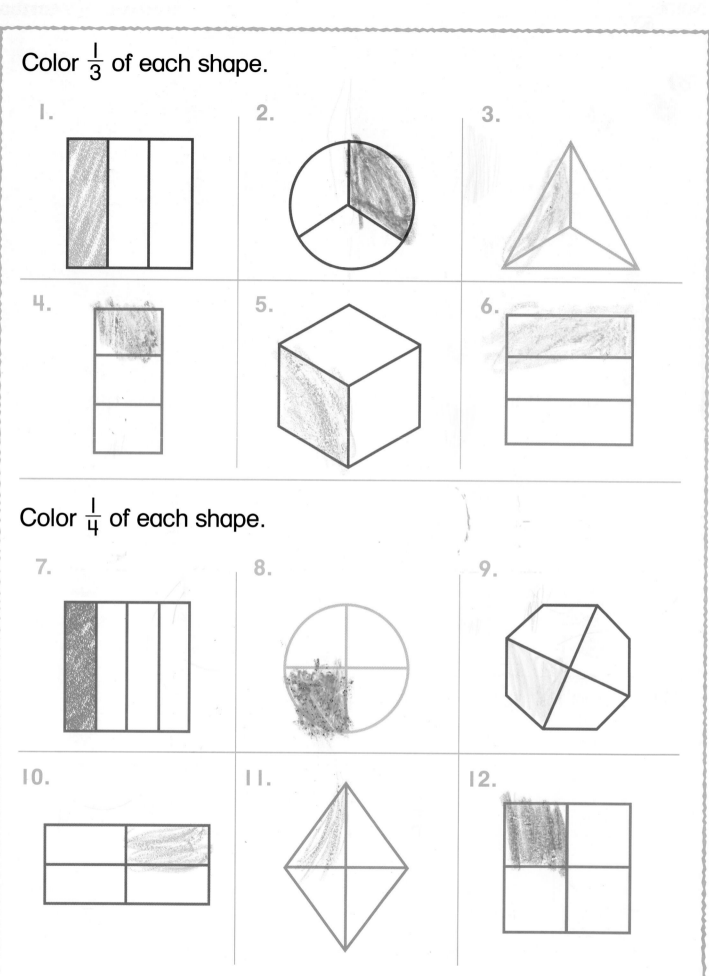

1.

2.

3.

4.

5.

6.

Color $\frac{1}{4}$ of each shape.

7.

8.

9.

10.

11.

12.

There are 3 pompoms.
One is blue.
One third of the group
is blue.

$\frac{1}{3}$ is blue.

What part is blue?
Circle the fraction.

1.

$\frac{1}{2}$ $\frac{1}{3}$ $\left(\frac{1}{4}\right)$

2.

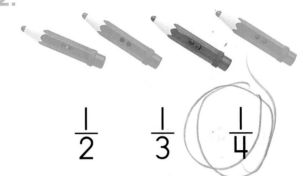

$\frac{1}{2}$ $\frac{1}{3}$ $\frac{1}{4}$

3.

$\left(\frac{1}{2}\right)$ $\frac{1}{3}$ $\frac{1}{4}$

4.

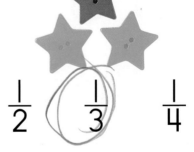

$\frac{1}{2}$ $\left(\frac{1}{3}\right)$ $\frac{1}{4}$

5.

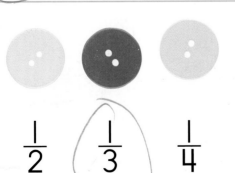

$\frac{1}{2}$ $\left(\frac{1}{3}\right)$ $\frac{1}{4}$

6.

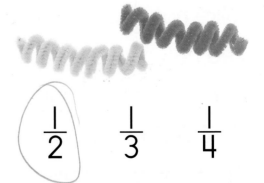

$\left(\frac{1}{2}\right)$ $\frac{1}{3}$ $\frac{1}{4}$

Home Connection Your child is learning to identify fractions of a group. Show your child 2, 3, or 4 identical objects. Have your child identify $\frac{1}{2}$, $\frac{1}{3}$, or $\frac{1}{4}$ of them.

one hundred fifty-five   **155**

Color to show each fraction.

1. $\frac{1}{3}$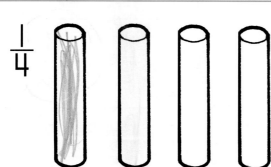

2. $\frac{1}{2}$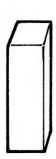

3. $\frac{1}{4}$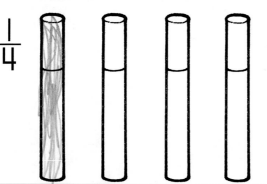

4. $\frac{1}{3}$

5. $\frac{1}{4}$

6. $\frac{1}{2}$

 Problem Solving

Solve.

7. Mike has $\frac{1}{3}$ of a jar of paint.

   Lee has $\frac{1}{4}$ of a jar of paint.

   The jars are the same size.

   Who has more paint? _____

   Tell how you know.

Name_____

Circle each child's fair share.
Use counters if you like.

1. 2 children

2. 4 children

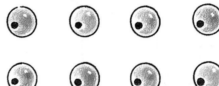

3. 3 children

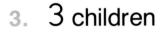
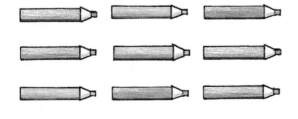

4. 6 children

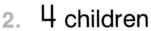
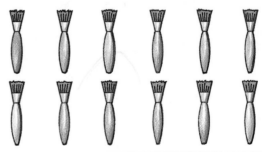

5. 4 children

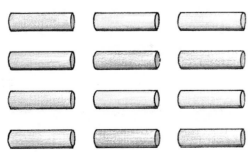

6. 5 children

Home Connection Your child is learning
how to share groups equally. Use food items
such as crackers or grapes to make fair shares.

one hundred fifty-seven   **157**

Does each picture show fair shares for two?
Circle **yes** or **no**.

1.
yes   no

2. 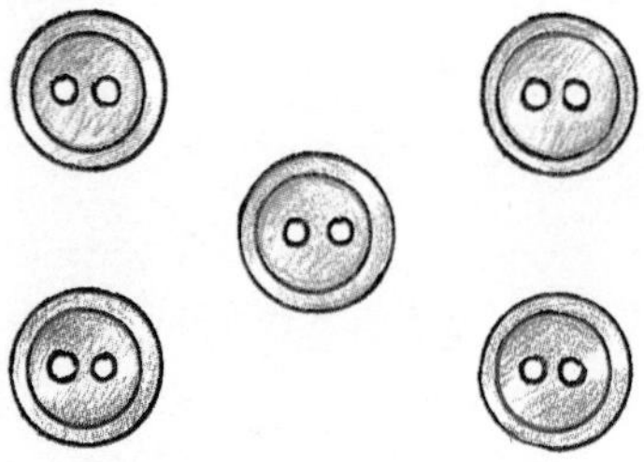
yes   no

3. 
yes   no

4. 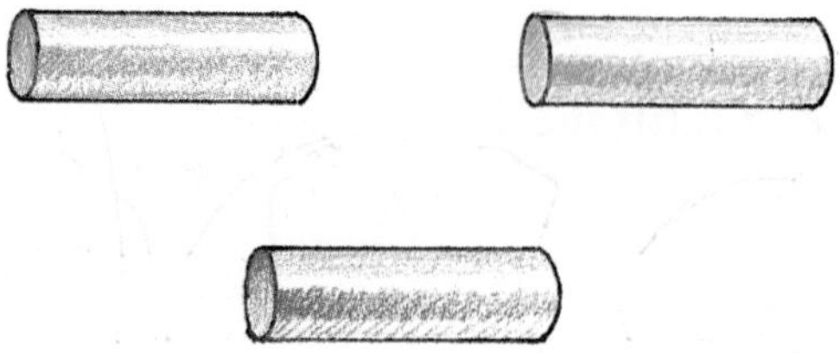
yes   no

5. 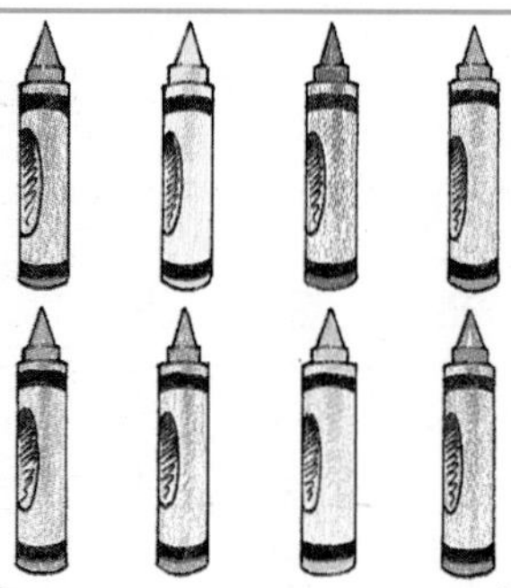
yes   no

6. 
yes   no

7. 
yes   no

8. 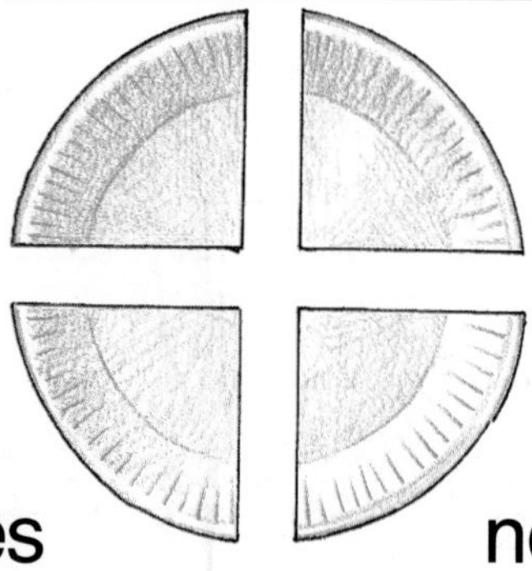
yes   no

Circle the objects with the same shape.

1.

Write the number of sides and corners.

2.  _____ sides
_____ corners

3.  _____ sides
_____ corners

Color inside the closed figures.

4.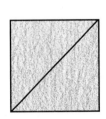

Write the number of equal parts.

5.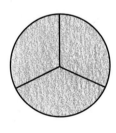
_____

6.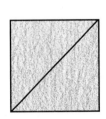
_____

7.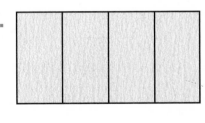
_____

Circle fair shares for 4 children.

8.

Name_____

What You Need

can    block

① Trace a face of each object.

② Look at the shape you made.

③ Write how many corners and sides.

_____ sides
_____ corners

_____ sides
_____ corners

④ Draw a line on one shape
to show 2 equal parts.
Color $\frac{1}{2}$.

⑤ Draw lines on the other shape
to show 4 equal parts.
Color $\frac{1}{4}$.

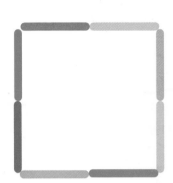

Count how many around.

1.

_____ around

2.

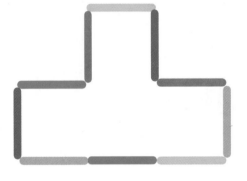

_____ around

3.

_____ around

4.

_____ around

5.

_____ around

6.

_____ around

Name_____

You can use the MathProcessor to show fractions.

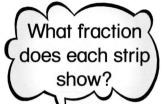

What fraction does each strip show?

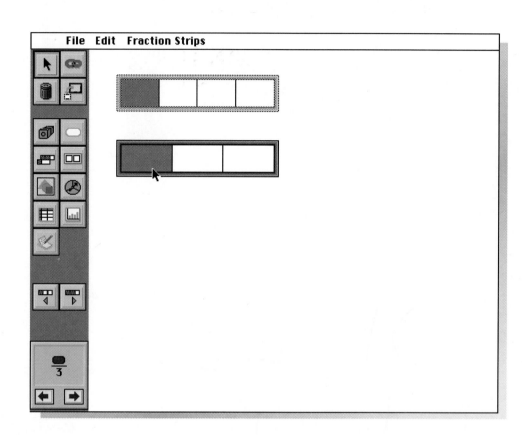

Work with a partner.

1 Click on the **fraction strip button** to show a fraction strip.

2 Click on the **arrow** to tell how many equal parts. Then click on the **number**.

3 Click on one part of the **fraction strip.** What fraction did you show?

Show other fractions.
Tell about the number of equal parts.

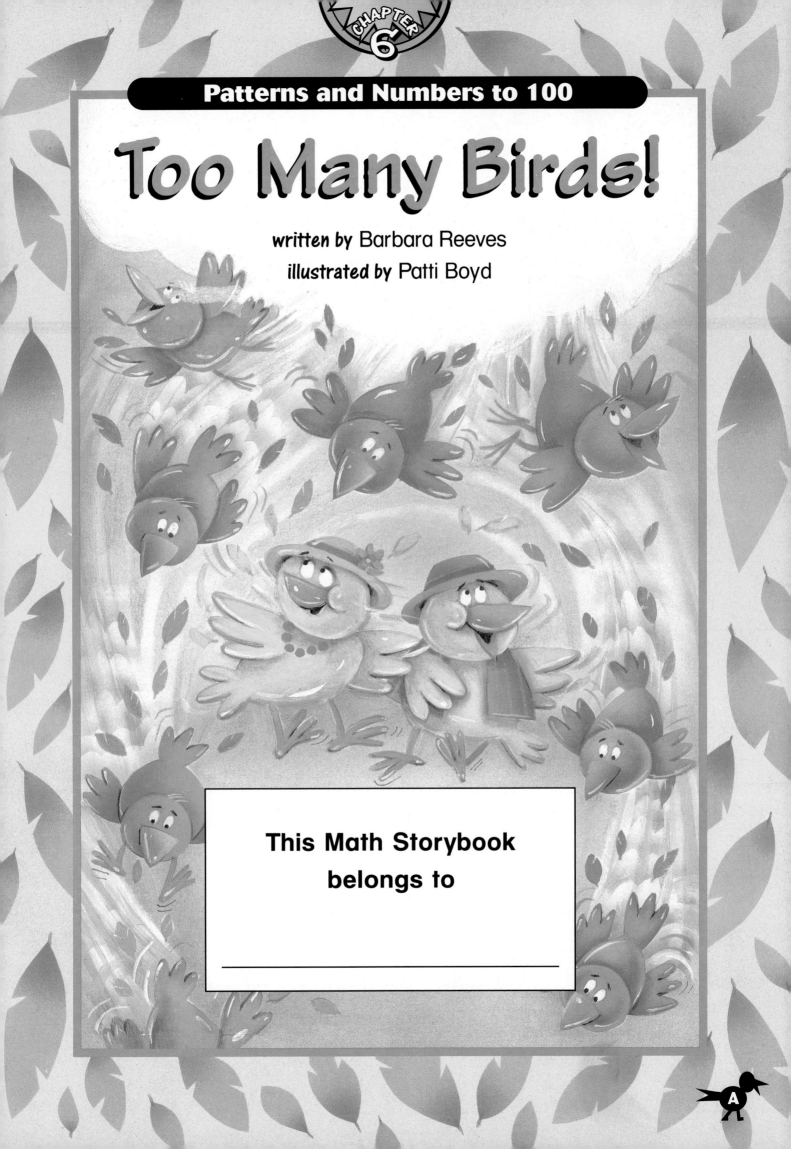

Too Many Birds!

written by Barbara Reeves

illustrated by Patti Boyd

This Math Storybook

belongs to

_____

Our tiny little treehouse
had lots of room for 2.

But when 10 friends moved in with us,
we looked for someplace new!

Our new two-story dream house
had room enough for 20.

When 10 more friends moved in with us,
there were 2 birds too many!

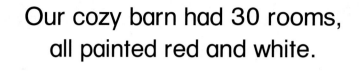

Our cozy barn had 30 rooms,
all painted red and white.

When 10 more friends moved in with us,
the space was very tight!

Our 50-room apartment house
has friends both up and down.

Now 10 more friends are on the way.
Maybe we'll leave town!

How many birds are in this house? _____

How many more will fit? _____

Draw some birds to fill the house.

Now how many birds are in it? _____

A Note to the Family

Here are some learning ideas you can share with your child.

Enjoy *Too Many Birds!* Together

- Read the story with your child. After sharing each page, count the number of birds in the birdhouse. Help your child recognize that there are ten birds in each row. Ask how many birds are left over.

- Your child can act out the story using counters, coins, or small pasta shapes to represent birds. Your child can fill the rooms in the story illustrations to show how the visiting birds fill the birdhouses and to demonstrate what happens to the two original birds.

- Discuss the questions on the last page of *Too Many Birds!* Ask your child how drawing the birds in the boxes helped him or her answer the questions.

At-Home Activity

- You and your child can begin a collection of hundreds. Pennies, milk caps, rubber bands, or bread tags are ideal choices. Encourage your child to make groups of ten to help make counting fun and easy.

Read More About It!

To continue to explore numbers to 100 with your child, look for the following books in your local library.

- *Anno's Counting Book* by Mitsumasa Anno (Harper, 1986)

- *One Watermelon Seed* by Celia Barker Lottridge (Oxford, 1986)

- *Richard Scarry's Best Counting Book Ever* by Richard Scarry (Random House, 1975)

Visit Our Web Site!

www.sbgmath.com

Use ▭▭▭▭▭▭▭▭▭, ▪, and Workmat 5.
Build and write each number.

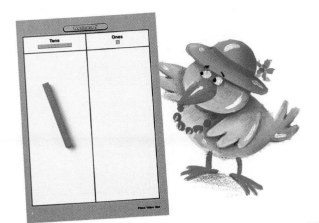

1. 1 ten 0 ones 10   ten

2. 1 ten 1 one ____   eleven

3. 1 ten 2 ones ____   twelve

4. 1 ten 3 ones ____   thirteen

5. 1 ten 4 ones ____   fourteen

6. 1 ten 5 ones ____   fifteen

7. 1 ten 6 ones ____   sixteen

8. 1 ten 7 ones ____   seventeen

9. 1 ten 8 ones ____   eighteen

10. 1 ten 9 ones ____   nineteen

Home Connection Your child is learning to show any number from 11–19 as one ten and some ones. Have your child use small objects to show the numbers on this page.

Write how many.

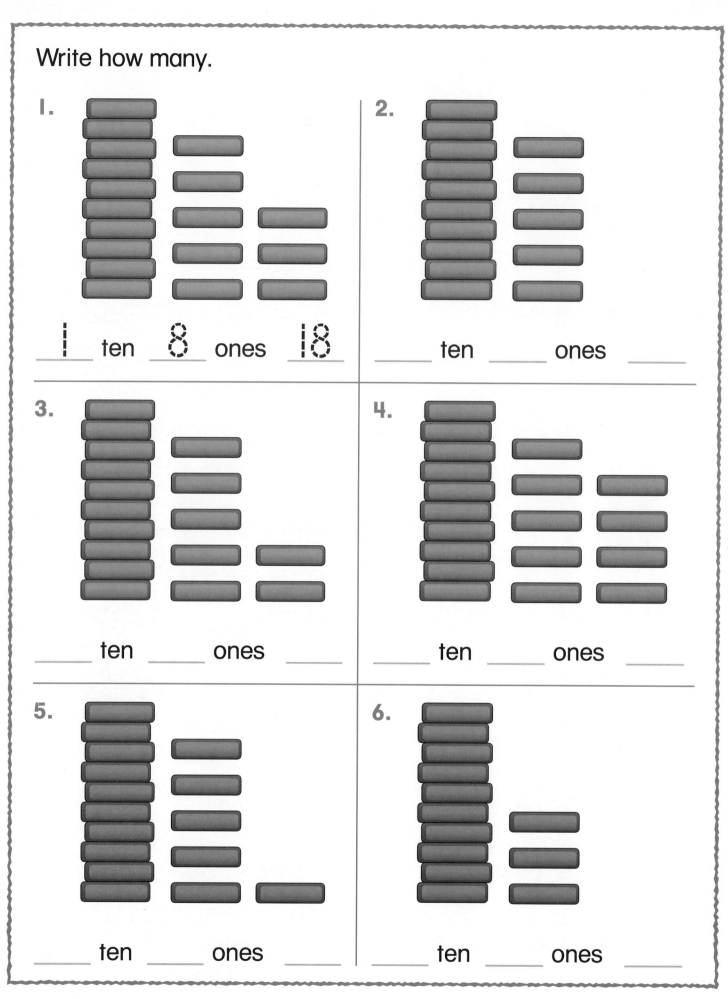

1. ___1___ ten ___8___ ones ___18___

2. _____ ten _____ ones _____

3. _____ ten _____ ones _____

4. _____ ten _____ ones _____

5. _____ ten _____ ones _____

6. _____ ten _____ ones _____

 **____** group of ten = **10**

Circle groups of ten.
Write how many.

1.

____ groups of ten = ____

2.

____ groups of ten = ____

3.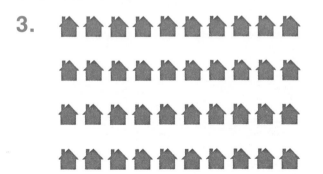

____ groups of ten = ____

4.

____ groups of ten = ____

Home Connection Have your child make groups of ten at home, using toys, coins, or crayons. Help your child count to see how many he or she has in all.

Circle groups of ten.
Write how many.

1.

_____

2.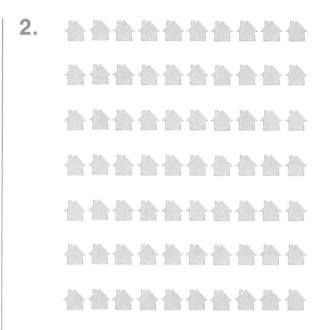

_____

3.

_____

4.

_____

Name_____

You can show numbers with tens and ones.

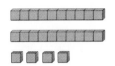

24 ones **=** **2** tens **4** ones

Use  , ▫ , and Workmat 5.
Build the number with ones.
Then regroup as tens. Write how many.

1.	15	I5 ones	I ten	5 ones
2.	22	_____ ones	_____ tens	_____ ones
3.	11	_____ ones	_____ ten	_____ one
4.	18	_____ ones	_____ ten	_____ ones
5.	20	_____ ones	_____ tens	_____ ones

Home Connection Regrouping 10 ones as 1 ten helps
children to understand two-digit numbers. Encourage your child
to tell you how he or she regrouped ones as tens on this page.

Write how many.

1.

Tens	Ones
1	2

= 12

2.

Tens	Ones

= _____

3.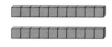

Tens	Ones

= _____

4.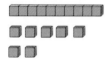

Tens	Ones

= _____

5.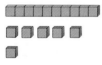

Tens	Ones

= _____

6.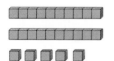

Tens	Ones

= _____

Problem Solving

Solve.

7. Jake has 2 tens and 4 ones.
   Ann has 2 more tens than Jake.
   How many does Ann have?   _____ tens _____ ones

Write how many.

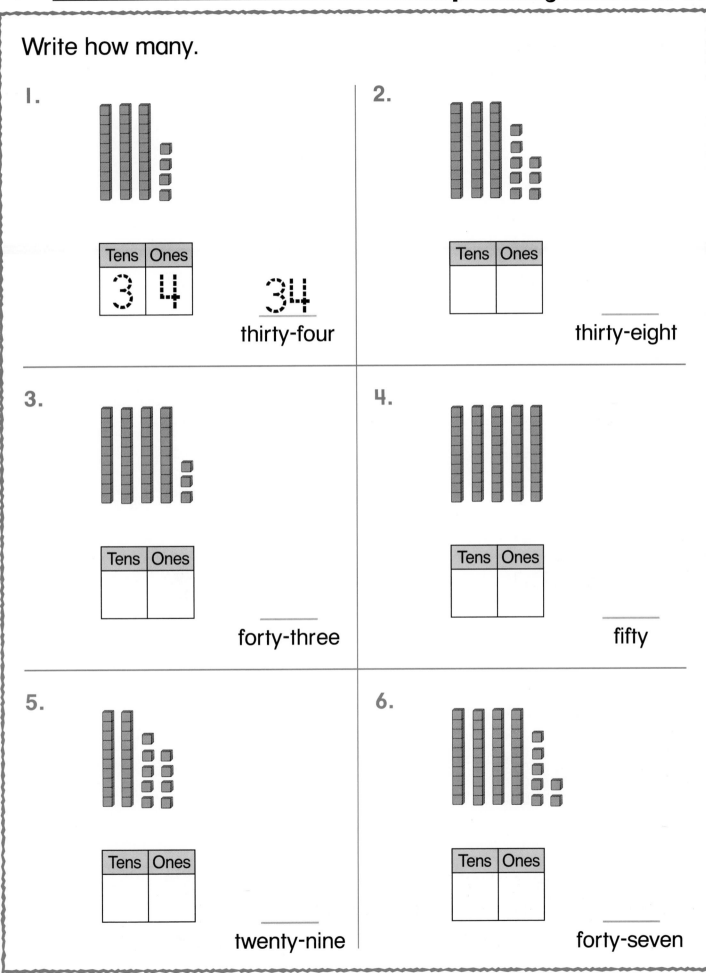

1.

Tens	Ones
3	4

34
thirty-four

2.

Tens	Ones

_____
thirty-eight

3.

Tens	Ones

_____
forty-three

4.

Tens	Ones

_____
fifty

5.

Tens	Ones

_____
twenty-nine

6.

Tens	Ones

_____
forty-seven

Home Connection It is important to know that two-digit numbers can be expressed as tens and ones. Ask your child to tell the number of tens and ones in numbers like 42 or 36.

one hundred seventy-one   **171**

Write how many.

1.

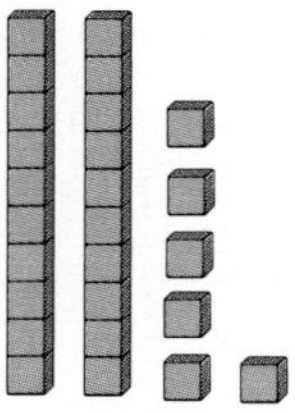

Tens	Ones
2	6

26

2.

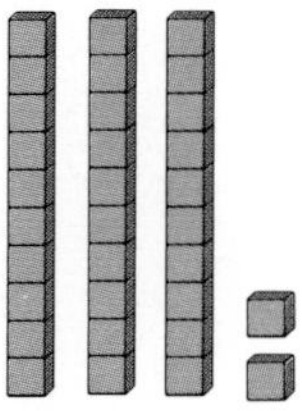

Tens	Ones

_____

3.

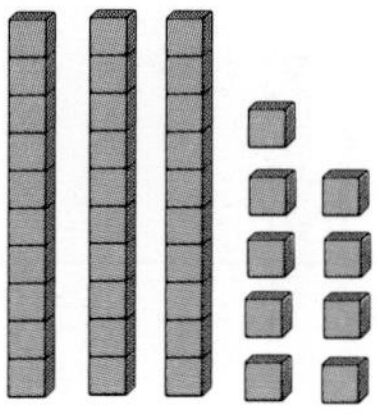

Tens	Ones

_____

4.

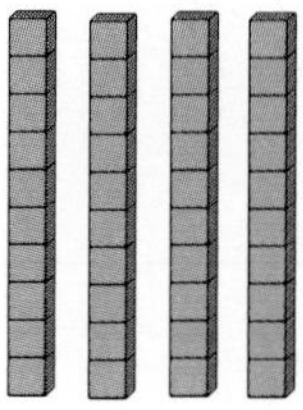

Tens	Ones

_____

5.

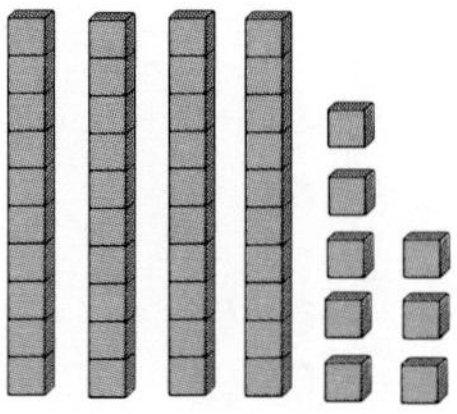

Tens	Ones

_____

6.

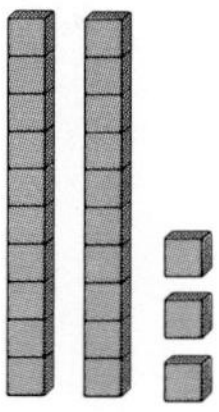

Tens	Ones

_____

There are 10 bees in each hive.

__5__ tens and __7__ ones is __57__.

fifty-seven

Write how many.

1.

Tens	Ones
6	4

64
sixty-four

2.

Tens	Ones

eighty-six

3.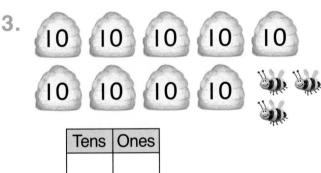

Tens	Ones

____
ninety-three

4.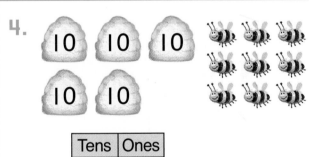

Tens	Ones

____
fifty-nine

5.

Tens	Ones

____
seventy-eight

6.

Tens	Ones

____
forty-five

Home Connection Tell your child a number of tens and ones and ask him or her to tell you the number in all. For example, "What is eight tens and three ones?" (83)

Write how many.

1.

Tens	Ones
5	3

53

2.

Tens	Ones

_____

3.

Tens	Ones

_____

4.

Tens	Ones

_____

5.

Tens	Ones

_____

6.

Tens	Ones

_____

I think 10 tens makes 100.
Do you agree? Tell why or why not.

174   one hundred seventy-four

Name _____

How can you show 33?

33

3 tens 3 ones

Use , , and Workmat 5.
Build and write each number.

1.	7 tens 6 ones	2.	1 ten 9 ones
	76		_____
3.	4 tens 0 ones	4.	5 tens 8 ones
	_____		_____
5.	8 tens 3 ones	6.	3 tens 5 ones
	_____		_____
7.	9 tens 6 ones	8.	2 tens 3 ones
	_____		_____

Home Connection Ask your child to use numbers or words to express two-digit numbers in ways illustrated on this page.

Match.

1.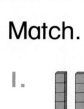
2.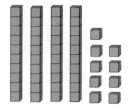
3.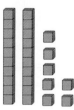

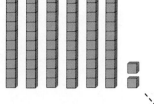 27

 62

Tens	Ones
6	2

Tens	Ones
4	9

 49

Tens	Ones
2	7

4.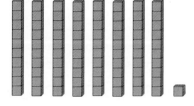
5.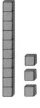
6.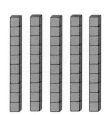

13

50

81

Tens	Ones
8	1

Tens	Ones
1	3

Tens	Ones
5	0

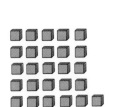  

You can show 26 in different ways.

26 ones $=$ 1 ten 16 ones $=$ 2 tens 6 ones

Use ▭▭▭▭▭ , ▫ , and Workmat 5.

Build each number one way.

Then regroup to show each number another way.

Record the ways.

1. 32	_3_ tens _2_ ones	_2_ tens _12_ ones
2. 25	____ tens ____ ones	____ tens ____ ones
3. 17	____ tens ____ ones	____ tens ____ ones
4. 28	____ tens ____ ones	____ tens ____ ones
5. 14	____ tens ____ ones	____ tens ____ ones
6. 33	____ tens ____ ones	____ tens ____ ones

Home Connection Children use models to show the same number different ways. Ask your child to draw models to show numbers like 36 or 59 in two ways.

one hundred seventy-seven   **177**

Use , 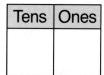 , and Workmat 5.

Build each number.

Regroup to show other ways.

Record the ways.

1. 32

Tens	Ones

Tens	Ones

Tens	Ones

2. 26

Tens	Ones

Tens	Ones

Tens	Ones

3. 45

Tens	Ones

Tens	Ones

Tens	Ones

Write how many.   **Checkpoint**

1.

_____ ten _____ ones _____

2.

_____ groups of ten = _____

3.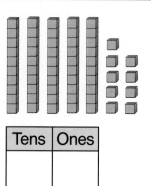

Tens	Ones

_____

4.

Tens	Ones

_____

Problem-Solving Strategy
Guess and Check

Understand
Plan
Solve
Look Back

Name_____

How many are there?

I guessed 20.
Then I
counted 23.

Guess how many.
Then circle tens
and count.

1.

Guess

Count

2.

Guess

Count

Home Connection Have your child estimate the number
of books on a shelf or pennies in a jar. Using 10 as a benchmark
will help your child make a better estimate.

Guess how many. Then circle tens and count.

1.

Guess

Count

2.

Guess

Count

3.

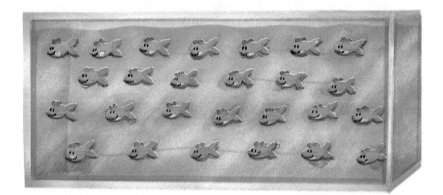

Guess

Count

Critical Thinking Corner

Mental Math

4. There are 5 .

Each has 10 🐭 .

How many 🐭 are there in all? _____ in all

Tell how you know.

35 is greater than 22.
22 is less than 35.

35

22

Use ⬛⬛⬛⬛⬛⬛⬛⬛⬛⬛ and ◼ to build each number.
Circle **greater than** or **less than**.

1.
44 is greater than 51.
(less than)

2.
67 is greater than 62.
less than

3.
87 is greater than 78.
less than

4.
30 is greater than 32.
less than

5.
23 is greater than 25.
less than

6.
54 is greater than 45.
less than

7.
36 is greater than 26.
less than

8.
74 is greater than 79.
less than

Home Connection Ask your child to give examples of numbers that are greater than 51 and numbers that are less than 78.

one hundred eighty-one   **181**

Circle the greater number.

Use ▭▭▭▭▭▭▭▭ and ▫ if you like.

1. 46   (51)

2. 82   75

3. 98   95

4. 65   56

5. 10   100

6. 39   40

Circle the number that is less.

7. (35)   52

8. 15   12

9. 98   89

10. 54   59

11. 20   28

12. 72   75

Problem Solving

13. Timmy has 8 🖍️[10] and 7 🖍️.

Alicia has 7 🖍️[10] and 8 🖍️.

Who has more crayons? _____

Tell how you know.

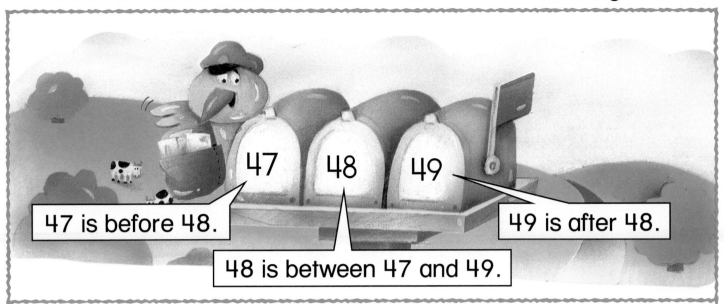

47 is before 48.

49 is after 48.

48 is between 47 and 49.

Write each number that comes after.

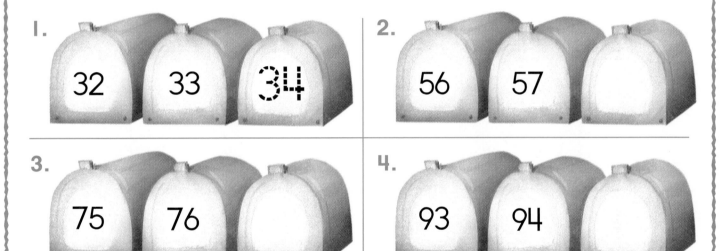

1. | 32 | 33 | 3̶4̶ |

2. | 56 | 57 | |

3. | 75 | 76 | |

4. | 93 | 94 | |

Write each number that comes before.

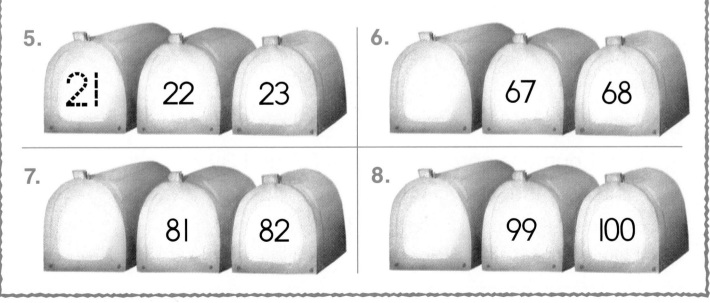

5. | 2̶1̶ | 22 | 23 |

6. | | 67 | 68 |

7. | | 81 | 82 |

8. | | 99 | 100 |

Home Connection Invite your child to count with you from 1 to 100. Talk about numbers that come before, after, and between other numbers.

one hundred eighty-three **183**

Write each number that comes between.

1.
45 | 46 | 47

2.
60 | | 62

3.
13 | | 15

4.
88 | | 90

Write each number that comes before and after.

5.
| 38 |

6.
| 72 |

7.
| 99 |

8.
| 50 |

Critical Thinking Corner

Number Sense

9. What number comes between 37 and 39? _____
   What number do you think
   comes between 137 and 139? _____
   Tell why you think that.

1. Write the missing numbers.

2. Color numbers with 9 ones 〔green〕.

3. Color numbers with 0 ones 〔blue〕.

4. Color numbers with 2 tens 〔red〕.

You can find patterns in numbers.

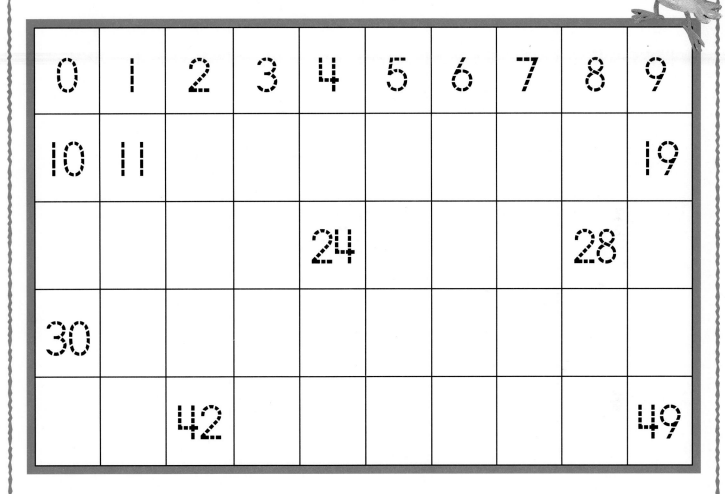

0	1	2	3	4	5	6	7	8	9
10	11								19
				24				28	
30									
		42							49

Use the chart to complete each pattern.

5. 🏠1 🏠3 🏠5 🏠7 🏠 🏠 🏠

6. 🏠5 🏠10 🏠15 🏠20 🏠 🏠 🏠

Home Connection Look at the chart with your child. Have your child tell you how numbers in one row change. Then talk about how numbers in one column change.

1. Write the missing numbers.

2. Color numbers with 3 ones red.

3. Color numbers with 6 tens blue.

4. Color numbers with 0 ones green.

50	51								
60									
				75					
80									
									99

Problem Solving

Solve.

5. Look for other patterns on the chart.
Use yellow to color one pattern.
Tell about your pattern.

Make Your Own

Name_____

1. Skip count by twos.

2   4   ___   ___   ___

2. Skip count by fives.

5   10   ___   ___   ___

3. Skip count by tens.

10   20   ___   ___   ___

Home Connection Invite your child to skip count aloud by twos, fives, and tens. Help your child count to 50 or above.

1. Skip count by twos. Circle the numbers.

2. Skip count by fives. Put an X on the numbers.

3. Skip count by tens. Color the numbers ⟨ red ⟩ .

0	1	2	3	4	5	6	7	8	9
10	11	12	13	14	15	16	17	18	19
20	21	22	23	24	25	26	27	28	29
30	31	32	33	34	35	36	37	38	39
40	41	42	43	44	45	46	47	48	49
50	51	52	53	54	55	56	57	58	59
60	61	62	63	64	65	66	67	68	69
70	71	72	73	74	75	76	77	78	79
80	81	82	83	84	85	86	87	88	89
90	91	92	93	94	95	96	97	98	99

4. Tell about the numbers that have only an X.

5. Tell about the numbers you colored ⟨ red ⟩ .

6. Tell about other patterns you see.

Problem-Solving Application
Choosing Reasonable Answers

Understand
Plan
Look Back
Solve

Name _____

This is Tiwa.
She lives here.

Circle the number that makes sense.

1. Tiwa's home has (6) or 60 rooms.

2. There are 4 or 45 chairs in the kitchen.

3. Tiwa's bedroom has 82 or 2 windows.

4. There are 3 or 33 lamps in the living room.

5. Grandfather is 7 or 75 years old.

6. Mom reads a newspaper with 2 or 72 pages.

Home Connection Your child is learning to choose reasonable answers. Ask your child similar word problems about your own home. Then invite your child to think of problems for you to answer.

one hundred eighty-nine **189**

This is Jordan. He lives in this apartment building.

Circle the number that makes sense.

1. This building has 3 or (30) rooms.

2. Jordan has 2 or 21 bathrooms in his apartment.

3. There are 49 or 4 beds in his home.

4. Jordan has 6 or 68 chairs in his living room.

5. Jordan shares his home with 3 or 93 people.

6. Jordan's little sister is 55 or 5 years old.

190 one hundred ninety

Circle the greater number.

1. ⟨86⟩   84 | 2.   63   69

Circle the number that is less.

3. ⟨74⟩   64 | 4.   32   23

Write the missing numbers.

5.  42 43 __

6.  __ 53 54

7.  36 __ 38

8. 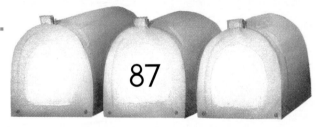 __ 87 __

Skip count by twos.

9.

2   4   __   __   __

Guess how many.
Then circle tens and count.

10.

Guess

Count

Connect the dots in order.
Start at 31.

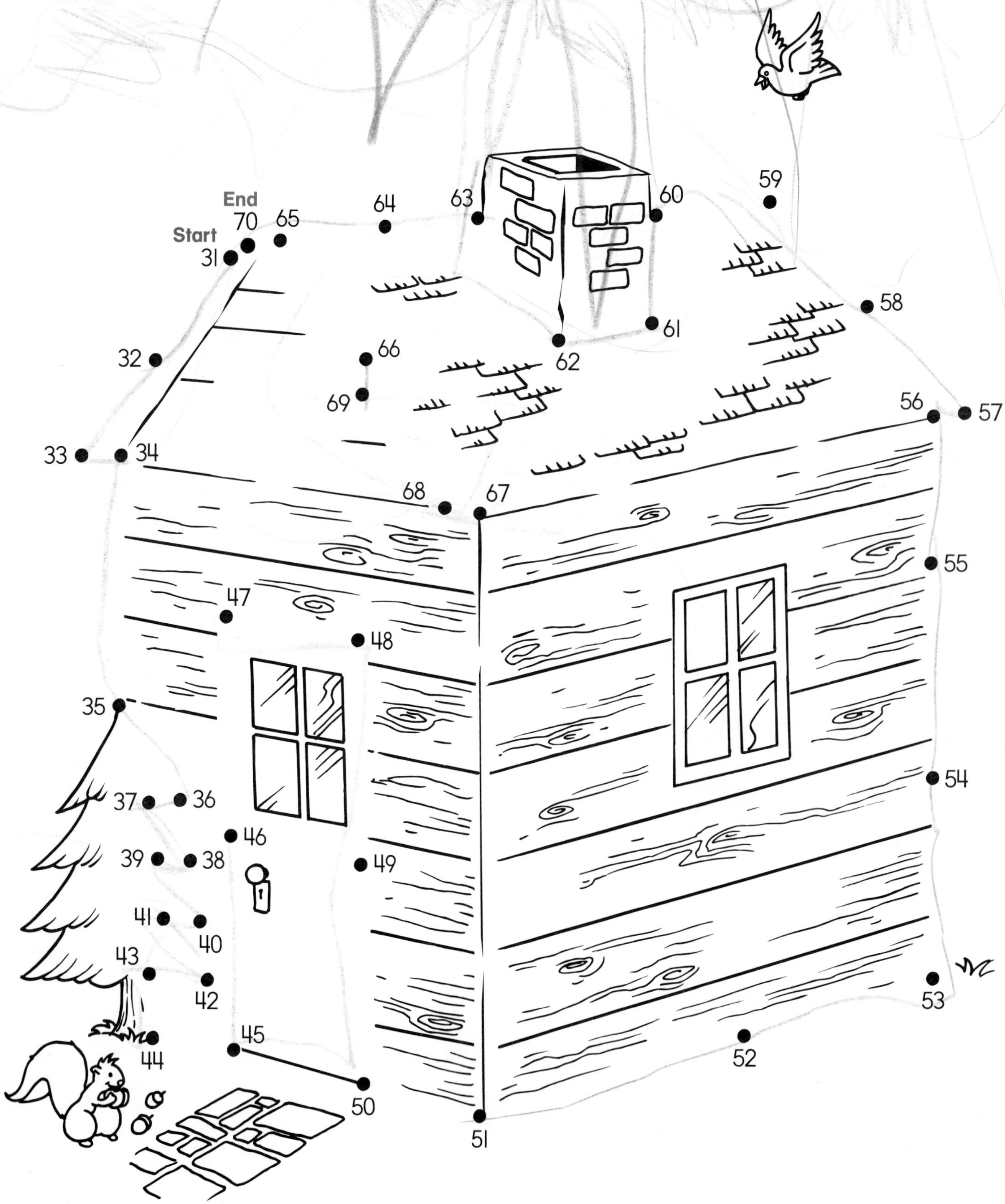

End
Start

64
63
59
60
70 65
31
58
32
66
61
69
62
33 34
56 57
68 67
55
47
48
35
54
37 36
46
39 38
49
41
40
53
43
42
52
45
44
51
50

Write how many.

1.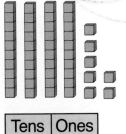

Tens	Ones

= _____

2.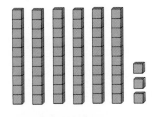

Tens	Ones

= _____

3. **46** _____ tens _____ ones

4. **89** _____ tens _____ ones

Write the missing numbers.

5.

25	26	

6.

	92	93

Circle **greater than** or **less than**.

7. 76 is   greater than / less than   79.

8. 32 is   greater than / less than   35.

Skip count by fives.

9.

5   10   ___   ___   ___   ___

Circle the number that makes sense.

10. Shannon drank   3   or   31   glasses of milk today.

Name_____

What You Need

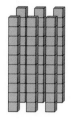

tens   ones

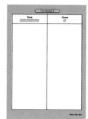

Workmat 5

number cube

① Roll the number cube. Show that many tens.

② Roll again. Show that many ones.

③ Write how many tens and ones.

④ Write the number in all.

1. _____ tens _____ ones _____ in all	2. _____ tens _____ ones _____ in all
3. _____ tens _____ ones _____ in all	4. _____ tens _____ ones _____ in all
5. _____ tens _____ ones _____ in all	6. _____ tens _____ ones _____ in all

Look at the numbers you recorded.

7. What is the greatest number? _____

8. What is the least number? _____

Use the number cards below to make numbers.
Use two cards to make each number.
Write the greatest number.
Write the least number.

1.

$$\underline{85}$$ $$\underline{45}$$
greatest   least

2.

_____ _____
greatest   least

3.

_____ _____
greatest   least

4.

_____ _____
greatest   least

5.

_____ _____
greatest   least

You can use a  to show two-digit numbers.

Remember to enter the tens first!

5 tens and 6 ones

Press ON/C

Show each number on the .

Record the keys. Write the number.

1. 7 tens and 2 ones

   Press ON/C

   72

2. 1 one and 4 tens

   Press ON/C

   ____

3. 9 tens and 7 ones

   Press ON/C

   ____

4. 4 ones and 6 tens

   Press ON/C

   ____

5.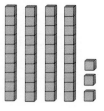

   Press ON/C

   ____

6.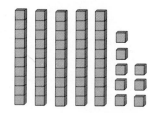

   Press ON/C

   ____

Name_____

Fill in the ⬭ for the correct answer.
How many are there?

1.

⬭	⬭	⬭	⬭
7	6	8	5

2.

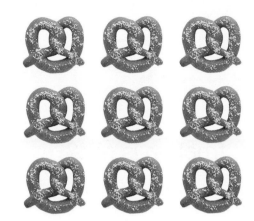

⬭	⬭	⬭	⬭
8	9	10	7

Add or subtract.

3.
$$\begin{array}{r} 3 \\ + 5 \\ \hline \end{array}$$
⬭ 6
⬭ 8
⬭ 9
⬭ 7

4.
$$\begin{array}{r} 4 \\ + 2 \\ \hline \end{array}$$
⬭ 5
⬭ 4
⬭ 6
⬭ 7

5.
$$\begin{array}{r} 7 \\ - 5 \\ \hline \end{array}$$
⬭ 1
⬭ 3
⬭ 2
⬭ 4

6.
$$\begin{array}{r} 6 \\ - 3 \\ \hline \end{array}$$
⬭ 5
⬭ 3
⬭ 4
⬭ 2

7.
$$\begin{array}{r} 5 \\ + 5 \\ \hline \end{array}$$
⬭ 0
⬭ 10
⬭ 12
⬭ 1

8.
$$\begin{array}{r} 8 \\ - 1 \\ \hline \end{array}$$
⬭ 6
⬭ 7
⬭ 9
⬭ 10

9.
$$\begin{array}{r} 6 \\ + 6 \\ \hline \end{array}$$
⬭ 10
⬭ 12
⬭ 11
⬭ 13

10.
$$\begin{array}{r} 7 \\ - 2 \\ \hline \end{array}$$
⬭ 8
⬭ 6
⬭ 4
⬭ 5

11.
$$\begin{array}{r} 9 \\ + 2 \\ \hline \end{array}$$
⬭ 8
⬭ 10
⬭ 11
⬭ 12

Which has the same shape?

12.

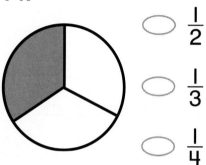

⬭ ⬭

⬭ ⬭

13.

⬭ ⬭

⬭ ⬭

What fraction is red?

14.

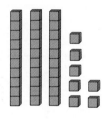

⬭ $\frac{1}{2}$

⬭ $\frac{1}{3}$

⬭ $\frac{1}{4}$

15.

⬭ $\frac{1}{2}$

⬭ $\frac{1}{3}$

⬭ $\frac{1}{4}$

16.

⬭ $\frac{1}{2}$

⬭ $\frac{1}{3}$

⬭ $\frac{1}{4}$

---

17. How many are there?

◯ 27

◯ 36

◯ 37

◯ 73

18. What number comes next?

72, 73, _____

◯ ◯ ◯ ◯

71 70 75 74

Solve.

19. I have curves.
I have faces.
What shape am I?

⬭ ⬭ ⬭

Which answer makes sense?

20. Franklin's family has
_____ cars.

⬭ ⬭ ⬭

2 25 52

Silly Sam

written by
Eric Michaels

illustrated by
Stephen Carpenter

This Math Storybook
belongs to

_____

seball
rds 5¢

Sam loves Saturdays.
He goes shopping with his brother.
Today, Sam has a quarter to spend.

Sam wants marbles.
He puts his quarter on the table.
"What a deal!" he says.

"Silly Sam!" says his brother.
"You forgot your change!
You paid 25¢, but the marbles only cost 15¢.
You get a dime back."

Sam wants a baseball card.
He puts his dime on the table.
"What a deal!" he says.

"Silly Sam!" says his brother.
"You forgot your change!
You paid 10¢, but the card only costs 5¢.
You get a nickel back."

Sam wants a silly sponge.
He puts his nickel on the table.
"What a deal!" he says.

"Silly Sam!" says his brother.
"You forgot your change!
You paid 5¢, but the sponge only costs 2¢.
You get 3 pennies back."

E

Sam wants a snack.
He puts his three pennies on the table.
The woman gives him two apples.

"Smart Sam!" says his brother.
"What a deal!" says Sam.

What if you had a quarter?
What would you buy?
Would you get change?

A Note to the Family

**Here are some learning ideas
you can share with your child.**

Enjoy *Silly Sam* Together

- Read the story with your child. If you wish, act out the story together. Your child can take the role of Sam while you play Sam's brother. Bring the dramatic reading to life by using real coins for the money transactions. Encourage your child to identify each coin by name.

- Discuss the last page of the story (page F). Ask your child why Sam didn't get any change this time.

At-Home Activity

- If your child has a coin bank at home, empty the contents and count the coins together. Encourage your child to group like coins together and begin counting with the coins of greatest value.

Read More About It!

To read more stories about money with your child, look for the following books in your local library.

- *Dollars and Cents for Harriet* by Betsy Maestro (Crown, 1988)

- *Money* by Benjamin Elkin (Childrens Press, 1983)

- *Why Money Was Invented* by Neale S. Godfrey (Silver Press, 1995)

Visit Our Web Site!

www.sbgmath.com

Name_____

What You Need

2 pennies

2 nickels

2 dimes

2 quarters

1. Use the boxes to sort the coins.
   Make as many groups as you like.

2. Then sort another way.
   Tell about ways to group the coins.
   Can you sort another way?

Home Connection Children learn that coins can be sorted by attributes such as size and color. Give your child a handful of coins and ask him or her to sort them in different ways.

one hundred ninety-nine   **199**

Put an X on the coins that are not the same kind.

1.

2.

3.

4.

or  or

penny
1¢

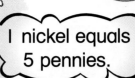
I nickel equals
5 pennies.

nickel
5¢

Word Bank

penny
nickel

Count on. Write how much in all.

1.

‾1¢‾ ‾2¢‾ ‾3¢‾ ‾4¢‾ ‾5¢‾

‾5¢‾
in all

2.

___¢ ___¢ ___¢ ___¢ ___¢

___¢
in all

3.

___¢ ___¢ ___¢ ___¢ ___¢

___¢
in all

4.

___¢ ___¢ ___¢ ___¢ ___¢

___¢
in all

 Home Connection Give your child a set of coins containing nickels and pennies. Have him or her determine the total value of each set.

two hundred one **201**

Circle the coins to match each price.

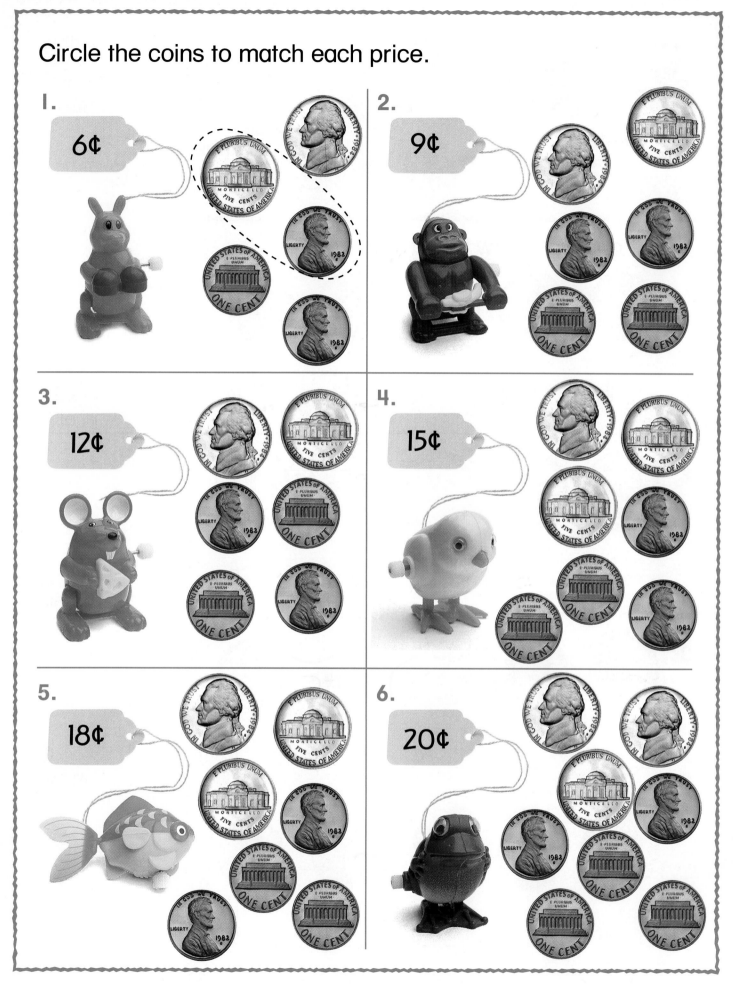

1. 6¢

2. 9¢

3. 12¢

4. 15¢

5. 18¢

6. 20¢

or

penny

1¢

I dime equals 10 pennies.

 or

dime

10¢

Word Bank

dime

Count on. Write how much in all.

1.

10¢ 20¢ 30¢ 40¢ 50¢   50¢
_____ _____ _____ _____ _____   _____
in all

2.   _____

____¢ ____¢ ____¢ ____¢ ____¢ ____¢   ____¢
in all

3.

____¢ ____¢ ____¢ ____¢ ____¢ ____¢   ____¢
in all

4.

____¢ ____¢ ____¢ ____¢ ____¢ ____¢   ____¢
in all

Home Connection Children learn to count coins by counting on from each coin. Give your child sets of coins containing pennies and dimes. Have your child count the coins.

Circle the coins to match each price.

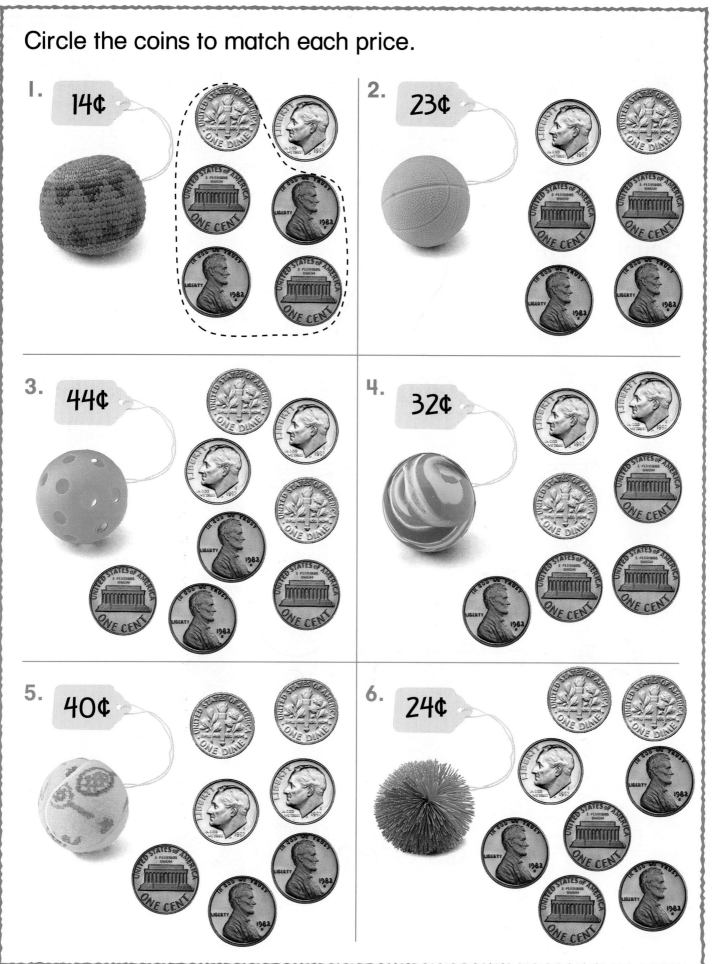

1. 14¢

2. 23¢

3. 44¢

4. 32¢

5. 40¢

6. 24¢

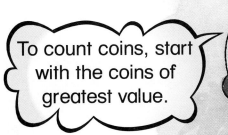

To count coins, start with the coins of greatest value.

22¢

Count on.
Write how much you have in all.

1.

5¢ 10¢ 15¢ 20¢ 21¢ 22¢   22¢
in all

2.

____¢ ____¢ ____¢ ____¢ ____¢   ____¢
in all

3.

____¢ ____¢ ____¢ ____¢ ____¢ ____¢   ____¢
in all

4.

____¢ ____¢ ____¢ ____¢ ____¢ ____¢   ____¢
in all

Home Connection Children learn that when counting a set of coins it is easier to start with the coin of greatest value. Have your child count sets of coins containing pennies, nickels, and dimes.

two hundred five   **205**

7/19/25

Remember to start with the coin of greatest value.

Write each amount.

1. 17¢

2. 23¢

3. 16¢

4. 22¢

5. 37¢

6. 27¢

Problem Solving

7. You have

Do you have enough money to buy the 🧸?

Circle **yes** or **no**.

yes   **no**

19¢

or

quarter

25¢

25¢

Circle the coins you could trade for a quarter.

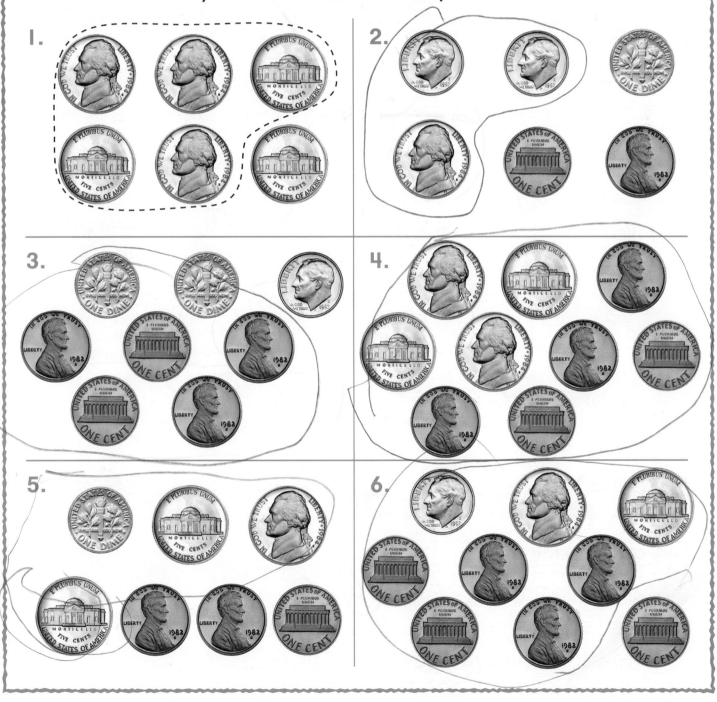

1.

2.

3.

4.

5.

6.

 Home Connection Have your child take and count a handful of coins. Encourage your child to explain the order in which he or she counted the coins and why.

two hundred seven   **207**

7/21/05

Circle the coins to match each price.

1. 25¢

2. 35¢

3. 26¢

4. 25¢

Critical Thinking Corner

Logical Thinking

5. You have 3 coins.
   They equal a quarter.
   Draw the coins you have.

⑩ ⑩ ⑤

Name _____ 7/21/05 _____

Count the coins.
Write how much in all.

1.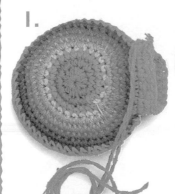

$\underset{\text{(dotted)}}{25¢}$ $30¢$ $31¢$ $32¢$ $32¢$
in all

2.

$25¢$ 30 $35¢$ $36¢$ $37¢$ $37¢$
in all

3.

$25¢$ $36¢$ $45¢$ $55¢$ $55¢$
in all

4.

$25¢$ $35¢$ $45¢$ $50¢$ $51¢$ $51¢$
in all

Home Connection Have your child empty a coin purse. Ask him or her to count five of the coins and tell you how much money there is.

two hundred nine   **209**

Circle the coins to show how much.

1. 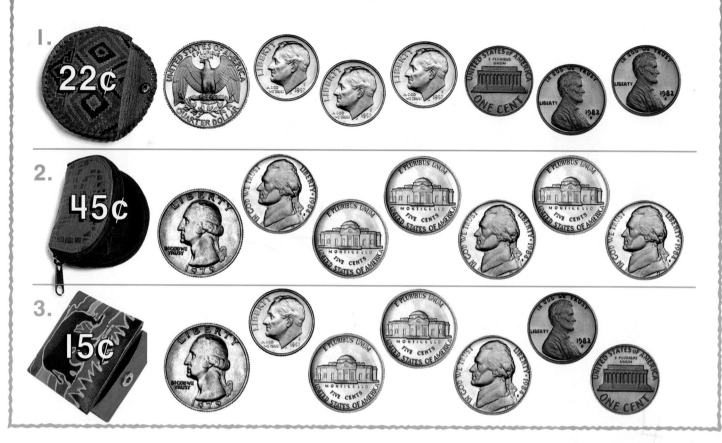 **22¢**

2. **45¢**

3. **15¢**

---

1. Count on.
Write how much in all.

_____ ¢   _____ ¢   _____ ¢   _____ ¢   _____ ¢   _____ ¢   _____ ¢
in all

---

2. Circle the coins to match the price.

 **41¢**

What coins could you use to buy one item?

I would use 2 dimes and 3 pennies!

I would use 4 nickels and 3 pennies!

23¢ each

Use coins.

Trace or draw coins to match each price.

1.  32¢

2.  48¢

3. 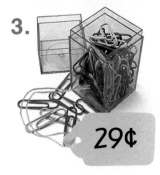 29¢

Home Connection Children need to practice combining different coins to get the same amount. Give your child a handful of coins to make a given amount.

Use coins to solve.
How much more money
do you need to buy each item?
Draw or trace the coins you need.

1.

 43¢

2.

 36¢

3.

 50¢

Critical Thinking Corner

Number Sense

4. Can every amount be shown in more than one way?
Tell why or why not.

Name_____ **Make a Table**

Use and to complete each table.

Look for patterns.

I have 2 coins. How much money could I have?

1.

		Amount
2	0	2¢
1		¢
0		¢

I have 3 coins. How much money could I have?

2.

		Amount
3	0	3¢
2		¢
1		¢
0		¢

Home Connection Your child is learning how to make a table to organize information. Discuss the tables above, and create more with your child. Observe if different patterns occur.

two hundred thirteen   **213**

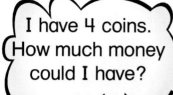

I have 4 coins.
How much money
could I have?

Use 🪙 and 🪙.

Complete the table.

Look for a pattern.

1.

🪙	🪙	Amount
4	0	4¢
	1	¢
2		¢
	3	¢
0		¢

Problem Solving

Solve.

2. You have 3 coins.

   None of the coins are greater than a dime.

   What is the greatest amount you could have? _____ ¢

   What is the least amount you could have? _____ ¢

35¢ is more than 24¢.

35¢

24¢

Count the coins.

Write each amount.

Circle the group that is worth more.

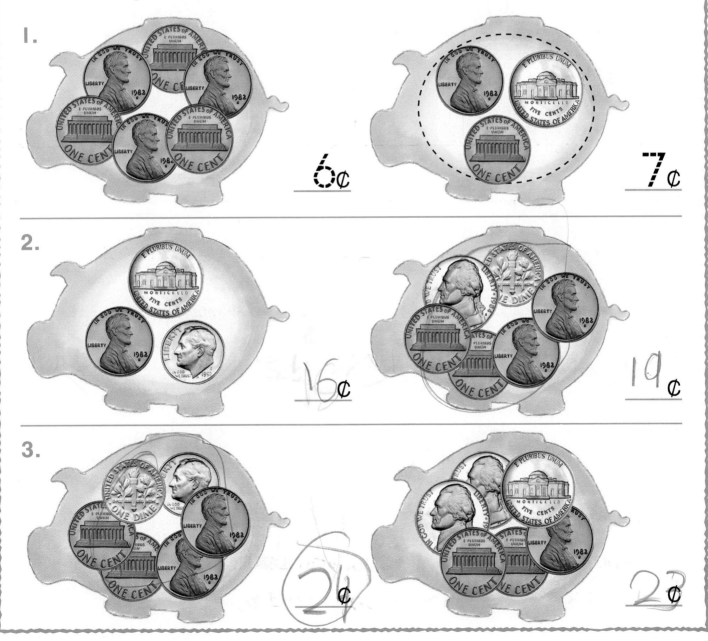

1.

6¢   7¢

2.

16¢   19¢

3.

21¢   23¢

 Home Connection As children compare groups of coins, they begin to understand that more coins do not necessarily mean greater value. Give your child groups of coins to compare values.

two hundred fifteen   **215**

Count the coins.
Write each amount.
Circle the group that shows less.

1.
 25¢

 18¢

2.
 51¢

 42¢

3.
 45¢

 50¢

© Silver Burdett Ginn Inc. All rights reserved.

What Do You Think?

I think having a dime is better than having a penny, even though a dime is smaller. What do you think?

Journal Idea

Name_____

Problem-Solving Application
Making Purchases

Understand
Plan
Look Back
Solve

9¢   11¢   18¢

20¢   30¢

Write how much money you have.
Circle what you would buy.

1.

_10_¢

2.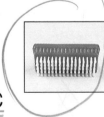

_2_¢

3.

_1_¢

4.

_3_¢

Home Connection Practice making purchases with
your child. Give your child a handful of money. Set up a
home store and have your child purchase different items.

two hundred seventeen   **217**

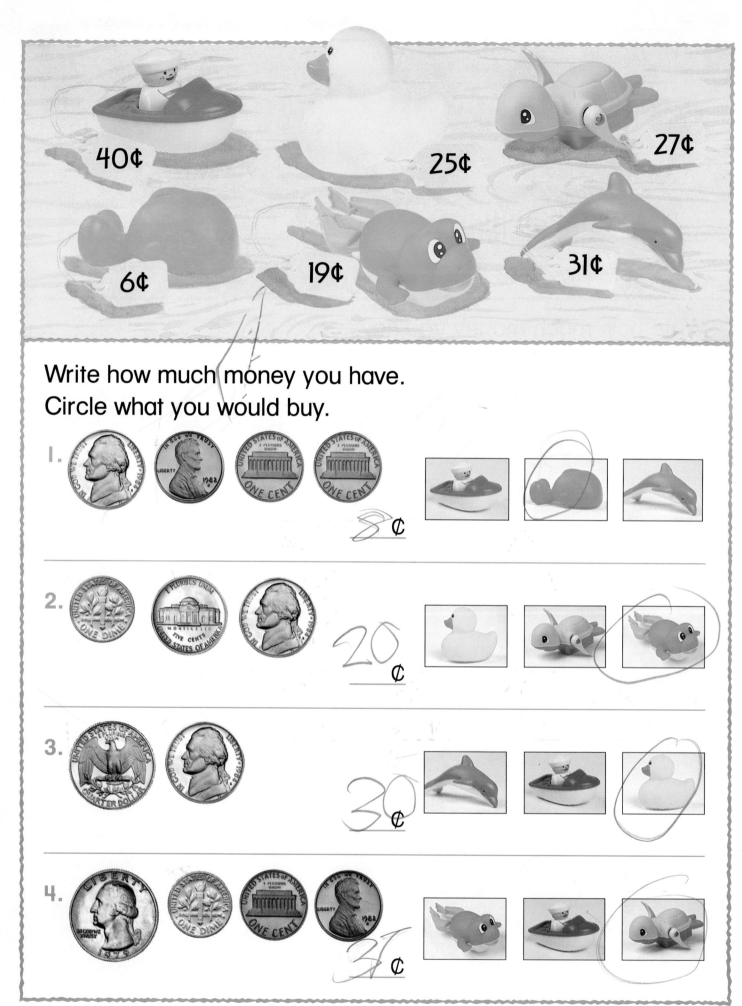

40¢ 25¢ 27¢

6¢ 19¢ 31¢

Write how much money you have.
Circle what you would buy.

1. ___ ¢

2. 20 ¢

3. 30 ¢

4. 37 ¢

6¢
+ 1¢
7¢

6¢
− 1¢
5¢

Add or subtract.
Use coins if you like.

1. 3¢      4¢
   +2¢   − 1¢
    5 ¢   3 ¢

2. 6¢   9¢   4¢   5¢   7¢   8¢
   +4¢   +2¢   −3¢   +4¢   −3¢   −3¢
    9 ¢   4 ¢   1 ¢   9 ¢   4 ¢   5 ¢

3. 8¢   9¢   6¢   3¢   9¢   6¢
   −4¢   −2¢   +6¢   +3¢   −9¢   +3¢
    4 ¢   7 ¢   12 ¢   6 ¢   0 ¢   9 ¢

4. 3¢   5¢   5¢   9¢   4¢   7¢
   +5¢   +6¢   −2¢   −8¢   +8¢   −2¢
    8 ¢   11 ¢   3 ¢   1 ¢   12 ¢   5 ¢

Home Connection Your child is learning to add and subtract different amounts. Give your child various amounts of pennies, and have him or her add or subtract. Ask your child to write the fact.

two hundred nineteen   **219**

Add or subtract.

1.
$\begin{array}{r} 3¢ \\ +\ 1¢ \\ \hline 4¢ \end{array}$
$\begin{array}{r} 5¢ \\ +\ 2¢ \\ \hline ¢ \end{array}$
$\begin{array}{r} 8¢ \\ -\ 2¢ \\ \hline ¢ \end{array}$
$\begin{array}{r} 9¢ \\ -\ 1¢ \\ \hline ¢ \end{array}$
$\begin{array}{r} 5¢ \\ -\ 3¢ \\ \hline ¢ \end{array}$
$\begin{array}{r} 2¢ \\ +\ 1¢ \\ \hline ¢ \end{array}$

2.
$\begin{array}{r} 9¢ \\ -\ 7¢ \\ \hline ¢ \end{array}$
$\begin{array}{r} 7¢ \\ +\ 4¢ \\ \hline ¢ \end{array}$
$\begin{array}{r} 8¢ \\ +\ 4¢ \\ \hline ¢ \end{array}$
$\begin{array}{r} 9¢ \\ +\ 1¢ \\ \hline ¢ \end{array}$
$\begin{array}{r} 5¢ \\ -\ 4¢ \\ \hline ¢ \end{array}$
$\begin{array}{r} 8¢ \\ -\ 5¢ \\ \hline ¢ \end{array}$

3.
$\begin{array}{r} 6¢ \\ -\ 4¢ \\ \hline ¢ \end{array}$
$\begin{array}{r} 9¢ \\ +\ 3¢ \\ \hline ¢ \end{array}$
$\begin{array}{r} 4¢ \\ +\ 4¢ \\ \hline ¢ \end{array}$
$\begin{array}{r} 2¢ \\ +\ 7¢ \\ \hline ¢ \end{array}$
$\begin{array}{r} 12¢ \\ -\ 6¢ \\ \hline ¢ \end{array}$
$\begin{array}{r} 3¢ \\ -\ 3¢ \\ \hline ¢ \end{array}$

4.
$\begin{array}{r} 7¢ \\ +\ 1¢ \\ \hline ¢ \end{array}$
$\begin{array}{r} 3¢ \\ +\ 4¢ \\ \hline ¢ \end{array}$
$\begin{array}{r} 7¢ \\ -\ 5¢ \\ \hline ¢ \end{array}$
$\begin{array}{r} 6¢ \\ -\ 5¢ \\ \hline ¢ \end{array}$
$\begin{array}{r} 8¢ \\ +\ 3¢ \\ \hline ¢ \end{array}$
$\begin{array}{r} 6¢ \\ -\ 2¢ \\ \hline ¢ \end{array}$

5.
$\begin{array}{r} 9¢ \\ -\ 6¢ \\ \hline ¢ \end{array}$
$\begin{array}{r} 8¢ \\ -\ 7¢ \\ \hline ¢ \end{array}$
$\begin{array}{r} 11¢ \\ -\ 9¢ \\ \hline ¢ \end{array}$
$\begin{array}{r} 8¢ \\ +\ 2¢ \\ \hline ¢ \end{array}$
$\begin{array}{r} 7¢ \\ +\ 5¢ \\ \hline ¢ \end{array}$
$\begin{array}{r} 4¢ \\ +\ 3¢ \\ \hline ¢ \end{array}$

Problem Solving

Solve.

6. One coin is a nickel. How many pennies are in the pocket?

8¢

_____ pennies

7. One coin is a nickel. How many pennies are in the pocket?

11¢

_____ pennies

I. Trace or draw coins to match the price.

47¢

2. Write each amount.
Circle the group that is worth less.

_____ ¢

_____ ¢

3. Write each amount.
Circle the group that is worth more.

_____ ¢

_____ ¢

4. Add or subtract.

7¢	8¢	9¢	4¢	9¢	7¢
+5¢	−6¢	−4¢	+0¢	+2¢	−4¢
___¢	___¢	___¢	___¢	___¢	___¢

5. Write the amount. Circle what you can buy.

_____ ¢

 40¢

  30¢

You want to buy each item.
How many of each coin would you use?
Use coins. Write how many.

Item	 (quarter)	 (dime)	 (nickel)	 (penny)
1. 46¢ 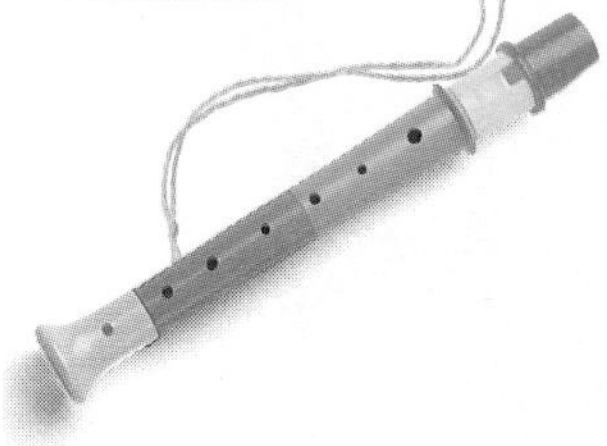	1	2	0	1
2. 32¢ 	0	2	0	2
3. 40¢ 	0	2	2	0
4. 33¢ 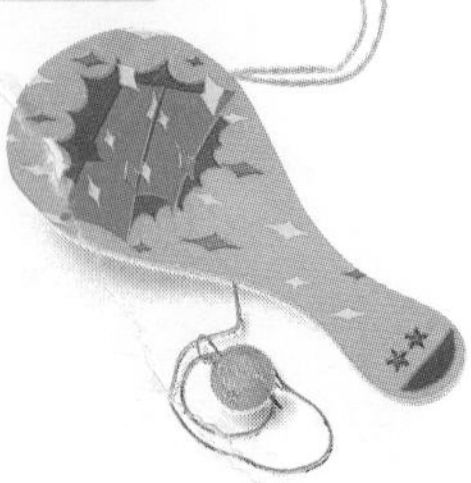	0	3	0	3

I. Circle the coins to match the price.

42¢

_____

2. Count the coins. Write how much in all.

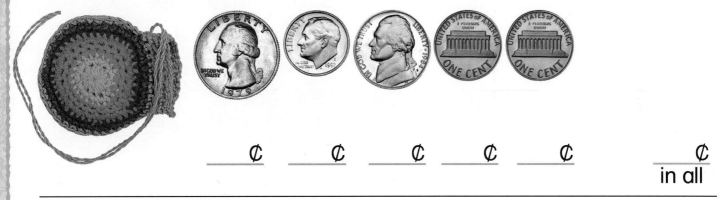

_____¢   _____¢   _____¢   _____¢   _____¢   _____¢
                                                            in all

_____

3. Write how much.
Circle the group that is worth more.

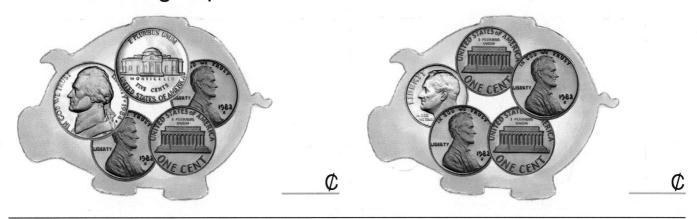

_____¢   _____¢

_____

4. Add or subtract.

7¢	8¢	10¢	4¢	9¢	7¢
+3¢	−6¢	−5¢	+4¢	−3¢	+4¢
___¢	___¢	___¢	___¢	___¢	___¢

Name_____

What coins could be in the ?

15¢

Use coins.
Write how many of each coin.

1. What if there are only pennies?

   _____ pennies

2. What if there are only nickels?

   _____ nickels

3. What if there are pennies and nickels?

   _____ pennies   _____ nickels

4. What if there are nickels and dimes?

   _____ nickel   _____ dime

5. What if there are pennies and dimes?

   _____ pennies   _____ dime

A dollar is equal to 100¢

or

100¢

Write how much.
Does it equal a dollar?
Circle **yes** or **no**.

1.

100 ¢

yes

no

2.

100 ¢

yes

no

3.

50 ¢

yes

no

Name_____

You can show amounts of money
with the MathProcessor.

I can show 49¢
in different ways.

① Click on the **money button** 2 times to show 2 workspaces.

② Click on the **arrow** to pick a coin.

③ Click on the **coin** to show a coin.

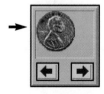

④ Click on one of the **trade buttons** to trade coins.

Show an amount in one workspace.
Have your partner show
the same amount another way
in the other workspace.

CHAPTER 8

Relating Addition and Subtraction

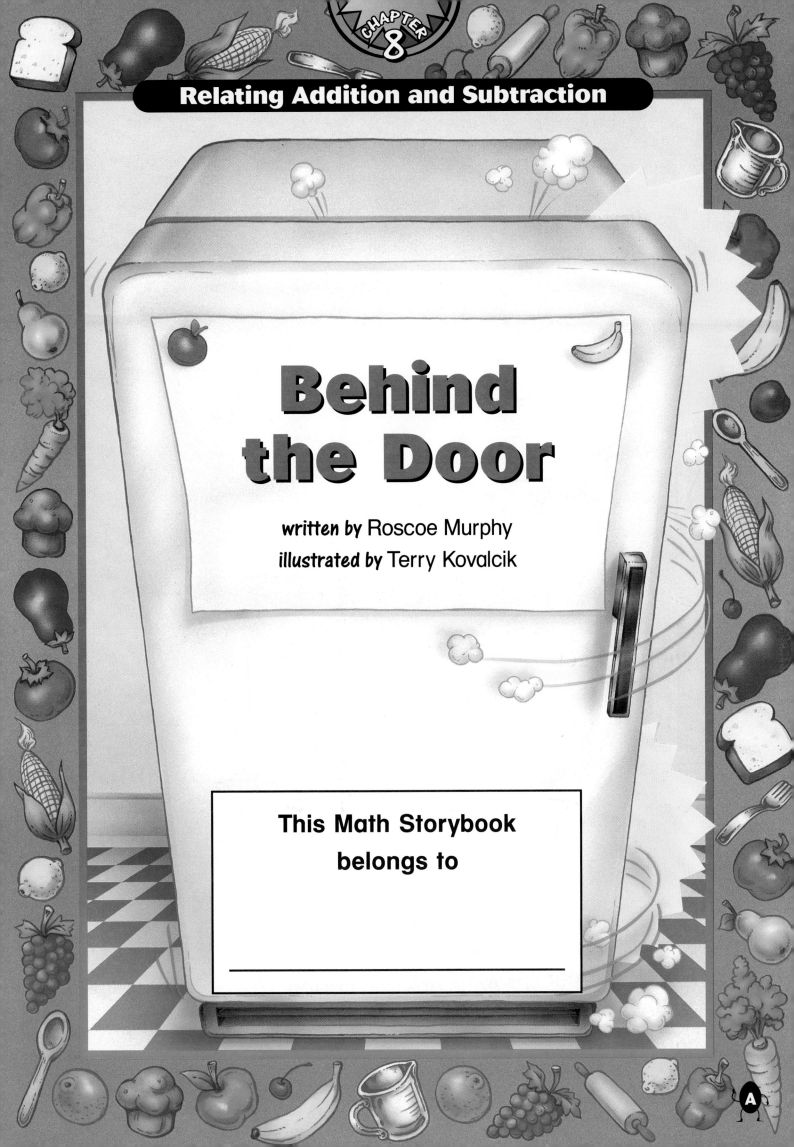

Behind the Door

written by Roscoe Murphy

illustrated by Terry Kovalcik

This Math Storybook

belongs to

_____

Behind the big white door,
it's time to start the day.
12 eggs are in a carton.
6 climb out to play.

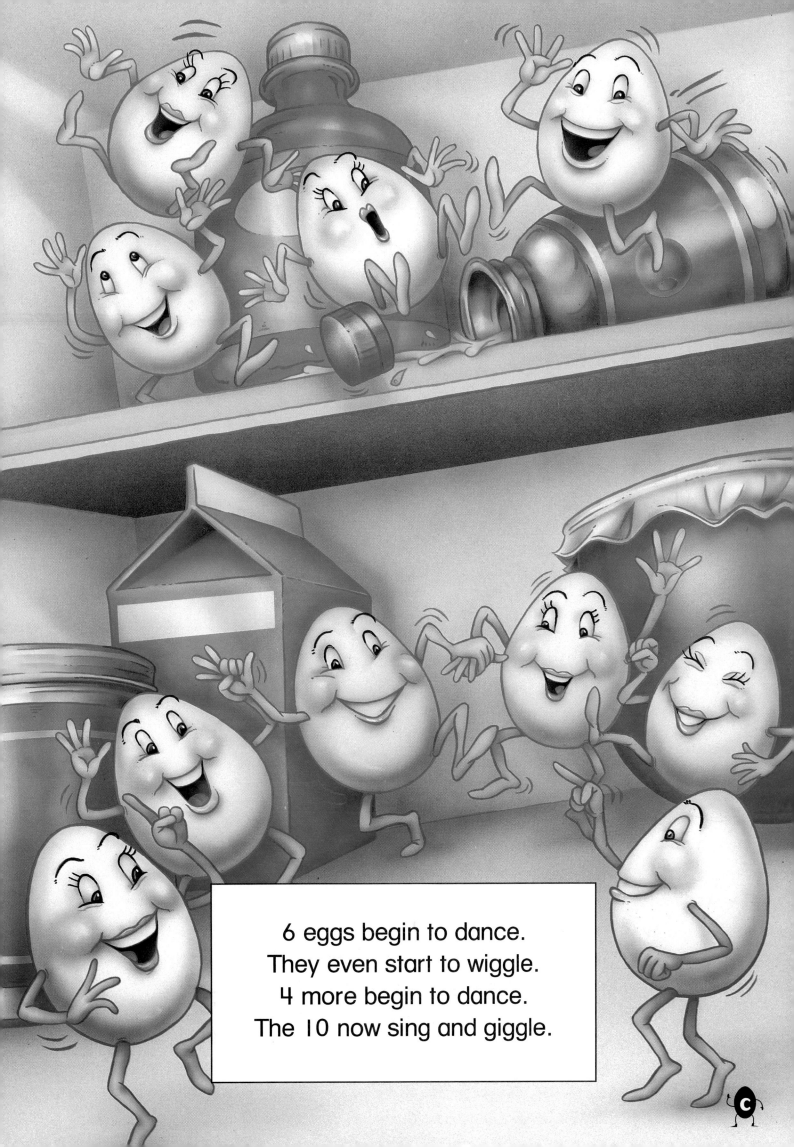

6 eggs begin to dance.
They even start to wiggle.
4 more begin to dance.
The 10 now sing and giggle.

8 eggs take turns jumping,
some are upside down.
Look at all the many ways
the 8 bounce up and down.

D

7 eggs use a carrot
to play on and to climb.
2 begin to slide right down.
How many wait in line?

Draw some eggs on the shelf
and some more just below.
Then tell a number story
of how eggs come and go.

A Note to the Family

Here are some learning ideas you can share with your child.

Enjoy *Behind the Door* Together

- Read the story aloud with your child. Talk about all the things the eggs do to have fun. Encourage your child to count the different groups of eggs on each page, then tell addition and subtraction stories about each picture.

- Encourage your child to show you what she or he drew on the last page of *Behind the Door*. Then work together to add and subtract the two groups of eggs. Have your child write the addition and subtraction sentences. For example, if your child drew a group of 6 eggs and a group of 4 eggs, he or she could write

$$6 + 4 = 10 \text{ and } 10 - 6 = 4.$$

At-Home Activity

- Have your child put 12 apples, oranges, pieces of play food, or other small items in different groups to practice adding and subtracting to and from 12. Write the addition or subtraction sentences as your child groups the objects. Then ask your child to complete each sentence.

Read More About It!

To read more about subtraction with your child, look for these books in your local library.

- *The Baker's Dozen: A Colonial American Tale* by Heather Forest (HarcourtBrace Juvenile Books, 1993)

- *Mr. Grumpy's Outing* by John Burningham (Holt, 1990)

- *12 Ways to Get to 11* by Eve Merriam (Simon & Schuster, 1993)

Visit Our Web Site!

www.sbgmath.com

H

$$5 + 2 = 7$$

$$7 - 2 = 5$$

Use two colors of cubes and
Workmat 4. Show each number.
Write an addition sentence.
Write a subtraction sentence.

1. 6 and 2 | $6 + 2 = 8$ | $8 - 2 = 6$

2. 4 and 3 | ___ + ___ = ___ | ___ - ___ = ___

3. 5 and 6 | ___ + ___ = ___ | ___ - ___ = ___

4. 8 and 4 | ___ + ___ = ___ | ___ - ___ = ___

5. 5 and 7 | ___ + ___ = ___ | ___ - ___ = ___

Home Connection It is important for children to understand that addition and subtraction are related. Ask your child to make up related addition and subtraction stories about 12 pennies.

two hundred twenty-seven   **227**

Add and subtract.

1.

$3 + 7 = \underline{10}$

$10 - 7 = \underline{}$

2.

$4 + 5 = \underline{}$

$9 - 5 = \underline{}$

3.

$6 + 3 = \underline{}$

$9 - 3 = \underline{}$

4.

$5 + 6 = \underline{}$

$11 - 6 = \underline{}$

5.

$5 + 5 = \underline{}$

$10 - 5 = \underline{}$

What addition fact can
help you find 11 − 7?

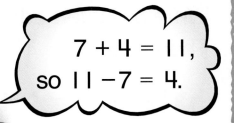

7 + 4 = 11,
so 11 − 7 = 4.

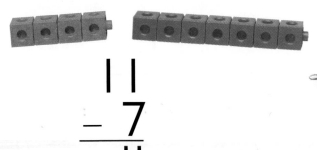

11
− 7
‾‾‾
4

Word Bank

related fact

Circle the related addition fact.
Then subtract.

1.
12
− 7
‾‾‾
5

7 + 3 = 10

7 + 4 = 11

(7 + 5 = 12)

2.
10
− 6
‾‾‾

6 + 4 = 10

6 + 5 = 11

6 + 6 = 12

3.
11
− 5
‾‾‾

5 + 5 = 10

5 + 6 = 11

5 + 7 = 12

4.
9
− 4
‾‾‾

4 + 5 = 9

5 + 3 = 8

5 + 5 = 10

5.
12
− 8
‾‾‾

8 + 2 = 10

8 + 3 = 11

8 + 4 = 12

6.
10
− 3
‾‾‾

3 + 9 = 12

3 + 7 = 10

3 + 8 = 11

Home Connection Your child is learning to use addition to
solve related subtraction problems. Give your child a subtraction
problem. Then challenge your child to think of a related addition fact.

two hundred twenty-nine **229**

7/21/05

Write a related addition fact.
Then subtract.

1. 12 − 8 = __4__   __8__ + __4__ = __12__

2. 7 − 3 = __4__   7 + 3 = __10__

3. 10 − 8 = __2__   10 + 8 = __18__

4. 8 − 6 = __3__   8 + 6 = __14__

5. 9 − 1 = __8__   9 + 1 = __10__

6. 11 − 3 = __8__   11 + 3 = __14__

Problem Solving

Solve.   10 − 2 − 3 + 5 = 10

7. Carolyn has 10 🥕 to feed the horses.

   One horse eats 2.

   Another horse eats 3.

   Erin gives Carolyn 5 more.

   How many 🥕 does Carolyn have now? __5__ 🥕

This is a fact family.

$3 + 7 = 10$ $10 - 7 = 3$

$7 + 3 = 10$ $10 - 3 = 7$

Complete each fact family.
Use counters if you like.

1.
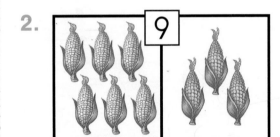
10

$6 + 4 = \underline{}$ $10 - 4 = \underline{}$

$4 + 6 = \underline{}$ $10 - 6 = \underline{}$

2.

9

$6 + 3 = \underline{}$ $9 - 3 = \underline{}$

$3 + 6 = \underline{}$ $9 - 6 = \underline{}$

3.
7

$4 + 3 = \underline{}$ $7 - 3 = \underline{}$

$3 + 4 = \underline{}$ $7 - 4 = \underline{}$

4.
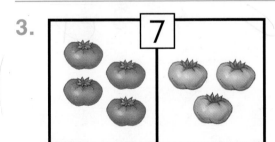
10

$5 + 5 = \underline{}$ $10 - 5 = \underline{}$

Add or subtract.
Use counters if you like.

1.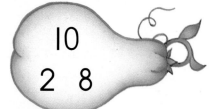

$2 + 8 = \underline{\hspace{1cm}}$ $10 - 8 = \underline{\hspace{1cm}}$

$8 + 2 = \underline{\hspace{1cm}}$ $10 - 2 = \underline{\hspace{1cm}}$

2.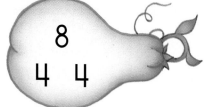

$4 + 4 = \underline{\hspace{1cm}}$ $8 - 4 = \underline{\hspace{1cm}}$

3.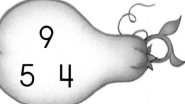

$5 + 4 = \underline{\hspace{1cm}}$ $9 - 4 = \underline{\hspace{1cm}}$

$4 + 5 = \underline{\hspace{1cm}}$ $9 - 5 = \underline{\hspace{1cm}}$

4.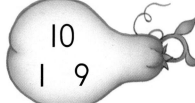

$9 + 1 = \underline{\hspace{1cm}}$ $10 - 1 = \underline{\hspace{1cm}}$

$1 + 9 = \underline{\hspace{1cm}}$ $10 - 9 = \underline{\hspace{1cm}}$

5.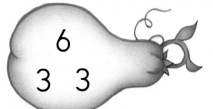

$3 + 3 = \underline{\hspace{1cm}}$ $6 - 3 = \underline{\hspace{1cm}}$

 Critical Thinking Corner

Number Sense

6. Look back at the exercises on this page.
Are there the same number of facts
in each fact family?
Tell why or why not.

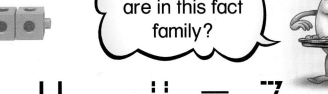

What numbers are in this fact family?

$$7 + 4 = 11 \qquad 11 - 4 = 7$$

$$4 + 7 = 11 \qquad 11 - 7 = 4$$

Complete each fact family.

1.

_____ + _____ = 11   11 − _____ = _____

_____ + _____ = 11   11 − _____ = _____

2.

_____ + _____ = 11   11 − _____ = _____

_____ + _____ = 11   11 − _____ = _____

3.

_____ + _____ = 11   11 − _____ = _____

_____ + _____ = 11   11 − _____ = _____

4.

_____ + _____ = 10   10 − _____ = _____

_____ + _____ = 10   10 − _____ = _____

Home Connection Give your child 11 household items. Ask him or her to make 2 groups and write the fact family to describe the groups.

two hundred thirty-three   **233**

Complete each fact family.

1.
$$\begin{array}{r} 8 \\ +\ 2 \\ \hline 10 \end{array}$$
$$\begin{array}{r} 2 \\ +\ 8 \\ \hline 10 \end{array}$$
$$\begin{array}{r} 10 \\ -\ 8 \\ \hline 2 \end{array}$$
$$\begin{array}{r} 10 \\ -\ 2 \\ \hline 8 \end{array}$$

2.
$$\begin{array}{r} 5 \\ +\ 4 \\ \hline 9 \end{array}$$
$$\begin{array}{r} 4 \\ +\ 5 \\ \hline 9 \end{array}$$
$$\begin{array}{r} 9 \\ -\ 5 \\ \hline 4 \end{array}$$
$$\begin{array}{r} 9 \\ -\ 4 \\ \hline 5 \end{array}$$

3.
$$\begin{array}{r} 2 \\ +\ 9 \\ \hline 11 \end{array}$$
$$\begin{array}{r} 9 \\ +\ 2 \\ \hline 11 \end{array}$$
$$\begin{array}{r} 11 \\ -\ 2 \\ \hline 9 \end{array}$$
$$\begin{array}{r} 11 \\ -\ 9 \\ \hline 2 \end{array}$$

4.
$$\begin{array}{r} 4 \\ +\ 6 \\ \hline 10 \end{array}$$
$$\begin{array}{r} 6 \\ +\ 4 \\ \hline 10 \end{array}$$
$$\begin{array}{r} 10 \\ -\ 4 \\ \hline 6 \end{array}$$
$$\begin{array}{r} 10 \\ -\ 6 \\ \hline 4 \end{array}$$

Problem Solving

Solve.

5. Jack had some .

He gave 6 to Mandy.

Then he gave Kevin the other 5.

How many did he have to start? _____

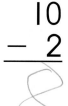

234   two hundred thirty-four

Name_____**Fact Families to 12**

Add or subtract.

1.
12
$7 \quad 5$

$\begin{array}{r} 7 \\ + 5 \\ \hline 12 \end{array}$
$\begin{array}{r} 5 \\ + 7 \\ \hline 12 \end{array}$
$\begin{array}{r} 12 \\ - 7 \\ \hline 5 \end{array}$
$\begin{array}{r} 12 \\ - 5 \\ \hline 7 \end{array}$

2.
12
$4 \quad 8$

$\begin{array}{r} 8 \\ + 4 \\ \hline 12 \end{array}$
$\begin{array}{r} 4 \\ + 8 \\ \hline 12 \end{array}$
$\begin{array}{r} 12 \\ - 8 \\ \hline 4 \end{array}$
$\begin{array}{r} 12 \\ - 4 \\ \hline 8 \end{array}$

3.
12
$3 \quad 9$

$\begin{array}{r} 9 \\ + 3 \\ \hline 12 \end{array}$
$\begin{array}{r} 3 \\ + 9 \\ \hline 12 \end{array}$
$\begin{array}{r} 12 \\ - 9 \\ \hline 3 \end{array}$
$\begin{array}{r} 12 \\ - 3 \\ \hline 4 \end{array}$

4.
11
$7 \quad 4$

$\begin{array}{r} 7 \\ + 4 \\ \hline 11 \end{array}$
$\begin{array}{r} 4 \\ + 7 \\ \hline 11 \end{array}$
$\begin{array}{r} 11 \\ - 7 \\ \hline 4 \end{array}$
$\begin{array}{r} 11 \\ - 4 \\ \hline 5 \end{array}$

5.
12
$6 \quad 6$

$\begin{array}{r} 6 \\ + 6 \\ \hline 12 \end{array}$
$\begin{array}{r} 12 \\ - 6 \\ \hline 6 \end{array}$

6 and 6 make one dozen.

Home Connection Give your child 12 pennies or other household items. Ask him or her to use the items to show several different fact families for 12.

two hundred thirty-five   **235**

Write the number sentences for each fact family.

1.

$5 + 6 = 11$ ___ − ___ = ___

___ + ___ = ___ ___ − ___ = ___

2.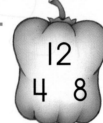

___ + ___ = ___ ___ − ___ = ___

___ + ___ = ___ ___ − ___ = ___

3.

___ + ___ = ___ ___ − ___ = ___

___ + ___ = ___ ___ − ___ = ___

Checkpoint

Circle the related addition fact. Then subtract.

1.
$$\begin{array}{r} 12 \\ -\ 6 \\ \hline \end{array}$$

$6 + 4 = 10$

$7 + 5 = 12$

$6 + 6 = 12$

2.
$$\begin{array}{r} 11 \\ -\ 9 \\ \hline \end{array}$$

$9 + 1 = 10$

$9 + 2 = 11$

$7 + 4 = 11$

3. Complete the fact family.

$3 + 7 = $ ___

$10 − 7 = $ ___

$7 + 3 = $ ___

$10 − 3 = $ ___

1. Use the picture to make a graph.
    Color one box for each bread or roll.

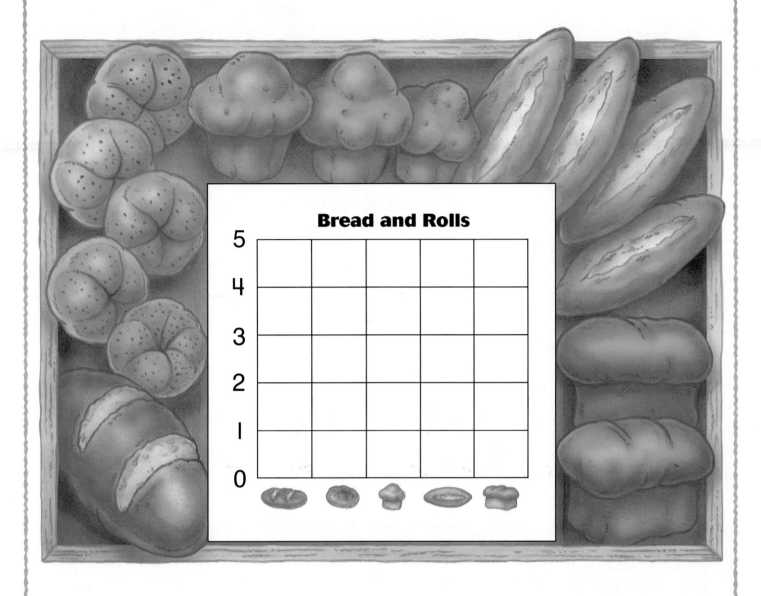

Bread and Rolls

Use the graph. Write how many.

2.  ____   ____   ____   ____   ____

3.  and ____

4. How many more are there than ? ____ more

5. How many fewer are there than ? ____ fewer

Home Connection Discuss this graph with your child. Ask him or her to explain what each box means.

two hundred thirty-seven   **237**

1. Use the picture to make a graph.
   Color one box for each food.

Healthful Foods

| | 0 | 1 | 2 | 3 | 4 | 5 | 6 |

Use the graph. Write how many.

2. _____ 🌽 _____ 🍅 _____ 🫑 _____ 🥕 _____

3. How many more are there than 🌽 ? _____

4. How many fewer are there than 🥕 ? _____

5. What if there were 2 more ?

   How many would there be? _____

 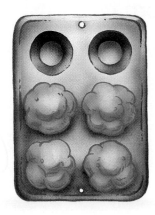 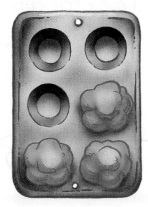 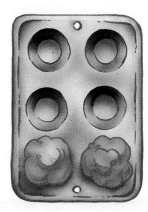

$$\begin{array}{r} 6 \\ -1 \\ \hline 5 \end{array} \qquad \begin{array}{r} 6 \\ -2 \\ \hline 4 \end{array} \qquad \begin{array}{r} 6 \\ -3 \\ \hline 3 \end{array} \qquad \begin{array}{r} 6 \\ -4 \\ \hline 2 \end{array}$$

Add or subtract.

Look for a pattern in each row.

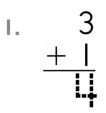

What pattern do you see? What comes next?

1.
$$\begin{array}{r} 3 \\ +1 \\ \hline 4 \end{array} \qquad \begin{array}{r} 3 \\ +2 \\ \hline \end{array} \qquad \begin{array}{r} 3 \\ +3 \\ \hline \end{array} \qquad \begin{array}{r} 3 \\ +4 \\ \hline \end{array} \qquad \begin{array}{r} 3 \\ +5 \\ \hline \end{array} \qquad \begin{array}{r} 3 \\ +6 \\ \hline \end{array}$$

2.
$$\begin{array}{r} 12 \\ -3 \\ \hline \end{array} \qquad \begin{array}{r} 12 \\ -4 \\ \hline \end{array} \qquad \begin{array}{r} 12 \\ -5 \\ \hline \end{array} \qquad \begin{array}{r} 12 \\ -6 \\ \hline \end{array} \qquad \begin{array}{r} 12 \\ -7 \\ \hline \end{array} \qquad \begin{array}{r} 12 \\ -8 \\ \hline \end{array}$$

3.
$$\begin{array}{r} 11 \\ -2 \\ \hline \end{array} \qquad \begin{array}{r} 10 \\ -2 \\ \hline \end{array} \qquad \begin{array}{r} 9 \\ -2 \\ \hline \end{array} \qquad \begin{array}{r} 8 \\ -2 \\ \hline \end{array} \qquad \begin{array}{r} 7 \\ -2 \\ \hline \end{array} \qquad \begin{array}{r} 6 \\ -2 \\ \hline \end{array}$$

Home Connection Your child is exploring and using number patterns. Make up addition or subtraction problems that follow a pattern and have your child solve them.

two hundred thirty-nine **239**

7/25/05

Add or subtract. Look for a pattern.
Write the next fact in the pattern.

1.
$$\begin{array}{r} 5 \\ +\ 1 \\ \hline 6 \end{array}$$
$$\begin{array}{r} 5 \\ +\ 2 \\ \hline 7 \end{array}$$
$$\begin{array}{r} 5 \\ +\ 3 \\ \hline 8 \end{array}$$
$$\begin{array}{r} 5 \\ +\ 4 \\ \hline 9 \end{array}$$
$$\begin{array}{r} 5 \\ +\ 5 \\ \hline 10 \end{array}$$
$$\begin{array}{r} 5 \\ +\ 6 \\ \hline 11 \end{array}$$

2.
$$\begin{array}{r} 7 \\ -\ 6 \\ \hline 1 \end{array}$$
$$\begin{array}{r} 7 \\ -\ 5 \\ \hline 2 \end{array}$$
$$\begin{array}{r} 7 \\ -\ 4 \\ \hline 3 \end{array}$$
$$\begin{array}{r} 7 \\ -\ 3 \\ \hline 4 \end{array}$$
$$\begin{array}{r} 7 \\ -\ 2 \\ \hline 5 \end{array}$$
$$\begin{array}{r} 7 \\ -\ 1 \\ \hline 6 \end{array}$$

3.
$$\begin{array}{r} 4 \\ +\ 1 \\ \hline 5 \end{array}$$
$$\begin{array}{r} 5 \\ +\ 1 \\ \hline 6 \end{array}$$
$$\begin{array}{r} 6 \\ +\ 1 \\ \hline 7 \end{array}$$
$$\begin{array}{r} 7 \\ +\ 1 \\ \hline 8 \end{array}$$
$$\begin{array}{r} 8 \\ +\ 1 \\ \hline 9 \end{array}$$
$$\begin{array}{r} 9 \\ +\ 1 \\ \hline 10 \end{array}$$

4.
$$\begin{array}{r} 5 \\ -\ 5 \\ \hline 0 \end{array}$$
$$\begin{array}{r} 6 \\ -\ 5 \\ \hline 1 \end{array}$$
$$\begin{array}{r} 7 \\ -\ 5 \\ \hline 2 \end{array}$$
$$\begin{array}{r} 8 \\ -\ 5 \\ \hline 3 \end{array}$$
$$\begin{array}{r} 9 \\ -\ 5 \\ \hline 4 \end{array}$$
$$\begin{array}{r} 10 \\ -\ 5 \\ \hline 5 \end{array}$$

 Critical Thinking Corner

Number Sense

 5. Tell about the patterns you see in each row.

7/25/05

4 + 4

9 - 1

10 − 2

16 − 8 = 8

6 + 2   8 − 0   5 + 3   7 + 1

I can name 8 in many ways. Can you think of another way?

Circle the names for each number.
Use counters if you like.

1.  3

   (4 − 1)   3 + 2   8 + 3

   2 + 2   (9 − 6)   (1 + 2)

2.  7

   10 − 2   (7 + 0)   (12 − 5)

   (3 + 4)   5 + 6   11 − 4

10 − 3

3.  6

   (3 + 3)   (12 − 6)   9 − 4

   (7 − 1)   6 + 3   (4 + 2)

4.  9

   (11 − 2)   (9 − 0)   5 + 3

   12 − 6   5 + 5   (4 + 5)

Home Connection Your child is learning different ways to name or make a number. Ask her or him to show different names for 10 and for 5. You may wish to use buttons or other household items to help.

Circle the names for each number.
Then write another name for each number.

1.  **9**

$(12 - 3)$ $(7 + 2)$ $9 - 3$

$4 + 4$ $(6 + 3)$ $(4 \;\oplus\; 5)$

2.  **5**

$8 + 4$ $8 - 3$ $9 + 3$

$6 - 1$ $4 + 1$ ___ $\bigcirc$ ___

3.  **8**

$8 + 0$ $6 + 5$ $11 - 3$

$4 + 3$ $12 - 4$ ___ $\bigcirc$ ___

4.  **11**

$11 - 4$ $12 - 9$ $7 + 4$

$9 + 2$ $3 + 8$ ___ $\bigcirc$ ___

What Do You Think?

 I can think of 6 names for 4.
How many can you think of?
Tell what they are.

242   two hundred forty-two

Should you add or subtract?

Jon has 6 . He eats 3.

How many are left?

$6 + 3 =$ ___

$6 - 3 = 3$

Circle the correct number sentence.
Then solve.

1. Chen has 3 .

   He picks 2 more.

   How many does
   he have now?

   $3 - 2 =$ ___

   $3 + 2 =$ ___

2. Marco has 9 .

   He gives 3 to Kyle.

   How many are left?

   $9 - 3 =$ ___

   $9 + 3 =$ ___

3. Jess makes 8 .

   She makes 1 more.

   How many does
   she make in all?

   $8 - 1 =$ ___

   $8 + 1 =$ ___

4. Julie has 9 .

   She gives 2 to Paul.

   How many does
   she have now?

   $2 + 9 =$ ___

   $9 - 2 =$ ___

Home Connection Tell your child an addition or
subtraction story. Ask him or her to decide whether to add
or subtract to solve the problem. Then change roles.

two hundred forty-three   **243**

Circle the correct number sentence. Then solve.

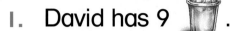

1. David has 9 .

   He sells 3.

   How many does he have now?

   $9 - 3 =$ _____ $9 + 3 =$ _____

2. Annie makes 5 .

   Betsy makes 5.

   How many are there altogether?

   $5 - 5 =$ _____ $5 + 5 =$ _____

3. Lisa makes 6 .

   She sells 1.

   How many does she have now?

   $6 - 1 =$ _____ $6 + 1 =$ _____

4. Make your own problem.
   Fill in the _____. Then solve.

   Make Your Own

   Tanya has _____ .

   She sells _____.

   How many does she have now?

   _____ + _____ = _____   _____ − _____ = _____

Fruits

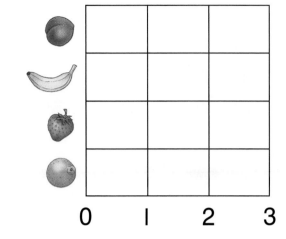

Use the picture. Complete the graph. Write how many.

1. and  ____

        0   I   2   3

2. How many more are there than ? ____

3. Subtract. Look for a pattern.

$$\begin{array}{cc}10\\-\ 1\\\hline\end{array}\quad\begin{array}{cc}10\\-\ 2\\\hline\end{array}\quad\begin{array}{cc}10\\-\ 3\\\hline\end{array}\quad\begin{array}{cc}10\\-\ 4\\\hline\end{array}\quad\begin{array}{cc}10\\-\ 5\\\hline\end{array}\quad\begin{array}{cc}10\\-\ 6\\\hline\end{array}$$

Circle the names for each number.

4.
    $12 - 3$ $6 + 3$ $6 + 5$

          $4 + 5$ $8 - 1$ $9 - 1$

5.
    $3 + 9$ $10 - 2$ $8 + 0$

        $12 - 4$ $6 + 4$ $11 - 4$

Circle the correct number sentence. Solve.

6. There are 8 at the store.

Molly buys 2.

How many are left?

$8 + 2 =$ ____

$8 - 2 =$ ____

What is my favorite time of day?

Add or subtract.
Write the letter that matches each sum
or difference in the box below.

$$\begin{array}{r} 0 \\ +\ 0 \\ \hline 0 \end{array}$$  L

$$\begin{array}{r} 11 \\ -\ 9 \\ \hline \end{array}$$  N

$$\begin{array}{r} 4 \\ +\ 2 \\ \hline \end{array}$$  I

$$\begin{array}{r} 5 \\ -\ 2 \\ \hline \end{array}$$  C

$$\begin{array}{r} 11 \\ -\ 2 \\ \hline \end{array}$$  X

$$\begin{array}{r} 7 \\ -\ 3 \\ \hline \end{array}$$  H

$$\begin{array}{r} 4 \\ +\ 4 \\ \hline \end{array}$$  E

$$\begin{array}{r} 9 \\ -\ 8 \\ \hline \end{array}$$  U

$$\begin{array}{r} 5 \\ +\ 5 \\ \hline \end{array}$$  Q

$$\begin{array}{r} 8 \\ +\ 4 \\ \hline \end{array}$$  Z

$$\begin{array}{r} 4 \\ +\ 1 \\ \hline \end{array}$$  T

$$\begin{array}{r} 12 \\ -\ 5 \\ \hline \end{array}$$  M

L	__	__	__	__	__	__	__	__ !
0	1	2	3	4	5	6	7	8

Add. Write a related subtraction sentence.

1.

$6 + 6 =$ ___

___ $-$ ___ $=$ ___

Solve. Complete each fact family.

2.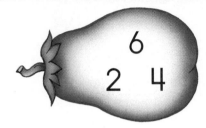

6
2 4

2	6	6	4
$+\ 4$	$-\ 2$	$-\ 4$	$+\ 2$

3.

12
4 8

8	4	12	12
$+\ 4$	$+\ 8$	$-\ 4$	$-\ 8$

Circle the names for the number.

4.

10

$11 - 3$ $10 - 2$ $4 + 6$

$3 + 7$ $9 + 1$ $12 - 4$

Use the picture.
Color one box for each food.

5.

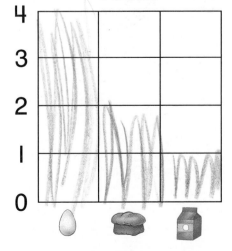

Foods

Name_____

What You Need

2 number cubes

① Roll the number cubes.

② Use the numbers to write an addition sentence.

③ Then write a related subtraction sentence.

_____

1.

___ + ___ = ___

___ − ___ = ___

2.

___ + ___ = ___

___ − ___ = ___

3.

___ + ___ = ___

___ − ___ = ___

4.

___ + ___ = ___

___ − ___ = ___

5.

___ + ___ = ___

___ − ___ = ___

6.

___ + ___ = ___

___ − ___ = ___

Name_____

Complete the addition table.
Tell about the patterns you see.

+	0	1	2	3	4	5	6	7	8	9
0	0	1	2	3	4	5	6	7	8	9
1	1	2	3	4	5	6	7	8	9	10
2	2	3	4	5	6	7	8	9	10	11
3	3	4	5	6	7	8	9	10	11	12
4	4	5	6	7	8	9	10	11	12	
5	5	6	7	8	9	10	11	12		
6	6	7	8	9	10	11	12			
7	7	8	9	10	11	12				
8	8	9	10	11	12					
9	9	10	11	12						

Name_____

Use a .

Circle + or −.

1. Press **5** + **3** **=** 2

2. Press **7** + **2** **=** 5

3. Press **3** + **7** **=** 10

4. Press **9** + **9** **=** 0

5. Press **8** + **5** **=** 3

6. Press **6** + **5** **=** 11

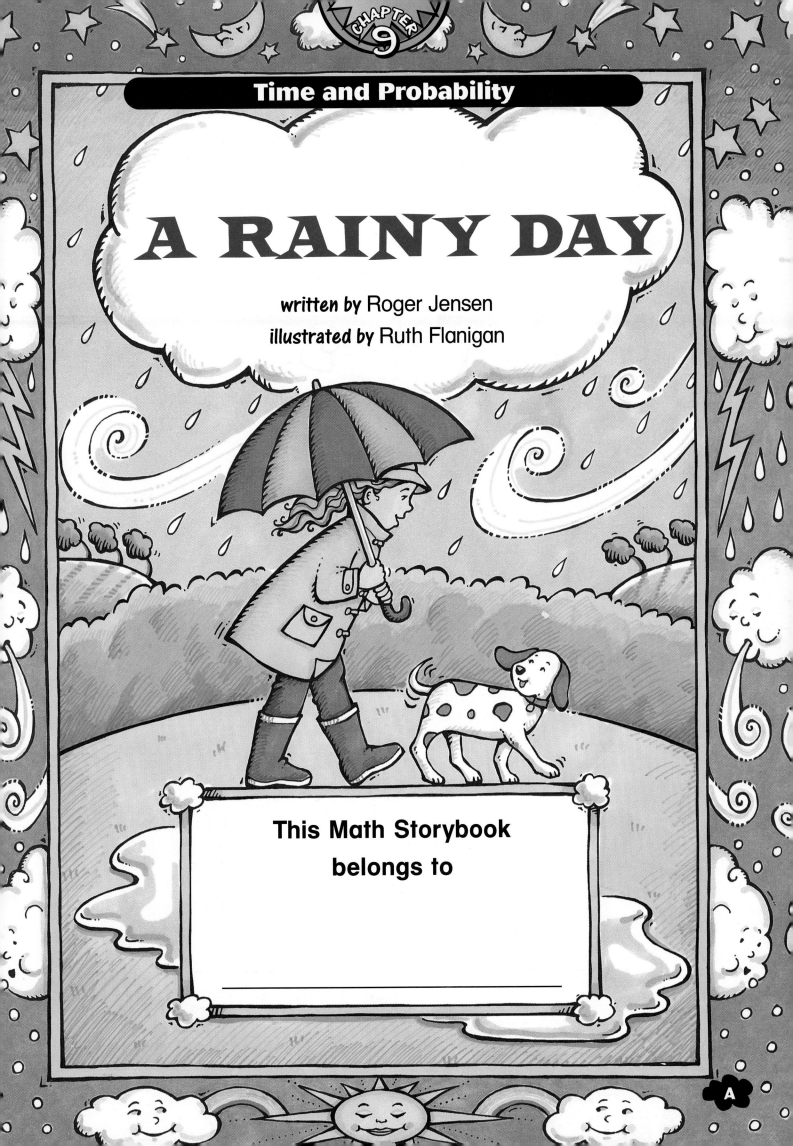

Rain is on the way.
What can I do today?
I'll have pancakes for breakfast.

Rain, rain, go away!
I guess I'll play inside today.
I'll play with Scooter.

The rain! The rain! It's gone away!
A rainbow has come out today.
Now I can go out and play!

Rain is on the way.
What can you do today?

Show a time on the clock.
Draw what you would do at that time.

A Note to the Family

Here are some learning ideas you can share with your child.

Enjoy *A Rainy Day* Together

- Read the story aloud with your child. Discuss the sequence of events and how the weather changes. Look at the clock on each page and ask your child to tell you the time. Ask your child what the girl in the story is doing at each time of day.

- Ask your child to show you what she or he has drawn on the last page of the story. Talk with your child about his or her favorite time of day and what she or he likes to do at that time.

At-Home Activities

- In the course of daily routines, encourage your child to look at the clock as you tell the time at which events are happening. For example, tell your child the time when he or she gets up, eats meals, and goes to bed.

- Make a schedule of your child's day and post it on the refrigerator. It might give times for getting up, having breakfast, going to school, playing after school, and so on.

Read More About It!

To read more about time with your child, look for these books in your local library.

- *Cookie's Week* by Cindy Ward (Putnam, 1992)

- *The Completed Hickory Dickory Dock* by Jim Aylesworth (Aladdin, 1994)

- *The Grouchy Ladybug* by Eric Carle (HarperCollins Children's Books, 1996)

- *Jasper's Beanstalk* by Nick Butterworth and Mick Inkpen (Simon & Schuster, 1993)

Visit Our Web Site!

 www.sbgmath.com

What happened first? What happened last?

3   1   2

Write **1**, **2**, and **3** to show the order.

1.

_____ _____ _____

2.

_____ _____ _____

3.

_____ _____ _____

Home Connection Discuss the events of the day with your child. Help your child to describe what happened first, next, and last.

Make Your Own

What do you do in a day?
Draw pictures to show your day.
Complete each sentence.

I.

First, I _____ .

2.

Next, I _____ .

3.

Last, I _____ .

What can you do in a minute?

I can count to 60.

I can tie my shoes.

Try each activity.
Can you do it in a minute?
Circle **yes** or **no**.

Word Bank

minute

1. Write your name 10 times.

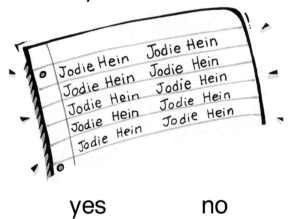

yes   no

2. Say the alphabet.

yes   no

3. Write 1 to 100.

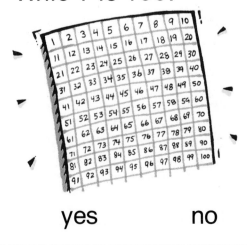

yes   no

4. Put on your coat.

yes   no

Home Connection Your child is learning the meaning of a minute. Ask your child to estimate how long a minute is. Does he or she come close to the real time?

two hundred fifty-three   **253**

Does each activity take more or less than a minute?
Circle **more** or **less**.

1. Eat lunch.

(more)   less

2. Brush your teeth.

more   less

3. Sharpen a pencil.

more   less

4. Read a book.

more   less

5. Wash a dog.

more   less

6. Take a drink.

more   less

minutes   hours

Word Bank

hour

About how long does each take?
Circle **minutes** or **hours**.

1. Get dressed.

(minutes)   hours

2. Watch a movie.

minutes   hours

3. Be at school.

minutes   hours

4. Set the table.

minutes   hours

Home Connection Your child is learning that some
activities take more time than others. Discuss activities that
take hours and activities that take minutes to complete.

7/17/05

Name_____ 7/17/-5 **Hour and Minute Hands**

The hour hand points to the 5. The minute hand points to the 12.

hour ➤ 5

minute ➤ 12

_5_ o'clock

Word Bank

hour hand
minute hand
o'clock

Where do the hands point?
Write each time.

1.

hour ➤ _9_

minute ➤ _12_

_9_ o'clock

2.

hour ➤ _11_

minute ➤ _12_

_11_ o'clock

3.

hour ➤ _12_

minute ➤ _12_

_12_ o'clock

4.

hour ➤ _4_

minute ➤ _12_

_4_ o'clock

5.

hour ➤ _6_

minute ➤ _12_

_6_ o'clock

6.

hour ➤ _____

minute ➤ _____

_____ o'clock

Home Connection Your child is learning about the hour and minute hands on the clock. Use a clock that has hour and minute hands, and discuss what each shows.

Write each time.

1.

___7___ o'clock

2.

___1___ o'clock

3.

___3___ o'clock

4.

___10___ o'clock

5.

___6___ o'clock

6.

___9___ o'clock

What Do You Think?

I think it is easy to tell time when the minute hand is on the 12. Do you agree? Why or why not?

7/17/05

5 o'clock

5:00

Draw the hour hand.
Write each time.

1. 3 o'clock

3:00

2. 6 o'clock

3. 8 o'clock

4. 1 o'clock

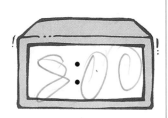

1 :00

5. 11 o'clock

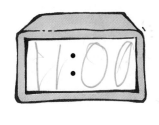

11:00

6. 12 o'clock

12:00

 Home Connection Your child is learning to tell time on analog and digital clocks. Help your child to tell the time on both kinds of clocks.

7/17/05

Write the time.
Draw the clock hands.

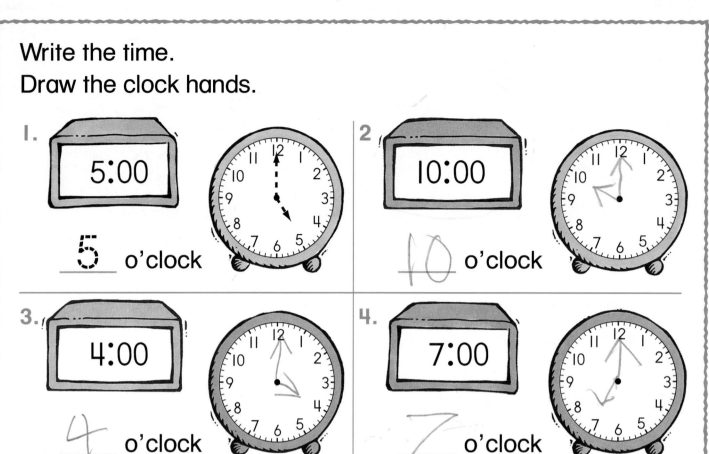

1. 5:00   __5__ o'clock

2. 10:00   __10__ o'clock

3. 4:00   __4__ o'clock

4. 7:00   __7__ o'clock

1. Write **1**, **2**, and **3** to show the order. **Checkpoint**

2. Does it take **more** or **less** than a minute? Circle.

more   less

3. Write the time.

9:00

260 two hundred sixty

7/17/05

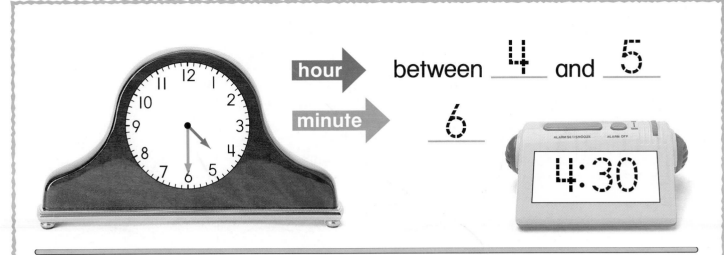

hour ➤ between __4__ and __5__

minute ➤ __6__

4:30

Where do the hands point?
Tell and write each time.

1.

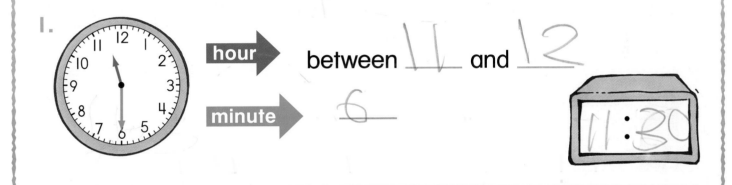

hour ➤ between __11__ and __12__

minute ➤ __6__

11:30

2.

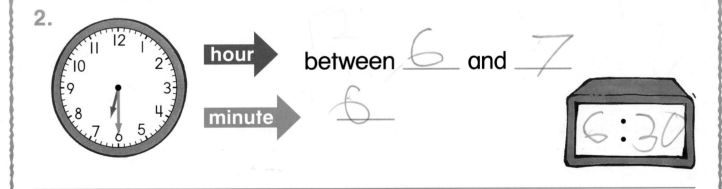

hour ➤ between __6__ and __7__

minute ➤ __6__

6:30

3.

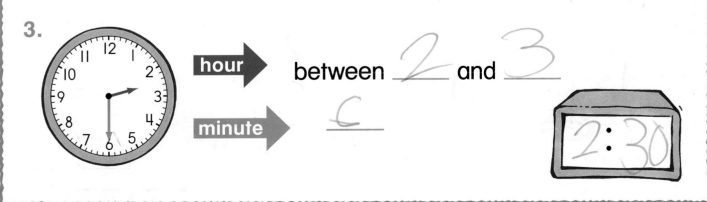

hour ➤ between __2__ and __3__

minute ➤ __6__

2:30

Home Connection Your child is learning to tell time to the half-hour. Use a clock from your house to practice telling time with your child.

2/28/05

Circle the clock that shows the same time.

1. 4:30

2. 11:30

3. 6:00

Problem Solving

Write each time.
Circle the clock that shows the earliest time.

4.

:

 5:30

Name_____

What time will it be in 1 hour?

It is 2:00.
One hour later
is 3:00.

Use a clock to act out the time.
Draw the clock hands.

Start	How long?	What time will it be?
1.	The boys play for 1 hour.	
2.	Maria weaves for 3 hours.	
3.	The men paint for 2 hours.	

Home Connection Have your child write down the start and stop times for an activity he or she has done. Ask how long the activity took.

What time will it be?
Use a clock.
Draw the clock hands.

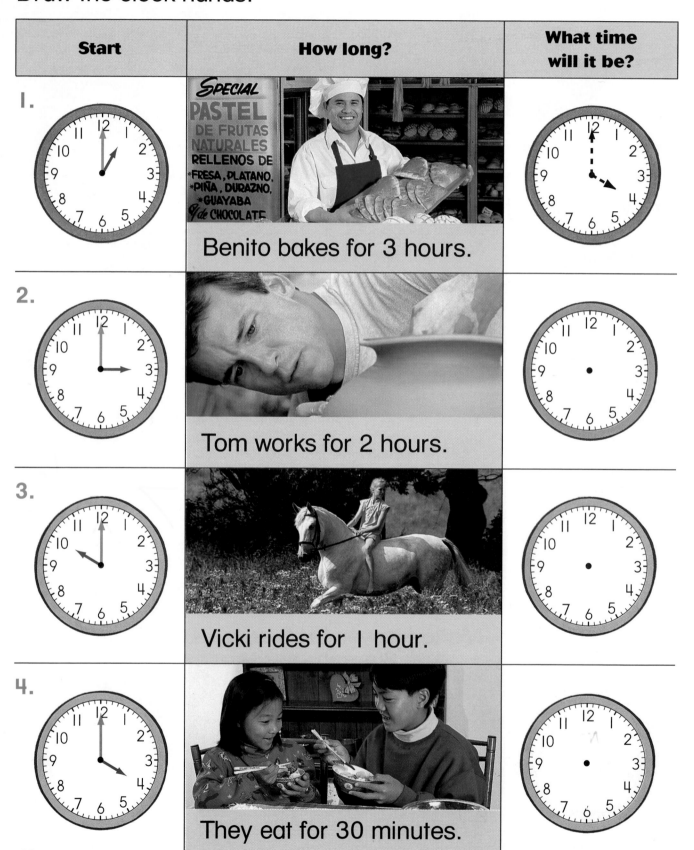

Start	How long?	What time will it be?
1.	SPECIAL PASTEL DE FRUTAS NATURALES RELLENOS DE *FRESA, PLATANO, *PIÑA, DURAZNO, *GUAYABA *Y de CHOCOLATE Benito bakes for 3 hours.	
2.	Tom works for 2 hours.	
3.	Vicki rides for 1 hour.	
4.	They eat for 30 minutes.	

July

Sunday	Monday	Tuesday	Wednesday	Thursday	Friday	Saturday
	1	2	3	4	5	6
7	8	9	10	11	12	13
14	15	16	17	18	19	20
21	22	23	24	25	26	27
28	29	30	31			

Use the calendar above.

Word Bank

calendar

1. How many days are
   in a week? _____

2. How many days are
   in this month? _____

3. How many Thursdays are
   in this month? _____

4. How many Mondays are
   in this month? _____

5. On what day is July 19? _____

Home Connection Show your child a calendar for the present month. Discuss the days that various dates fall on. Have your child mark family birthdays, holidays, or events.

Sunday	Monday	Tuesday	Wednesday	Thursday	Friday	Saturday

Create a calendar for this month.
Use your calendar to answer each question.

1. On what day of the week
   does this month start? _____

2. What is the date of
   the first Tuesday? _____

3. What is today's date? _____

4. What date is tomorrow? _____

5. What date was yesterday? _____

Morning Schedule

Time	Subject	
9:00	Reading	
10:00	Math	
11:00	Lunch	
11:30	Recess	

Use the schedule.

Circle the correct activity for each time.

1.

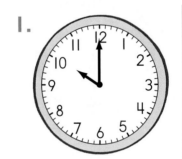

 Reading Math   Lunch

2.

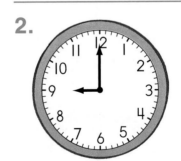

 Lunch   Reading  Recess

3.

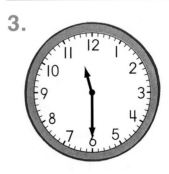

 Recess Lunch  Math

 Home Connection Have your child make a schedule of his or her day. Read the schedule with your child and discuss the day's events.

After-School Schedule

Time	Event
3:00	Leave school.
3:30	Have a snack.
4:00	Play.
5:30	Eat dinner.

Use the schedule.

Circle the correct time for each activity.

1. Play.

2. Leave school.

3. Eat dinner.

4. Have a snack.

Use a counter like above.
Toss it a few times.
Which side will it land on?
Circle **yes**, **no**, or **maybe**.

I.	●	yes	no	(maybe)
2.	●	yes	no	maybe
3.	●	yes	no	maybe
4.	● or ●	yes	no	maybe
5.	● or ●	yes	no	maybe

Home Connection Your child is learning about probability. Ask him or her to think about some events that definitely happen, some events that cannot happen, and some events that might happen.

Will it happen?

Circle **yes**, **no**, or **maybe**.

1.

It will rain tomorrow.

yes no (maybe)

2.

A dog will talk.

yes no maybe

3.

I will get mail today.

yes no maybe

4.

A cat will fly.

yes no maybe

5.

A kangaroo will hop.

yes no maybe

Tallies can help you record how many.

1	2	3	4	5	6
one	two	three	four	five	six
I	II	III	IIII	⊬⊬⊬	⊬⊬⊬ I

Use a 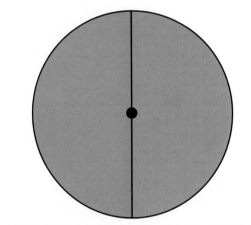 and your pencil to make each spinner.
Spin each 10 times.
Tally to show your results.
Write the totals.

Word Bank
tally

1.

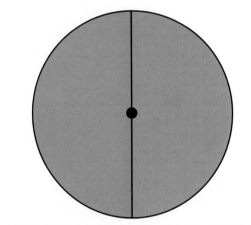

	Tally	Total
Red		
Blue		

2.

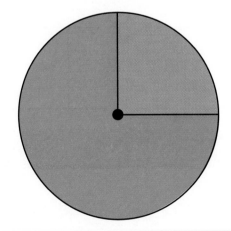

	Tally	Total
Red		
Blue		

3.   Did both spinners give you the same results?
Tell why or why not.

Home Connection Your child is learning that some events are more likely to happen than others. Encourage your child to talk about the results of the experiments on this page.

Use a and your pencil to make each spinner.
Spin each 10 times.
Tally to show your results.
Write the totals.

1.

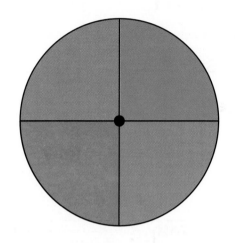

	Tally	Total
Red		
Blue		
Green		

2.

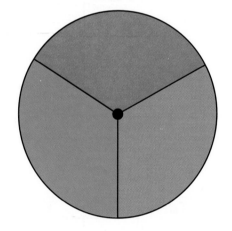

	Tally	Total
Red		
Blue		
Green		

Critical Thinking Corner

Logical Thinking

3. Which spinner would be more likely to land on blue?
Tell why.

Where do the hands point?
Write the time.

1.    **hour** ▶ between ____ and ____

   minute ▶ ____

Will it happen?
Circle **yes**, **no**, or **maybe**.

2.

   The ice cream will melt.

   yes   no   maybe

3.

   A fish will play ball.

   yes   no   maybe

What time will it be?
Draw the clock hands.

Start	How long?	What time will it be?
4. 	Zach naps for 2 hours.	

Name_____ **Extra Practice**

Connect the dots in order of time.

Start
12:00   6:00

12:30   5:30

1:00   5:00

2:30
3:00   1:30
    2:00   4:30
3:30   4:00

274   two hundred seventy-four

7/21/05

Count by 5s to find the time.

60   5   10   15   20   25   30   35   40   45   50   55

<u>10</u> minutes after <u>3</u>

What time is it? Write the numbers.

1.

20 minutes after 11

2.

40 minutes after 4

3.

15 minutes after 9

4.

50 minutes after 12

How many times will the spinner land on 1?

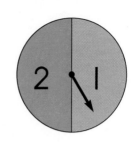

You can use the MathProcessor to find out.

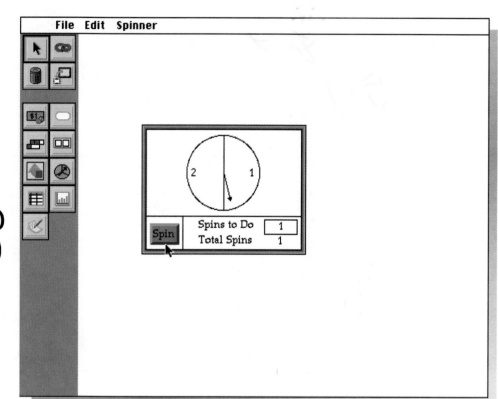

Take turns with a partner.

1 Click on the **spinner button** to show a spinner.

2 Circle the number you think will be spun more.

1   2

3 Click on the word .
Spin 20 times.

4 Tally the number for each spin.
Write the totals.

Compare your results with those of your classmates.

	Tally	Total
1		
2		

Name_____

Fill in the ⬭ for the correct answer.

1. Find how many.

⬭ 7   ⬭ 6   ⬭ 9   ⬭ 10

2. Which number comes between?

9, ____, 11

⬭ 8   ⬭ 12   ⬭ 5   ⬭ 10

Add or subtract.

3. 9
     + 3
⬭ 11
⬭ 12
⬭ 6
⬭ 7

4. 7
     − 4
⬭ 9
⬭ 11
⬭ 3
⬭ 0

5. 5
     − 5
⬭ 10
⬭ 7
⬭ 0
⬭ 11

6. 6
     + 5
⬭ 10
⬭ 1
⬭ 11
⬭ 12

7. 8
     − 3
⬭ 4
⬭ 12
⬭ 11
⬭ 5

8. 4
     + 2
⬭ 6
⬭ 2
⬭ 8
⬭ 10

9. 4
     + 7
⬭ 11
⬭ 12
⬭ 9
⬭ 8

10. 12
      − 6
⬭ 4
⬭ 10
⬭ 6
⬭ 7

11. 11
      − 5
⬭ 5
⬭ 12
⬭ 7
⬭ 6

---

12. Choose the correct number sentence.

⬭ 5 + 3 = 8   ⬭ 5 − 2 = 3

⬭ 7 + 2 = 9   ⬭ 7 − 5 = 2

13. Which object has the same shape?

◯ ◯ ◯ ◯

14. What fraction is blue?

◯ $\frac{1}{3}$ ◯ $\frac{1}{2}$ ◯ $\frac{1}{4}$

15. What number comes before?

_____, 98, 99

◯ ◯ ◯ ◯

89   97   100   96

16. How many are there?

◯ ◯ ◯ ◯

71   62   51   80

17. What can you buy?

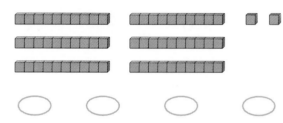  

47¢   40¢   44¢

◯   ◯   ◯

18. What time is it?

◯ 7:00

◯ 8:30

◯ 8:00

◯ 12:00

19. What time is it?

◯ 1:00

◯ 4:00

◯ 2:00

◯ 9:00

20. What time will it be in 1 hour?

4:30

◯   ◯   ◯

CHAPTER 10

Measurement

HOW DO YOU MEASURE A PIG?

written by Teri Jones

illustrated by Rosanne Litzinger

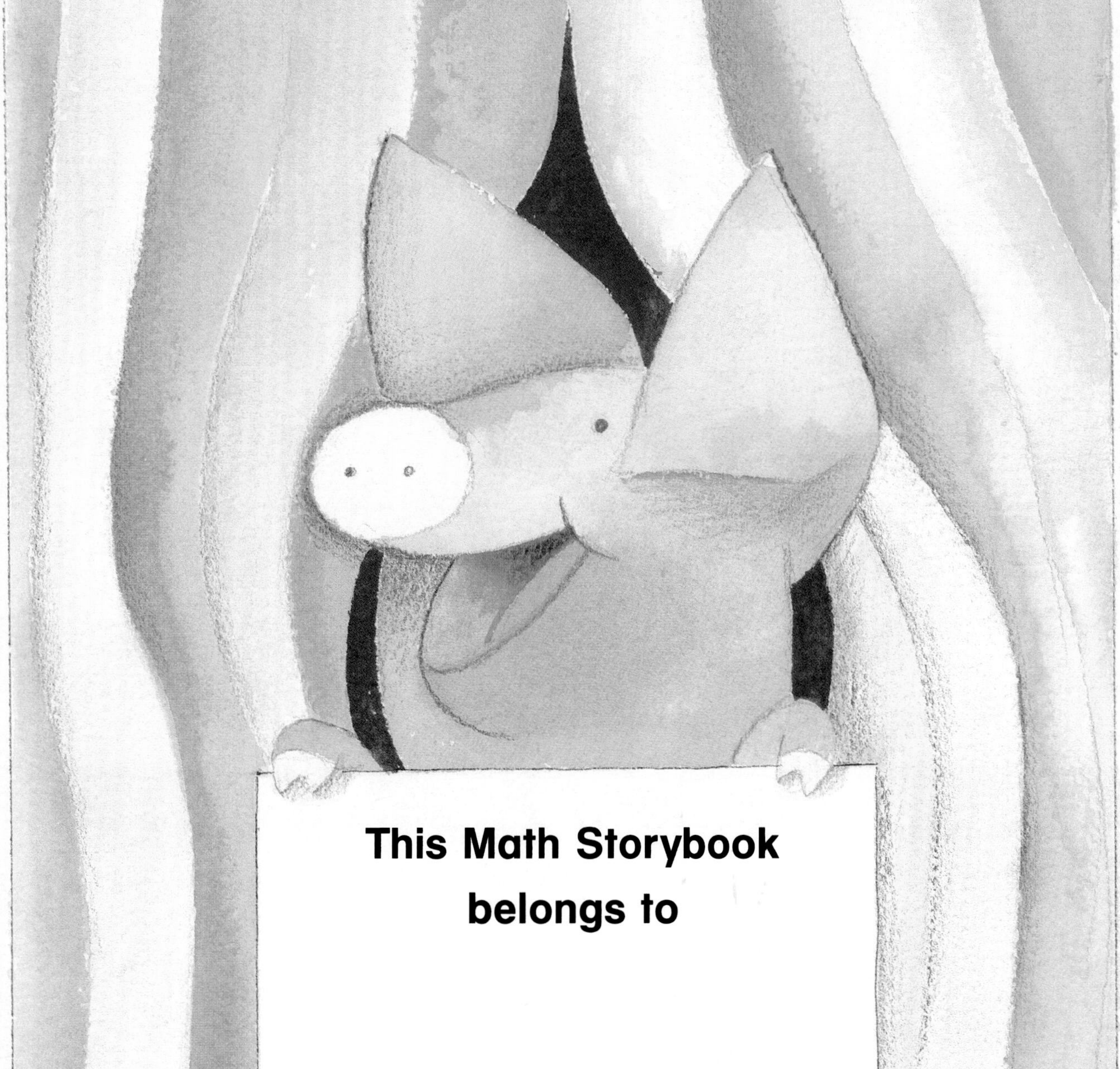

This Math Storybook

belongs to

_____

Come to the pig fair and win a prize.
Pigs of all sizes are welcome.
We'll have fun as we find out
how to measure a pig!

Slim is the winner of a prize.
He's the tallest pig of all!
Slim is 30 inches from head to foot.
That's how you measure a pig.

Oink is the winner of a prize.
She's the longest pig of all!
Oink is 36 inches from snout to tail.
That's how you measure a pig.

Big Bert is the winner of a prize.
He's the heaviest pig of all!
Big Bert weighs 300 pounds.
That's how you measure a pig.

Little Gert is the winner of a prize.
She is the nicest pig of all!
She measures up in a special way.
Is that how you measure a pig?

How many ways can you measure Little Gert?
Use a ruler.
Tell what you find.

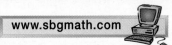

A Note to the Family

Here are some learning ideas you can share with your child.

Enjoy *How Do You Measure a Pig?* Together

- Read the story aloud together. Talk about the prize each pig won.

- On the last page of the story, talk about different ways a pig could be measured, such as its length from snout to tail or its height from head to foot. Work with your child to measure the parts of Little Gert with a ruler. Write down each part and the measurement.

At-Home Activities

- Using a tape measure, a ruler, and/or a yardstick, measure different objects in your home. For example, you could measure the height of a table, the height of a glass, the length of a shoe, and the width of a window. You might also measure around a lamp or other circular objects. Help your child compare measurements to decide what items are the tallest, longest, and widest.

- In the kitchen, select several empty containers and have your child guess how many 8-oz cups of water each container will hold. Then use a measuring cup to see how much water is needed to fill each container. Then compare the guesses with the actual amounts.

Read More About It!

To read more about measurement with your child, look for these books in your local library.

- *The Carrot Seed* by Ruth Krauss
  (HarperCollins Children's Books, 1989)

- *Farmer Mack Measures His Pig* by Tony Johnston
  (HarperCollins Children's Books, 1986)

- *How Big Is a Foot?* by Rolf Myller (Dell, 1991)

- *How to Weigh an Elephant* by Bob Barner (Bantam, 1995)

Visit Our Web Site!

www.sbgmath.com

H

Are you shorter or taller than the real object? Compare to find out. Circle **shorter** or **taller**.

Word Bank

shorter
taller
longer

1.

   shorter

   (taller)

   trash can

2.

   shorter

   taller

   door

3.

   shorter

   taller

   closet

4.

   shorter

   taller

   desk

5.

   shorter

   taller

   watering can

6.

   shorter

   taller

   bookshelf

 Home Connection Children are learning to compare lengths and heights of objects. Encourage your child to compare objects at home, using the words "shorter", "longer", and "taller."

Circle the longer object.

Put an **X** on the shorter object.

1.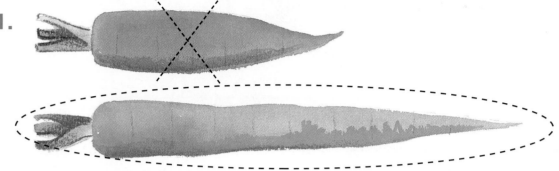

2.

3.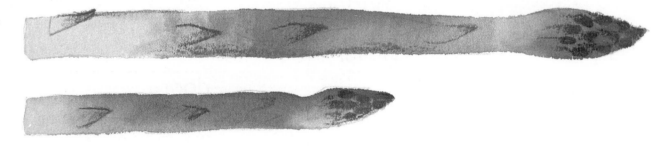

4.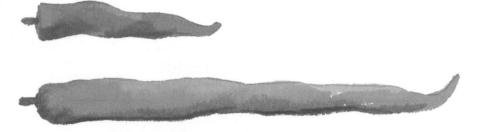

 Look at all the objects on this page.
Which one is the longest?
Tell how you know.

Name_____

The worm is about 4 cubes long.

About how long is each one?
Use cubes.
Guess and then measure.

1.

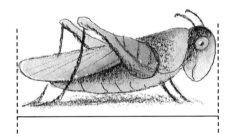

Guess
about _____ cubes

Measure
about _____ cubes

2.

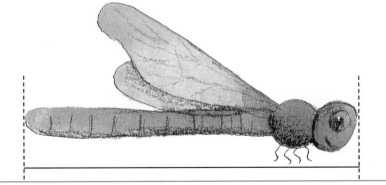

Guess
about _____ cubes

Measure
about _____ cubes

3.

Guess
about _____ cubes

Measure
about _____ cubes

Home Connection Your child is learning how to measure length, using a nonstandard unit such as cubes. Ask your child to measure things at home with items like paper clips.

Use cubes.

Find objects that are about each length.

Draw to show what you find.

1.

    about 6 cubes long
___

2.

    about 2 cubes long
___

3.

    about 10 cubes long

Critical Thinking Corner

Visual Thinking

4. Kelly used cubes to measure this pencil.
   What is wrong with the way she measured?

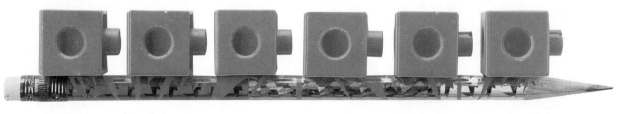

The pencil is about 5 inches long.

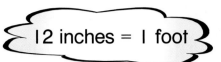

12 inches = 1 foot

1 inch

| | | | | | |
|inches|1|2|3|4|5|6|

About how long is the real object?
Use an inch ruler to measure.

Word Bank

inch
foot

1. crayon

about _____ inches

2. paper clip

about _____ inches

3. 3 cubes

about _____ inches

4. eraser

about _____ inches

5. marker

about _____ inches

6. book

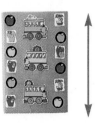

about _____ inches

Home Connection Children are learning to measure in inches. Ask your child to use a ruler to measure common items at home, such as spoons, toys, pencils, and books.

two hundred eighty-five　**285**

Use an inch ruler.
Write how many inches long or tall.

1.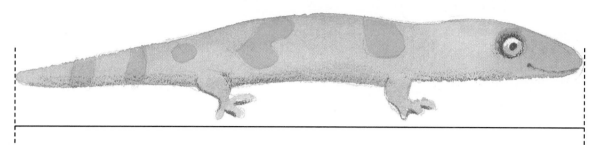

   about __6__ inches long

2.

   about _____ inches long

3.

4.

   about _____ inch tall

   about _____ inches tall

5. Draw your own object.
   About how long is it?
   About how tall is it?

   about _____ inches long

   about _____ inches tall

About how long is the mouse's tail?

10 centimeters = 1 decimeter

1 centimeter

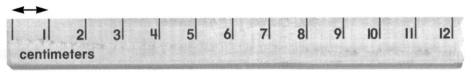

centimeters

Word Bank

centimeter
decimeter

Work with a partner.
Use a centimeter ruler to measure.

1. Your ear
   about _____
   centimeters

2. Your thumb
   about _____
   centimeters

3. Your hand
   about _____
   centimeters

4. Your forearm
   about _____
   centimeters

5. Your foot
   about _____
   centimeters

Home Connection Invite your child to find things at home that are about 10 centimeters long. Help your child check the measurements with a centimeter ruler.

Use a centimeter ruler to measure.

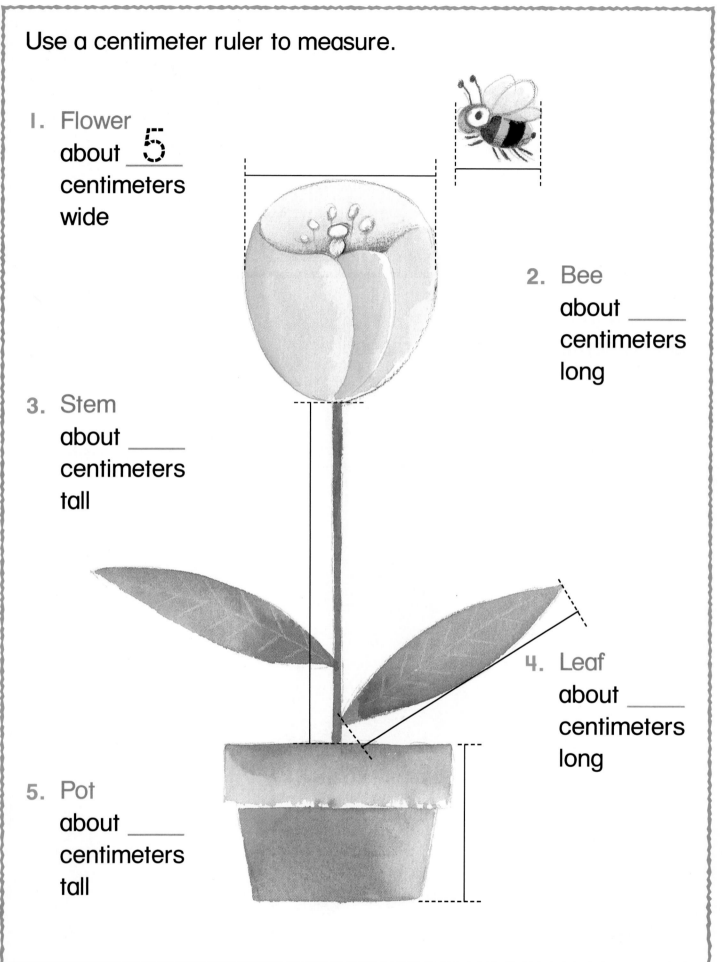

1. Flower
   about __5__
   centimeters
   wide

2. Bee
   about ____
   centimeters
   long

3. Stem
   about ____
   centimeters
   tall

4. Leaf
   about ____
   centimeters
   long

5. Pot
   about ____
   centimeters
   tall

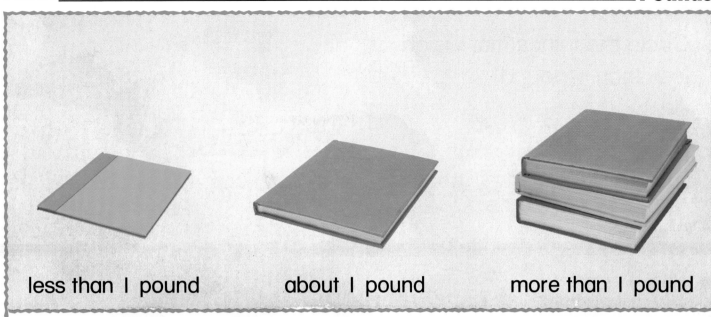

less than 1 pound   about 1 pound   more than 1 pound

Does each weigh **more** or **less** than 1 pound?
Circle **more** or **less**.

Word Bank

pound

1. pencil

     more

     (less)

2. backpack

     more

     less

3. chalk

     more

     less

4. globe

     more

     less

Home Connection Help your child find food products in your home that are less than, more than, and about 1 pound.

two hundred ninety-one   **291**

Circle the things that weigh less than 1 pound.

1. Circle the longer object.

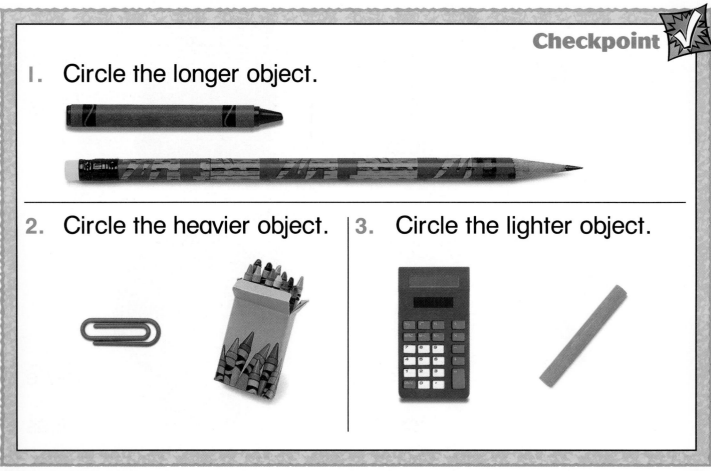

2. Circle the heavier object.

3. Circle the lighter object.

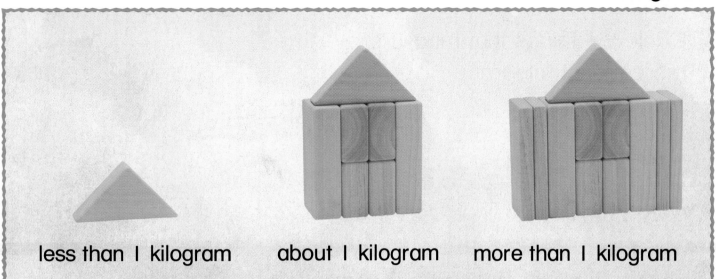

less than 1 kilogram   about 1 kilogram   more than 1 kilogram

Does each thing measure **more** or **less** than a kilogram?
Circle **more** or **less**.

Word Bank
kilogram

1. plant

(more)

less

2. 3 books

more

less

3. folder

more

less

4. shoe

more

less

Home Connection Work with your child to practice measuring 1-kilogram amounts (about 2.2 pounds) of dry materials, such as beans, pebbles, or marbles, on a household scale.

Circle the things that measure
more than 1 kilogram.

1.

Problem Solving

Solve.

2. Tara's rabbit measures 2 kilograms.
Ricardo's rabbit measures 3 kilograms.
Color Ricardo's rabbit.

 =

2 cups fill 1 pint.   2 pints fill 1 quart.

How many can you fill?
Circle to show how many.

1.

2.

3.
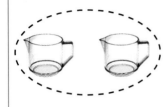   

4.

Home Connection Your child is learning about cups, pints, and quarts. On a trip to the supermarket, have your child identify containers and compare the quantities each holds.

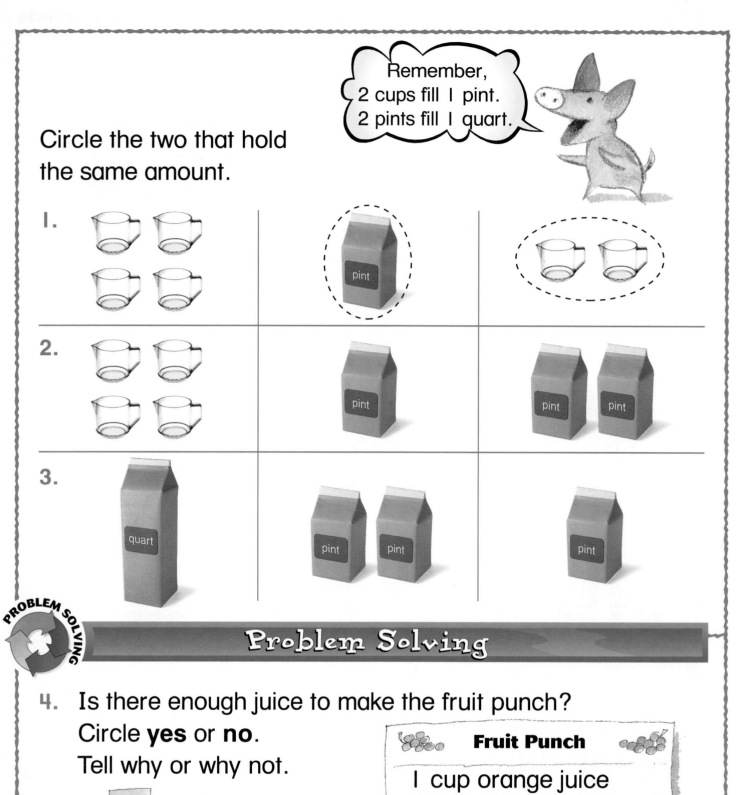

Remember,
2 cups fill 1 pint.
2 pints fill 1 quart.

Circle the two that hold
the same amount.

1. | | pint | cups |

2. | | pint | pint pint |

3. | quart | pint pint | pint |

PROBLEM SOLVING

Problem Solving

4. Is there enough juice to make the fruit punch?
Circle **yes** or **no**.
Tell why or why not.

Fruit Punch

1 cup orange juice

1 quart pineapple juice

1 pint cranberry juice

yes   no

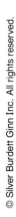

© Silver Burdett Ginn Inc. All rights reserved.

less than I liter

I liter

more than I liter

Circle the things that hold more than I liter.

Word Bank
liter

Home Connection Children are learning about liters. Display a I-liter bottle at home and help your child find containers that hold more than, less than, and about I liter.

two hundred ninety-nine   **299**

1. Color the things that hold less than 1 liter.

I liter

Solve.

2. Each jar holds 4 liters.
About how many more liters do
you need to fill each jar?

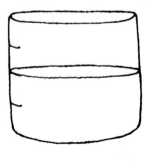

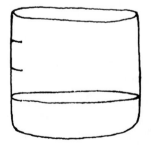

about _____ liters   about _____ liters

Use the right tool to measure.

 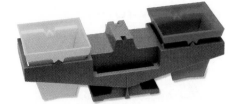

How long is it?   How much does it hold?   How heavy is it?

Circle the tool you would use.

1. How long is it?

2. How heavy is it?

3. How much does it hold?

4. How tall is it?

Home Connection Invite your child to name things in your home that he or she would measure with a ruler, a measuring cup, and a scale.

Circle the correct measurement.

1. How long is it?

3 inches

3 pounds

3 cups

2. How much does it hold?

1 inch

1 pound

1 quart

3. How heavy is it?

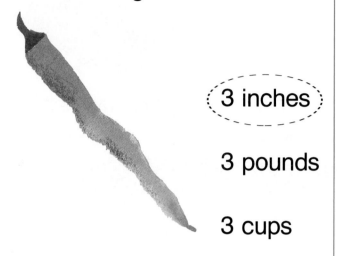

5 inches

5 pounds

5 pints

4. How much does it hold?

1 inch

1 pound

1 cup

5. How tall is it?

2 inches

2 pounds

2 cups

6. How heavy is it?

4 inches

4 pounds

4 cups

Does it weigh **more** or **less**
than a kilogram?
Circle **more** or **less**.

1.

2.

less   more   less   more

Circle the container that holds the most.
Order the containers from most to least.

3.

_____   _____   _____

Circle the containers that hold less than a liter.

4.

How long is it?
Circle the tool you would use.

5.

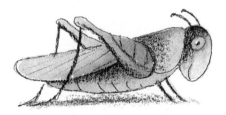    

Name_____

Use a centimeter ruler to measure.

1. The 🚐 is about ___9___ centimeters long.

2. The 🌳 is about _____ centimeters tall.

3. The 🦆 is about _____ centimeters tall.

4. The 🐷 is about _____ centimeters long.

5. The 🐤 is about _____ centimeter tall.

Name_____

About how long is each one?
Circle the better answer.

1.

   2 inches   6 inches

2.

   3 centimeters   5 centimeters

Does it weigh more or less
than 1 pound?
Circle **more** or **less**.

3.

   more

   less

Does it weigh more or less
than 1 kilogram?
Circle **more** or **less**.

4.

   more

   less

How many cups can you fill?
Circle to show how many.

5.

6.

Circle the containers that hold
more than a liter.

7.

How much does it hold?
Circle the tool you would use.

8.

Name____________________________ **Performance Assessment**

Pick an object. Draw it.
Measure to tell about it.

1. It weighs more than ____________________.

2. It weighs less than ____________________.

3. It is about ____________________ tall.

4. It is about ____________________ long.

5. What tools did you use to measure?

____

____

90° F

90 degrees

20° F

20 degrees

Circle the picture
that shows each temperature.

1. 80° F

2. 60° F

3. 30° F

About how many cubes
will cover a workspace?

You can use the
MathProcessor
to find out.

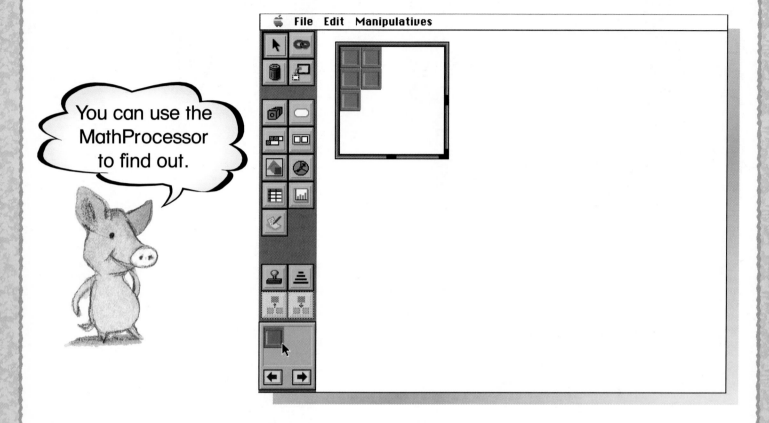

Take turns with a partner.

1 Click on the **cube button**
to show a workspace.

2 Click on the **arrow**
to pick a cube color.

3 Click on the **cube** 5
times to show 5 cubes.
Guess how many cubes
will cover the workspace.

4 Click on the **cube** to
cover the workspace.
Stop to guess again.
Then count.

Change the size of the workspace.
How many cubes cover it now?

Addition and Subtraction to 18

Look Who's Here!

written by Roxane Fox

illustrated by Rose Mary Berlin

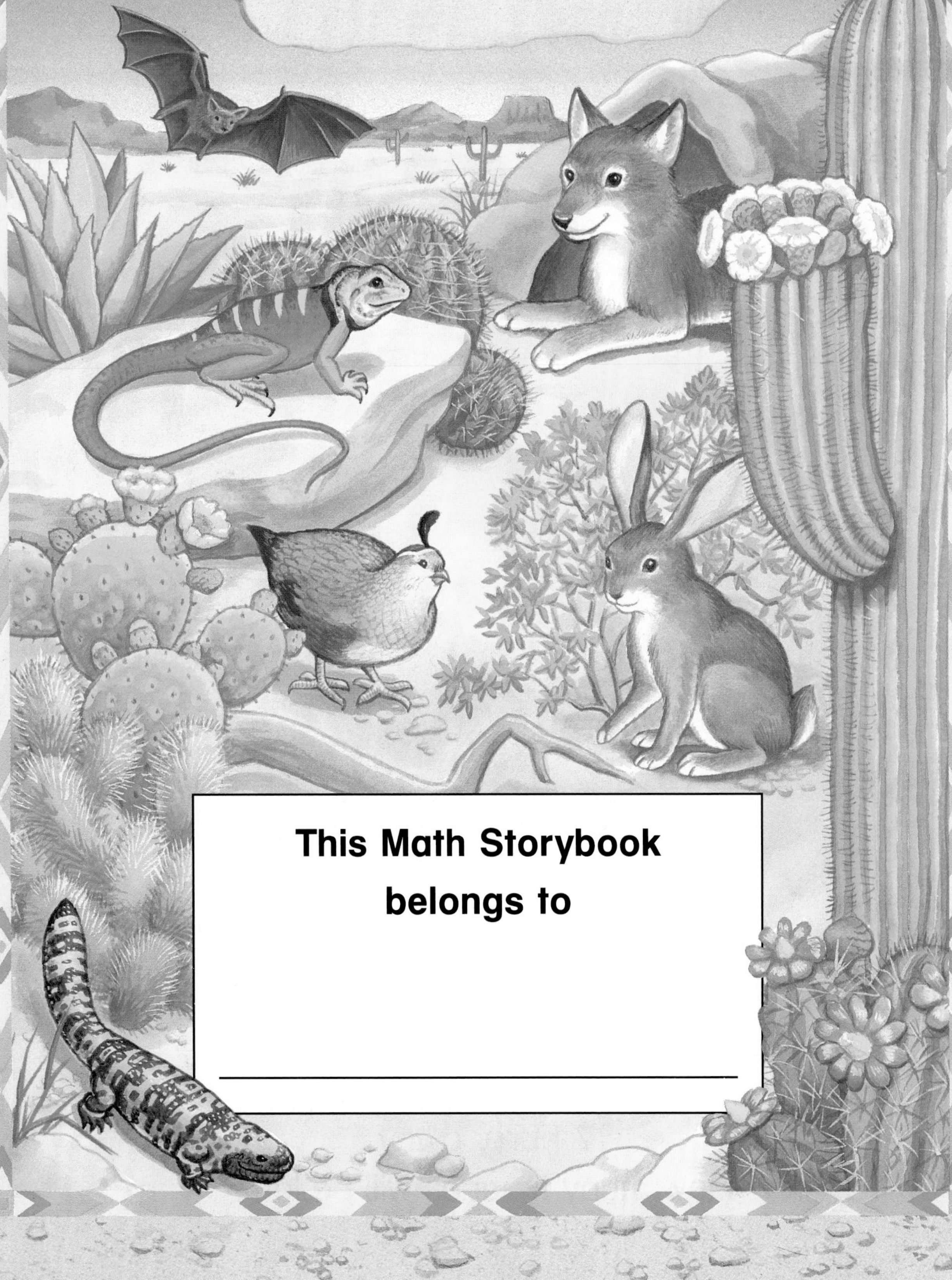

This Math Storybook belongs to

____

It is springtime in the desert.
Many animals wake up from a long winter rest.
Look who's here!

There are 10 iguanas.
7 hurry away.
How many iguanas will be left?

The desert air is hot and dry.
Animals look for water.
Look who's here!

9 rabbits drink.
Here come 9 quails.
How many animals are there in all?

In springtime the cactuses bloom.
Many animals walk near the cactuses.
Look who's here!

There are 13 Gila monsters.
4 walk away.
How many Gila monsters will be left?

The air gets cool when the sun goes down.
This is when some animals look for food.
Look who's here!

4 coyotes watch their pups.
8 pups play.
How many coyotes are there in all?

It is nighttime in the desert.
Some animals come out at night.
Look who's here!

17 bats hunt for food.
9 fly back to their cave.
How many bats will be left?

Color the desert animals.
What if there were 4 more?
What if there were 5 fewer?
Tell how many there will be.

G

A Note to the Family

**Here are some learning ideas
you can share with your child.**

Enjoy *Look Who's Here!* Together

- Read each page of the story with your child. Ask whether he or she needs to add or subtract in order to find the answer to the question on each page. Help your child write addition or subtraction sentences to find how many there are in all or how many are left.

  For example: 4 big coyotes and 8 little coyotes are 12 in all
  $$4 + 8 = 12$$

- Ask your child to tell how many animals are on the last page of the story. Encourage him or her to tell number stories about more animals coming along or some going away.

At-Home Activity

- Use peanuts, raisins, grapes, or any other small snack food. To practice addition, give your child 2 groups of snacks and have him or her tell you an addition sentence that shows how many there are in all. To practice subtraction, begin with a single group and tell your child that she or he may eat a specified number. Before he or she eats, ask your child to say a subtraction sentence that describes how many will be left.

Read More About It!

To read more stories about the desert or addition and subtraction, look for these books in your local library.

- *Desert Giant: The World of the Saguaro Cactus* by Barbara Bash (Sierra Club Books/Little, Brown, 1989)
- *Caps for Sale* by Esphyr Slobodkina (HarperCollins, 1987)
- *Eat Up, Gemma* by Sarah Hayes (Harcourt Brace, 1993)

Visit Our Web Site!

www.sbgmath.com

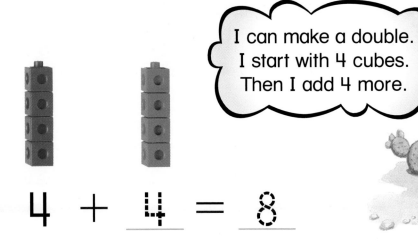

I can make a double.
I start with 4 cubes.
Then I add 4 more.

$4 + \underline{4} = \underline{8}$

Use two colors of cubes and Workmat 4.
Show each number. Then show the double.
Complete the addition sentence.

1. Show 3.

   $3 + \underline{} = \underline{}$

2. Show 5.

   $5 + \underline{} = \underline{}$

3. Show 2.

   $2 + \underline{} = \underline{}$

4. Show 7.

   $7 + \underline{} = \underline{}$

5. Show 6.

   $6 + \underline{} = \underline{}$

6. Show 9.

   $9 + \underline{} = \underline{}$

7. Show 8.

   $8 + \underline{} = \underline{}$

8. Show 1.

   $1 + \underline{} = \underline{}$

Home Connection Use buttons or other household
items to practice doubles with your child.

three hundred nine **309**

Add. Circle the doubles.
Use cubes if you like.

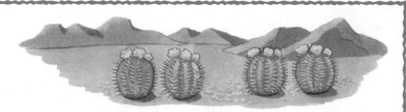

1. $(2 + 2 = \underline{4})$ $7 + 3 = \underline{}$ $0 + 8 = \underline{}$

2. $3 + 5 = \underline{}$ $5 + 5 = \underline{}$ $6 + 6 = \underline{}$

3. $7 + 7 = \underline{}$ $3 + 9 = \underline{}$ $8 + 8 = \underline{}$

4.
$$\begin{array}{cccccc} 8 & 5 & 0 & 1 & 2 & 6 \\ +2 & +4 & +0 & +1 & +6 & +1 \end{array}$$

5.
$$\begin{array}{cccccc} 3 & 4 & 7 & 4 & 5 & 6 \\ +3 & +8 & +1 & +4 & +6 & +4 \end{array}$$

6.
$$\begin{array}{cccccc} 8 & 6 & 7 & 9 & 3 & 7 \\ +3 & +0 & +4 & +9 & +6 & +2 \end{array}$$

How can you use doubles to add 5 + 6?

Think 5 + 5 and I more is 11.

$5 + 5 =$ 10

$5 + 6 =$ 11

Use cubes. Write each sum.

1.
$3 + 3 =$ ___
$3 + 4 =$ ___

2.
$4 + 4 =$ ___
$4 + 5 =$ ___

3.
$7 + 7 =$ ___
$7 + 8 =$ ___

4.
$1 + 1 =$ ___
$2 + 1 =$ ___

5.
$5 + 5 =$ ___
$5 + 6 =$ ___

6.
$8 + 8 =$ ___
$9 + 8 =$ ___

7.
$6 + 6 =$ ___
$6 + 7 =$ ___

8.
$2 + 2 =$ ___
$2 + 3 =$ ___

Home Connection Ask your child to use household items such as pennies or buttons to show doubles. Then add one item to the number and ask what the new sum is.

Use cubes.
Write each sum.

1.
$$\begin{array}{r} 3 \\ + 3 \\ \hline 6 \end{array}$$
$$\begin{array}{r} 3 \\ + 4 \\ \hline 7 \end{array}$$

2.
$$\begin{array}{r} 0 \\ + 0 \\ \hline \end{array}$$
$$\begin{array}{r} 0 \\ + 1 \\ \hline \end{array}$$

3.
$$\begin{array}{r} 6 \\ + 6 \\ \hline \end{array}$$
$$\begin{array}{r} 6 \\ + 7 \\ \hline \end{array}$$

4.
$$\begin{array}{r} 2 \\ + 2 \\ \hline \end{array}$$
$$\begin{array}{r} 2 \\ + 3 \\ \hline \end{array}$$

5.
$$\begin{array}{r} 5 \\ + 5 \\ \hline \end{array}$$
$$\begin{array}{r} 5 \\ + 6 \\ \hline \end{array}$$

6.
$$\begin{array}{r} 8 \\ + 8 \\ \hline \end{array}$$
$$\begin{array}{r} 8 \\ + 9 \\ \hline \end{array}$$

7.
$$\begin{array}{r} 4 \\ + 4 \\ \hline \end{array}$$
$$\begin{array}{r} 4 \\ + 5 \\ \hline \end{array}$$

8.
$$\begin{array}{r} 1 \\ + 1 \\ \hline \end{array}$$
$$\begin{array}{r} 1 \\ + 2 \\ \hline \end{array}$$

Problem Solving

Solve.

9. There are 7 owls on a cactus.
There are double that many
and one more flying away.
How many owls are flying away? _____ owls

Use counters and the ten-frame below.
Find each sum. Look for a pattern.

1. 10 + 1 = 11

2. 10 + 2 = ____

3. 10 + 3 = ____

4. 10 + 4 = ____

5. 10 + 5 = ____

6. 10 + 6 = ____

7. 10 + 7 = ____

8. 10 + 8 = ____

9. 10 + 9 = ____

Home Connection Encourage your
child to talk about patterns when adding ones
to 10. Ask how the sum changes each time.

three hundred thirteen   **313**

Draw more dots to add.

1. 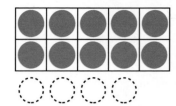 $\begin{array}{r} 4 \\ +\ 10 \\ \hline 14 \end{array}$

2. 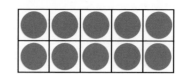 $\begin{array}{r} 10 \\ +\ 7 \\ \hline \end{array}$

3. 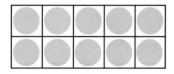 $\begin{array}{r} 10 \\ +\ 5 \\ \hline \end{array}$

4. 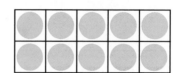 $\begin{array}{r} 6 \\ +\ 10 \\ \hline \end{array}$

5. 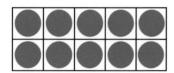 $\begin{array}{r} 10 \\ +\ 2 \\ \hline \end{array}$

6. 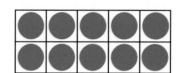 $\begin{array}{r} 3 \\ +\ 10 \\ \hline \end{array}$

Critical Thinking Corner

Mental Math

Complete each pattern.

7.
$10 + 6 = \underline{\hspace{1cm}}$

$10 + 7 = \underline{\hspace{1cm}}$

$10 + 8 = \underline{\hspace{1cm}}$

$10 + 9 = \underline{\hspace{1cm}}$

8.
$20 + 6 = \underline{\hspace{1cm}}$

$20 + 7 = \underline{\hspace{1cm}}$

$20 + 8 = \underline{\hspace{1cm}}$

$20 + 9 = \underline{\hspace{1cm}}$

9 + 3

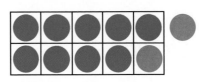

10 + 2 = 12

so 9 + 3 = 12

Make 10.
Then add 2.

Use counters and Workmat 2.
Show 9 in the ten-frame.
Make 10. Add.

1. ┃ 9 + 6 ┃

10 + 5 = ____

so 9 + 6 = ____

2. ┃ 9 + 4 ┃

10 + 3 = ____

so 9 + 4 = ____

3. ┃ 9 + 8 ┃

10 + 7 = ____

so 9 + 8 = ____

4. ┃ 9 + 2 ┃

10 + 1 = ____

so 9 + 2 = ____

5. ┃ 9 + 7 ┃

10 + 6 = ____

so 9 + 7 = ____

6. ┃ 9 + 5 ┃

10 + 4 = ____

so 9 + 5 = ____

Home Connection Making 10 can help children find
sums where one number is 9. Ask your child to explain
how making 10 can help find sums on this page.

three hundred fifteen   **315**

Make 10.

Draw dots to add.

1.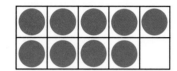
$$\begin{array}{r} 9 \\ +\ 7 \\ \hline 16 \end{array}$$

2.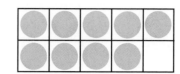
$$\begin{array}{r} 9 \\ +\ 3 \\ \hline \end{array}$$

3.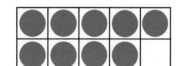
$$\begin{array}{r} 9 \\ +\ 5 \\ \hline \end{array}$$

4.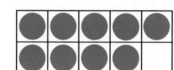
$$\begin{array}{r} 9 \\ +\ 8 \\ \hline \end{array}$$

5.
$$\begin{array}{r} 9 \\ +\ 6 \\ \hline \end{array}$$

6.
$$\begin{array}{r} 9 \\ +\ 9 \\ \hline \end{array}$$

Problem Solving

Use counters to solve.

9. The sum of two numbers fits in a ten-frame with 3 left over.

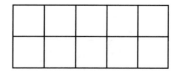

What two numbers could they be? _____ and _____

Tell other numbers that could also solve the problem.

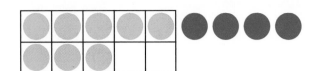

$8 + 4$

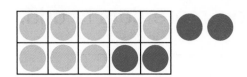

$10 + 2 = 12$

so $8 + 4 = 12$

Make 10. Then add the others.

Draw more dots to add.

1.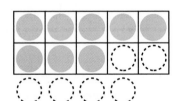
$$\begin{array}{r} 8 \\ + 6 \\ \hline 14 \end{array}$$

2.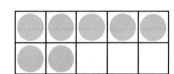
$$\begin{array}{r} 7 \\ + 4 \\ \hline \end{array}$$

3.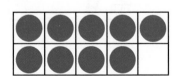
$$\begin{array}{r} 9 \\ + 7 \\ \hline \end{array}$$

4.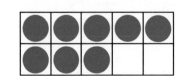
$$\begin{array}{r} 8 \\ + 5 \\ \hline \end{array}$$

5.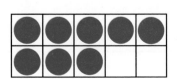
$$\begin{array}{r} 8 \\ + 7 \\ \hline \end{array}$$

6.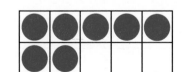
$$\begin{array}{r} 7 \\ + 5 \\ \hline \end{array}$$

Home Connection Have your child use pennies, buttons, or other household items to add. Ask your child to show a fact like 8 + 5. Then have him or her make 10 and find the sum.

Draw more dots to add.

1.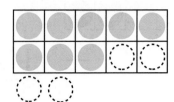
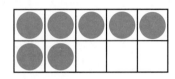
$$\begin{array}{r} 8 \\ + 4 \\ \hline 12 \end{array}$$

2.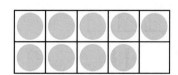
$$\begin{array}{r} 9 \\ + 5 \\ \hline \end{array}$$

3.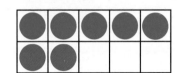
$$\begin{array}{r} 7 \\ + 5 \\ \hline \end{array}$$

4.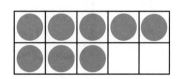
$$\begin{array}{r} 8 \\ + 6 \\ \hline \end{array}$$

5.
$$\begin{array}{r} 7 \\ + 9 \\ \hline \end{array}$$

6.
$$\begin{array}{r} 8 \\ + 5 \\ \hline \end{array}$$

Add. Circle the doubles.

1.
$$\begin{array}{r} 8 \\ + 5 \\ \hline \end{array}$$
$$\begin{array}{r} 6 \\ + 5 \\ \hline \end{array}$$
$$\begin{array}{r} 4 \\ + 7 \\ \hline \end{array}$$
$$\begin{array}{r} 6 \\ + 6 \\ \hline \end{array}$$
$$\begin{array}{r} 5 \\ + 4 \\ \hline \end{array}$$
$$\begin{array}{r} 8 \\ + 8 \\ \hline \end{array}$$

2.
$$\begin{array}{r} 5 \\ + 5 \\ \hline \end{array}$$
$$\begin{array}{r} 8 \\ + 7 \\ \hline \end{array}$$
$$\begin{array}{r} 8 \\ + 9 \\ \hline \end{array}$$
$$\begin{array}{r} 9 \\ + 6 \\ \hline \end{array}$$
$$\begin{array}{r} 9 \\ + 9 \\ \hline \end{array}$$
$$\begin{array}{r} 9 \\ + 7 \\ \hline \end{array}$$

3. $6 + 7 =$ ___ $9 + 4 =$ ___ $4 + 4 =$ ___

You can add three numbers in many ways.

You can make 10.

You can look for doubles.

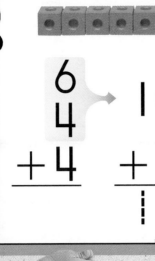

$$\begin{array}{r} 6 \\ 4 \\ +4 \\ \hline \end{array} \quad \begin{array}{r} 10 \\ +4 \\ \hline 14 \end{array} \quad \begin{array}{r} 6 \\ 4 \\ +4 \\ \hline \end{array} \quad \begin{array}{r} 6 \\ +8 \\ \hline 14 \end{array}$$

Find each sum.

1.
$$\begin{array}{r} 6 \\ 5 \\ +5 \\ \hline \end{array} \boxed{10} \qquad \begin{array}{r} 7 \\ 3 \\ +1 \\ \hline \end{array} \boxed{} \qquad \begin{array}{r} 2 \\ 2 \\ +8 \\ \hline \end{array} \boxed{} \qquad \begin{array}{r} 6 \\ 3 \\ +3 \\ \hline \end{array} \boxed{}$$

2.
$$\begin{array}{r} 4 \\ 4 \\ +5 \\ \hline \end{array} \qquad \begin{array}{r} 6 \\ 3 \\ +7 \\ \hline \end{array} \qquad \begin{array}{r} 9 \\ 1 \\ +5 \\ \hline \end{array} \qquad \begin{array}{r} 7 \\ 7 \\ +1 \\ \hline \end{array} \qquad \begin{array}{r} 7 \\ 4 \\ +6 \\ \hline \end{array} \qquad \begin{array}{r} 6 \\ 6 \\ +2 \\ \hline \end{array}$$

3.
$$\begin{array}{r} 8 \\ 1 \\ +1 \\ \hline \end{array} \qquad \begin{array}{r} 4 \\ 3 \\ +7 \\ \hline \end{array} \qquad \begin{array}{r} 2 \\ 2 \\ +5 \\ \hline \end{array} \qquad \begin{array}{r} 8 \\ 8 \\ +1 \\ \hline \end{array} \qquad \begin{array}{r} 6 \\ 1 \\ +9 \\ \hline \end{array} \qquad \begin{array}{r} 5 \\ 5 \\ +7 \\ \hline \end{array}$$

Home Connection Children can add three numbers in any order. Ask your child how he or she found each sum on this page. Ask which numbers he or she added first and why.

three hundred nineteen   **319**

Find each sum.

1.
$$\begin{array}{r} 4 \\ 6 \\ + 7 \\ \hline 17 \end{array}$$
$$\begin{array}{r} 2 \\ 2 \\ + 9 \\ \hline \end{array}$$
$$\begin{array}{r} 6 \\ 7 \\ + 3 \\ \hline \end{array}$$
$$\begin{array}{r} 2 \\ 9 \\ + 1 \\ \hline \end{array}$$
$$\begin{array}{r} 3 \\ 4 \\ + 4 \\ \hline \end{array}$$

2.
$$\begin{array}{r} 7 \\ 3 \\ + 2 \\ \hline \end{array}$$
$$\begin{array}{r} 5 \\ 6 \\ + 4 \\ \hline \end{array}$$
$$\begin{array}{r} 2 \\ 8 \\ + 4 \\ \hline \end{array}$$
$$\begin{array}{r} 0 \\ 9 \\ + 9 \\ \hline \end{array}$$
$$\begin{array}{r} 4 \\ 8 \\ + 2 \\ \hline \end{array}$$

3. $5 + 3 + 3 = \underline{}$ $\qquad$ $6 + 6 + 4 = \underline{}$

4. $8 + 2 + 7 = \underline{}$ $\qquad$ $1 + 6 + 6 = \underline{}$

Problem Solving

Add across. Add down.

The sum is the same. Complete each ⊞ .

5.

4	9	
	5	7
8		

Each sum is 15.

6.

7		3
	4	
5	6	

Each sum is 12.

You can add in many ways.

$$\begin{array}{r} 4 \\ + 5 \\ \hline 9 \end{array}$$

Use doubles.

$$\begin{array}{r} 9 \\ + 5 \\ \hline 14 \end{array}$$

Make 10.

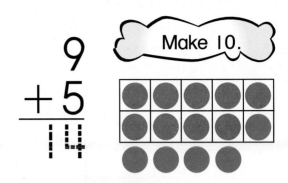

$$\begin{array}{r} 3 \\ + 8 \\ \hline 11 \end{array}$$

Count on.

8, 9, 10, 11

Sometimes one way is easier than another.

Add. Tell how you found each sum.

1.
$$\begin{array}{r} 5 \\ + 6 \\ \hline \end{array}$$
$$\begin{array}{r} 9 \\ + 4 \\ \hline \end{array}$$
$$\begin{array}{r} 7 \\ + 3 \\ \hline \end{array}$$
$$\begin{array}{r} 8 \\ + 8 \\ \hline \end{array}$$
$$\begin{array}{r} 9 \\ + 2 \\ \hline \end{array}$$
$$\begin{array}{r} 4 \\ + 8 \\ \hline \end{array}$$

2.
$$\begin{array}{r} 6 \\ + 7 \\ \hline \end{array}$$
$$\begin{array}{r} 9 \\ + 6 \\ \hline \end{array}$$
$$\begin{array}{r} 8 \\ + 2 \\ \hline \end{array}$$
$$\begin{array}{r} 4 \\ + 3 \\ \hline \end{array}$$
$$\begin{array}{r} 9 \\ + 8 \\ \hline \end{array}$$
$$\begin{array}{r} 8 \\ + 5 \\ \hline \end{array}$$

3.
$$\begin{array}{r} 9 \\ + 3 \\ \hline \end{array}$$
$$\begin{array}{r} 8 \\ + 1 \\ \hline \end{array}$$
$$\begin{array}{r} 7 \\ + 8 \\ \hline \end{array}$$
$$\begin{array}{r} 4 \\ + 9 \\ \hline \end{array}$$
$$\begin{array}{r} 9 \\ + 9 \\ \hline \end{array}$$
$$\begin{array}{r} 9 \\ + 7 \\ \hline \end{array}$$

Home Connection Have your child tell how he or she found each sum on this page.

three hundred twenty-one **321**

Follow each rule.

1.

Make the double	
4	8
5	
6	
7	
8	
9	

2.

Count on 3	
4	
5	
6	
7	
8	
9	

3.

Add 7	
9	
6	
7	
8	
4	
5	

4.

Add 8	
3	
6	
9	
4	
8	
7	

5.

Add 9	
2	
6	
4	
8	
5	
7	

Subtraction is the opposite of addition.

Use two colors of counters and Workmat 4.
Show each number.
Add. Then subtract.

1. Start with 6. Add 4.

    Then take away 4.

    $6 + 4 = 10$

    $10 - 4 = 6$

2. Start with 7. Add 6.

    Then take away 6.

    ___ + ___ = ___

    ___ − ___ = ___

3. Start with 8. Add 8.

    Then take away 8.

    ___ + ___ = ___

    ___ − ___ = ___

4. Start with 6. Add 9.

    Then take away 9.

    ___ + ___ = ___

    ___ − ___ = ___

Home Connection Choose an addition fact. Ask your child to use pennies or other household items to show the fact and the related subtraction fact. Then write both number sentences.

Use two colors of counters and Workmat 4.
Show each number. Add. Then subtract.

	Add	Subtract
1. 4 9	$4 + 9 = 13$	$13 - 9 = 4$
2. 5 8	___ + ___ = ___	___ − ___ = ___
3. 9 9	___ + ___ = ___	___ − ___ = ___
4. 7 8	___ + ___ = ___	___ − ___ = ___
5. 5 9	___ + ___ = ___	___ − ___ = ___

Problem Solving

Use counters to solve.

6. The sum of two numbers is 8.
   The difference of the numbers is 2.
   What are the numbers?   _____ and _____

There are 9 snakes.
2 hide under a rock.
How many snakes are left?

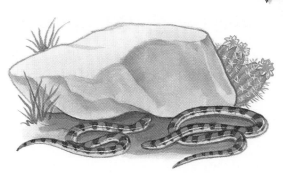

  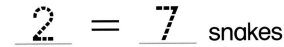 snakes

___

Write a number sentence. Solve.

1. 6 deer eat.
    6 more join them.
    How many are there now?

    _____ ◯ _____ = _____ deer

2. There are 13 rabbits.
    6 of them leave.
    How many are there now?

    _____ ◯ _____ = _____ rabbits

3. 14 bats are in a cave.
    7 fly away.
    How many bats are there now?

    _____ ◯ _____ = _____ bats

4. 8 owls are on a cactus.
    7 more join them.
    How many owls are there?

    _____ ◯ _____ = _____ owls

Home Connection Use 18 or fewer household items such
as pennies or paper clips. Make up addition or subtraction stories.
Ask your child to write a number sentence for each story.

three hundred twenty-five   **325**

Write a number sentence. Solve.

1. 4 big bears play.
   2 little bears play.
   How many are playing?

   _____ ◯ _____ = _____ bears

2. 8 rabbits hop.
   4 rabbits eat.
   How many rabbits are there?

   _____ ◯ _____ = _____ rabbits

3. 12 owls sleep.
   4 of them fly away.
   How many are left?

   _____ ◯ _____ = _____ owls

4. 9 deer drink.
   6 of them race away.
   Now how many are drinking?

   _____ ◯ _____ = _____ deer

What Do You Think?

When you subtract, is the difference always less than the number you started with? Tell why or why not.

Journal Idea

$$7 + 5 = 12 \qquad 12 - 5 = 7$$
$$5 + 7 = 12 \qquad 12 - 7 = 5$$

Every fact has the same numbers. This must be a fact family.

Add or subtract.
Write the numbers for each fact family.

1.  **14 8 6**

$8 + 6 = \underline{\quad}$ $14 - 6 = \underline{\quad}$

$6 + 8 = \underline{\quad}$ $14 - 8 = \underline{\quad}$

2.  **13 6 7**

$6 + 7 = \underline{\quad}$ $13 - 7 = \underline{\quad}$

$7 + 6 = \underline{\quad}$ $13 - 6 = \underline{\quad}$

3.  **16 9 7**

$9 + 7 = \underline{\quad}$ $16 - 7 = \underline{\quad}$

$7 + 9 = \underline{\quad}$ $16 - 9 = \underline{\quad}$

4.  **13 8 5**

$8 + 5 = \underline{\quad}$ $13 - 5 = \underline{\quad}$

$5 + 8 = \underline{\quad}$ $13 - 8 = \underline{\quad}$

Home Connection Fact families are number facts that use the same numbers. Ask your child to write number sentences for a fact family like 3, 9, and 12.

three hundred twenty-seven   **327**

Add and subtract.
Write the numbers for each fact family.

1.

$3 + 9 = \underline{12}$ $12 - 9 = \underline{3}$

$9 + 3 = \underline{12}$ $12 - 3 = \underline{9}$

2.

$9 + 4 = \underline{\hphantom{00}}$ $13 - 4 = \underline{\hphantom{00}}$

$4 + 9 = \underline{\hphantom{00}}$ $13 - 9 = \underline{\hphantom{00}}$

3.

$7 + 8 = \underline{\hphantom{00}}$ $15 - 8 = \underline{\hphantom{00}}$

$8 + 7 = \underline{\hphantom{00}}$ $15 - 7 = \underline{\hphantom{00}}$

4.

$9 + 8 = \underline{\hphantom{00}}$ $17 - 8 = \underline{\hphantom{00}}$

$8 + 9 = \underline{\hphantom{00}}$ $17 - 9 = \underline{\hphantom{00}}$

5.

$5 + 9 = \underline{\hphantom{00}}$ $14 - 9 = \underline{\hphantom{00}}$

$9 + 5 = \underline{\hphantom{00}}$ $14 - 5 = \underline{\hphantom{00}}$

6. Make your own fact family.
Write the number sentences.

$\underline{\hphantom{00}} + \underline{\hphantom{00}} = \underline{\hphantom{00}}$ $\underline{\hphantom{00}} - \underline{\hphantom{00}} = \underline{\hphantom{00}}$

$\underline{\hphantom{00}} + \underline{\hphantom{00}} = \underline{\hphantom{00}}$ $\underline{\hphantom{00}} - \underline{\hphantom{00}} = \underline{\hphantom{00}}$

You can subtract in many ways.

$$\begin{array}{r} 12 \\ -\ 9 \\ \hline 3 \end{array}$$

Think addition.

$3 + 9 = 12$

$$\begin{array}{r} 16 \\ -\ 8 \\ \hline 8 \end{array}$$

Use 10.

$$\begin{array}{r} 10 \\ -\ 2 \\ \hline 8 \end{array}$$

Use counters.

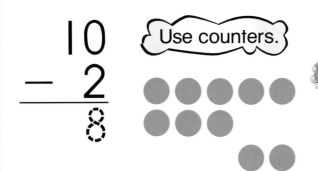

Sometimes one way is easier than another.

Subtract. Tell how you found each difference.

1.
$$\begin{array}{r} 12 \\ -\ 4 \\ \hline \end{array}$$
$$\begin{array}{r} 10 \\ -\ 7 \\ \hline \end{array}$$
$$\begin{array}{r} 17 \\ -\ 9 \\ \hline \end{array}$$
$$\begin{array}{r} 14 \\ -\ 6 \\ \hline \end{array}$$
$$\begin{array}{r} 7 \\ -\ 3 \\ \hline \end{array}$$
$$\begin{array}{r} 13 \\ -\ 4 \\ \hline \end{array}$$

2.
$$\begin{array}{r} 18 \\ -\ 9 \\ \hline \end{array}$$
$$\begin{array}{r} 8 \\ -\ 2 \\ \hline \end{array}$$
$$\begin{array}{r} 13 \\ -\ 5 \\ \hline \end{array}$$
$$\begin{array}{r} 14 \\ -\ 5 \\ \hline \end{array}$$
$$\begin{array}{r} 16 \\ -\ 7 \\ \hline \end{array}$$
$$\begin{array}{r} 12 \\ -\ 7 \\ \hline \end{array}$$

3.
$$\begin{array}{r} 16 \\ -\ 9 \\ \hline \end{array}$$
$$\begin{array}{r} 15 \\ -\ 6 \\ \hline \end{array}$$
$$\begin{array}{r} 12 \\ -\ 6 \\ \hline \end{array}$$
$$\begin{array}{r} 10 \\ -\ 4 \\ \hline \end{array}$$
$$\begin{array}{r} 14 \\ -\ 9 \\ \hline \end{array}$$
$$\begin{array}{r} 9 \\ -\ 0 \\ \hline \end{array}$$

Home Connection Write 2 or 3 problems similar to the ones on this page. Ask your child to solve the problems and describe the strategy he or she used to find each answer.

Follow the path to add and subtract.
Write the missing numbers.

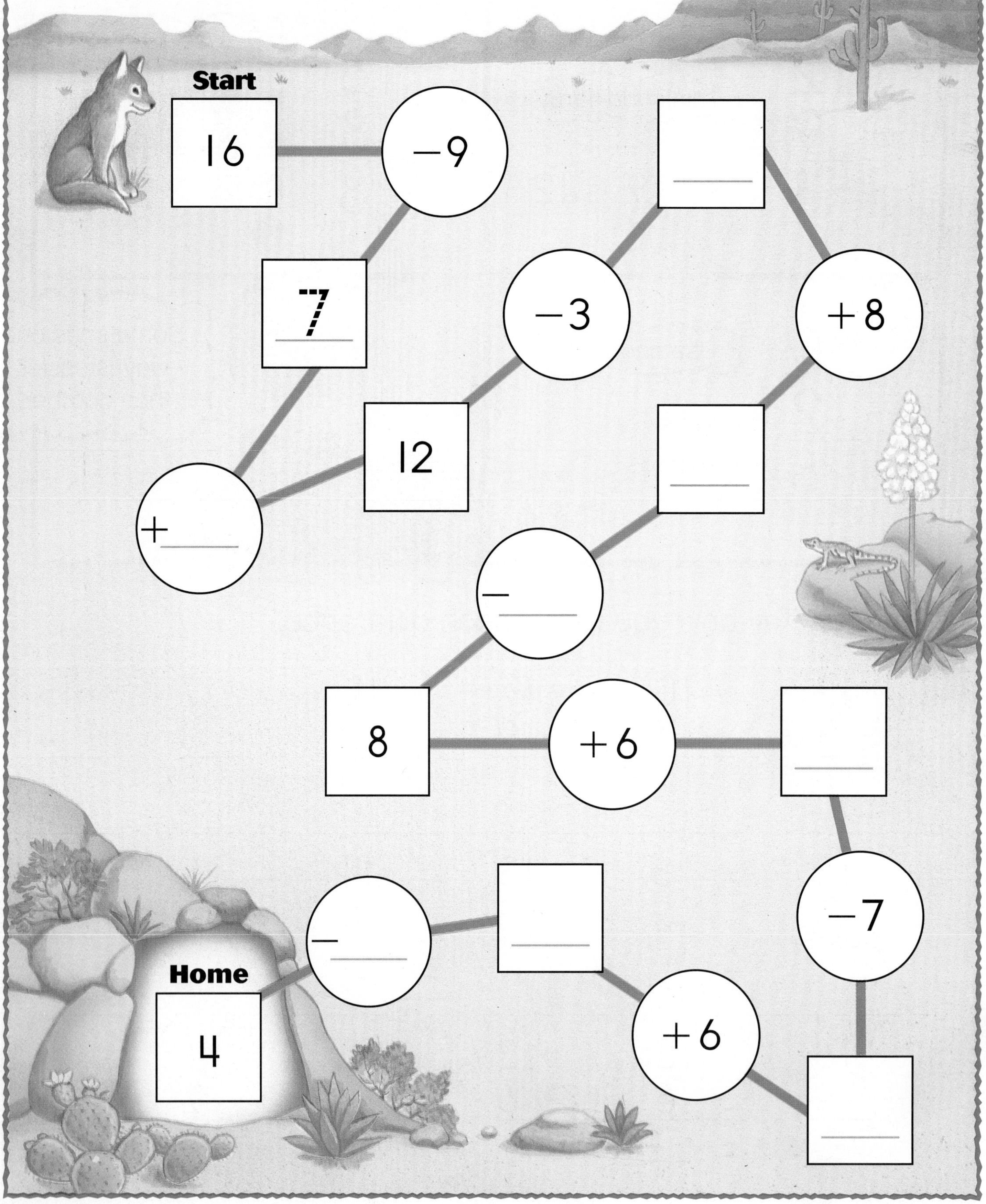

Start

16 — −9 — [___]

7 ___ — −3 — +8

+ ___ — 12 — [___]

− ___

8 — +6 — [___]

Home

4 — − ___ — [___] — +6 — −7

[___]

Name_____

Cross out the information you do not need.
Write the number sentence.

1. Nancy sees 7 white flowers.
    ~~She sees 6 lizards.~~
    She sees 8 red flowers.
    How many flowers does she see?

    7 ⊕ 8 = 15 flowers

2. Kurt counts 17 butterflies.
    9 fly away.
    Kurt sees 6 beetles.
    How many butterflies are there now?

    $\begin{array}{r} 1 \\ 0 \\ +7 \\ \hline \\ -9 \\ \hline 7 \\ 2 \end{array}$ 9=7+2

    17 ⊖ 9 = 8 butterflies

    8 + 9 = 17

    10 7
    8 7

    17 − 9 = ?
    ? + 9 = 17

3. Jenny sees 8 deer.
    She sees 2 cactuses.
    Jenny sees 6 more deer.
    How many deer does she see?

    8 ⊕ 6 = 14 deer

4. Alex sees 2 hawks.
    He sees 18 lizards.
    9 lizards hide.
    How many lizards are there now?

    18 ⊖ 9 = 9 lizards

Home Connection Make up word problems with extra
information or facts. Ask your child to decide what information is
unnecessary and then solve the problem. Then change roles.

Cross out the information you do not need.
Write the number sentence.

1. Rachel has 13 pieces of fruit.
    She has 2 baskets.
    She gives 8 pieces of fruit to friends.
    How many pieces of fruit does she have now?

    _____ ◯ _____ = _____ pieces of fruit

2. Cody's family sees 16 deer.
    8 deer run away.
    Cody sees 2 bobcats.
    How many deer are there now?

    _____ ◯ _____ = _____ deer

3. José sees 4 owls.
    He sees 6 bats.
    He sees 8 deer.
    How many bats and owls does José see?

    _____ ◯ _____ = _____ bats and owls

4. Sara sees 7 birds.
    Then she sees 4 more.
    Sara sees 8 squirrels.
    How many birds does she see?

    _____ ◯ _____ = _____ birds

Add.

1.
$$\begin{array}{r} 6 \\ 4 \\ +\ 2 \\ \hline \end{array}$$
$$\begin{array}{r} 7 \\ 5 \\ +\ 5 \\ \hline \end{array}$$
$$\begin{array}{r} 4 \\ 4 \\ +\ 5 \\ \hline \end{array}$$
$$\begin{array}{r} 9 \\ 2 \\ +\ 2 \\ \hline \end{array}$$
$$\begin{array}{r} 8 \\ 2 \\ +\ 1 \\ \hline \end{array}$$
$$\begin{array}{r} 7 \\ 3 \\ +\ 2 \\ \hline \end{array}$$

Subtract.

2. $14 - 9 =$ ___ $13 - 8 =$ ___ $16 - 7 =$ ___

3. $15 - 7 =$ ___ $17 - 8 =$ ___ $14 - 6 =$ ___

Add or subtract.

4.  $4 + 9 =$ ___ $13 - 9 =$ ___

    $9 + 4 =$ ___ $13 - 4 =$ ___

5.  $9 + 6 =$ ___ $15 - 6 =$ ___

    $6 + 9 =$ ___ $15 - 9 =$ ___

Cross out the information you do not need.
Write a number sentence.

6. Toby sees 5 deer.
    She sees 14 cactuses.
    She sees 9 more deer.
    How many deer does Toby see?

    ____ ◯ ____ = ____ deer

Where is the largest desert in the world?

Add or subtract to find out.
Color each sum or difference.   less than 9 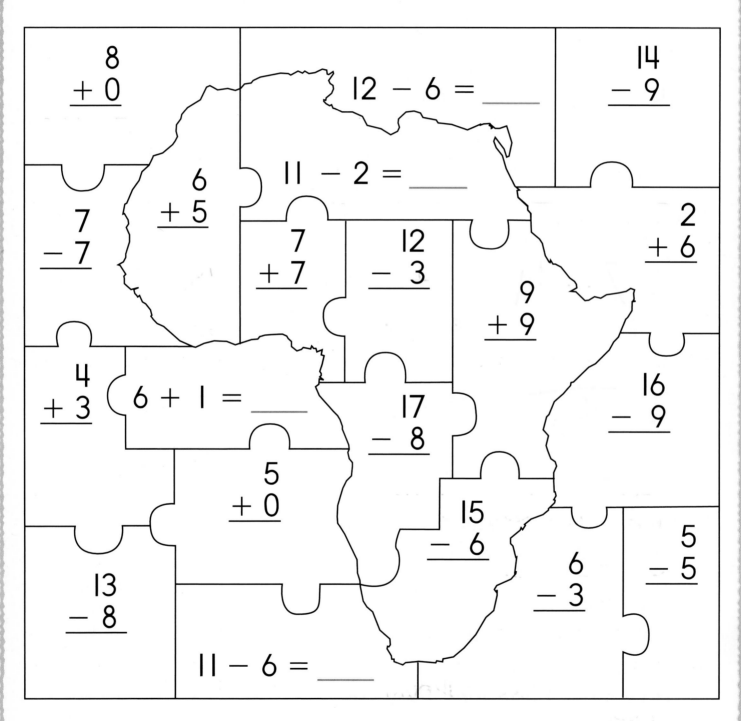 blue

9 or greater green

$$8 + 0$$

$$12 - 6 = \underline{\quad}$$

$$14 - 9$$

$$6 + 5$$

$$11 - 2 = \underline{\quad}$$

$$7 - 7$$

$$2 + 6$$

$$7 + 7$$

$$12 - 3$$

$$9 + 9$$

$$4 + 3$$

$$6 + 1 = \underline{\quad}$$

$$17 - 8$$

$$16 - 9$$

$$5 + 0$$

$$15 - 6$$

$$5 - 5$$

$$13 - 8$$

$$6 - 3$$

$$11 - 6 = \underline{\quad}$$

Add or subtract.

1.

$$\begin{array}{r} 9 \\ + 5 \\ \hline \end{array} \qquad \begin{array}{r} 8 \\ + 8 \\ \hline \end{array} \qquad \begin{array}{r} 9 \\ + 9 \\ \hline \end{array} \qquad \begin{array}{r} 8 \\ + 9 \\ \hline \end{array} \qquad \begin{array}{r} 4 \\ 1 \\ + 9 \\ \hline \end{array} \qquad \begin{array}{r} 5 \\ 5 \\ + 3 \\ \hline \end{array}$$

2.

$$\begin{array}{r} 10 \\ - 5 \\ \hline \end{array} \qquad \begin{array}{r} 12 \\ - 7 \\ \hline \end{array} \qquad \begin{array}{r} 13 \\ - 9 \\ \hline \end{array} \qquad \begin{array}{r} 17 \\ - 8 \\ \hline \end{array} \qquad \begin{array}{r} 11 \\ - 9 \\ \hline \end{array} \qquad \begin{array}{r} 12 \\ - 6 \\ \hline \end{array}$$

3. $15 - 7 =$ ____ $12 - 8 =$ ____ $17 - 9 =$ ____

Add or subtract.

4.  15 8 7

$8 + 7 =$ ____ $15 - 7 =$ ____

$7 + 8 =$ ____ $15 - 8 =$ ____

5. 12 9 3

$9 + 3 =$ ____ $12 - 3 =$ ____

$3 + 9 =$ ____ $12 - 9 =$ ____

Write a number sentence.

6. 3 hawks rest in a tree.
   9 hawks join them.
   How many are there now? ____ ____ = ____ hawks

7. 12 foxes drink at a stream.
   8 run away.
   How many are there now? ____ ____ = ____ foxes

What You Need

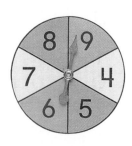

spinner

1 Spin the spinner 2 times.
   Record each number.

2 Use the numbers to write an addition sentence.
   Then write a related subtraction sentence.

	Spin 1	Spin 2	Number Sentences
1.			___ + ___ = ___ ___ − ___ = ___
2.			___ + ___ = ___ ___ − ___ = ___
3.			___ + ___ = ___ ___ − ___ = ___

4. Look at the sentences you wrote.
   Tell other related number sentences.

Complete each table.
Look for a pattern.

1.

foxes	1	2	3	4	5	6
legs	4	8	12			

2.

rabbits	1	2	3	4	5	6
ears	2	4				

3.

cactuses	1	2	3	4	5	6
flowers	3	6				

4.

feet	1	2	3	4	5	6
toes	5	10				

Use a .

Circle + or − .

1. **8** $\overset{+}{\underset{-}{}}$ **7** $\overset{+}{\underset{-}{}}$ **9** **=** 10

2. **6** $\overset{+}{\underset{-}{}}$ **5** $\overset{+}{\underset{-}{}}$ **7** **=** 18

3. **1** $\overset{+}{\underset{-}{}}$ **8** $\overset{+}{\underset{-}{}}$ **3** **=** 6

4. **9** $\overset{+}{\underset{-}{}}$ **4** $\overset{+}{\underset{-}{}}$ **8** **=** 13

5. **7** $\overset{+}{\underset{-}{}}$ **6** $\overset{+}{\underset{-}{}}$ **7** **=** 8

6. **4** $\overset{+}{\underset{-}{}}$ **9** $\overset{+}{\underset{-}{}}$ **2** **=** 11

7. **5** $\overset{+}{\underset{-}{}}$ **9** $\overset{+}{\underset{-}{}}$ **5** **=** 9

8. **9** $\overset{+}{\underset{-}{}}$ **3** $\overset{+}{\underset{-}{}}$ **8** **=** 14

Po Lan's Pocket

written by Jerry Melvin

illustrated by Judy Moffatt

This Math Storybook

belongs to

_____

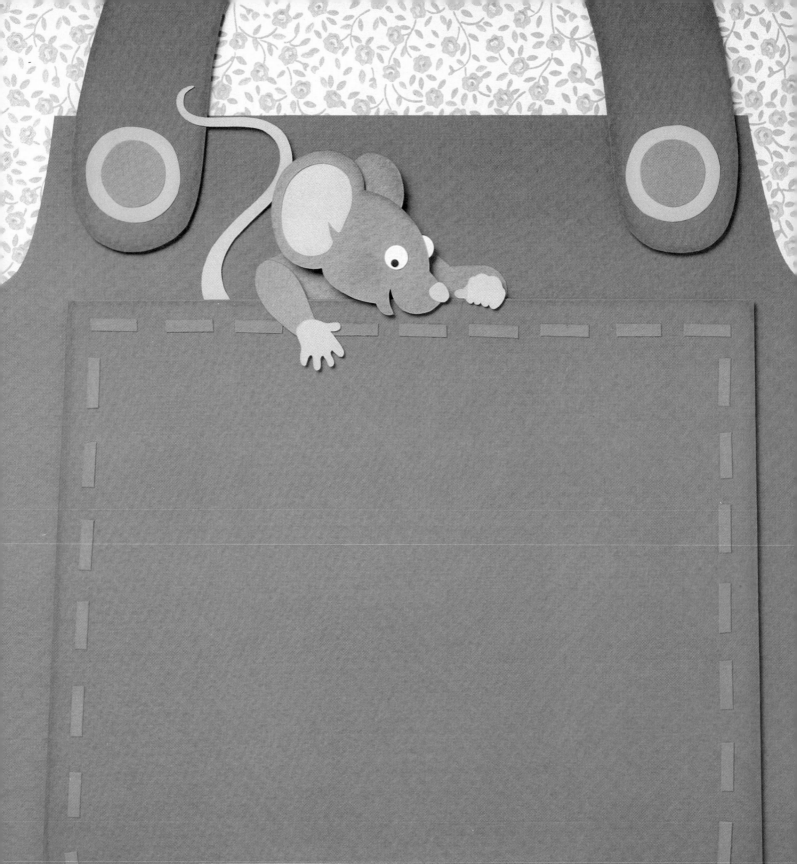

Po Lan has a pocket.
It's a very special kind.
It can fit most anything
that she seems to find.

In come 10 small pebbles
and 10 beads that she sees.
Add them all together.
How many will there be?

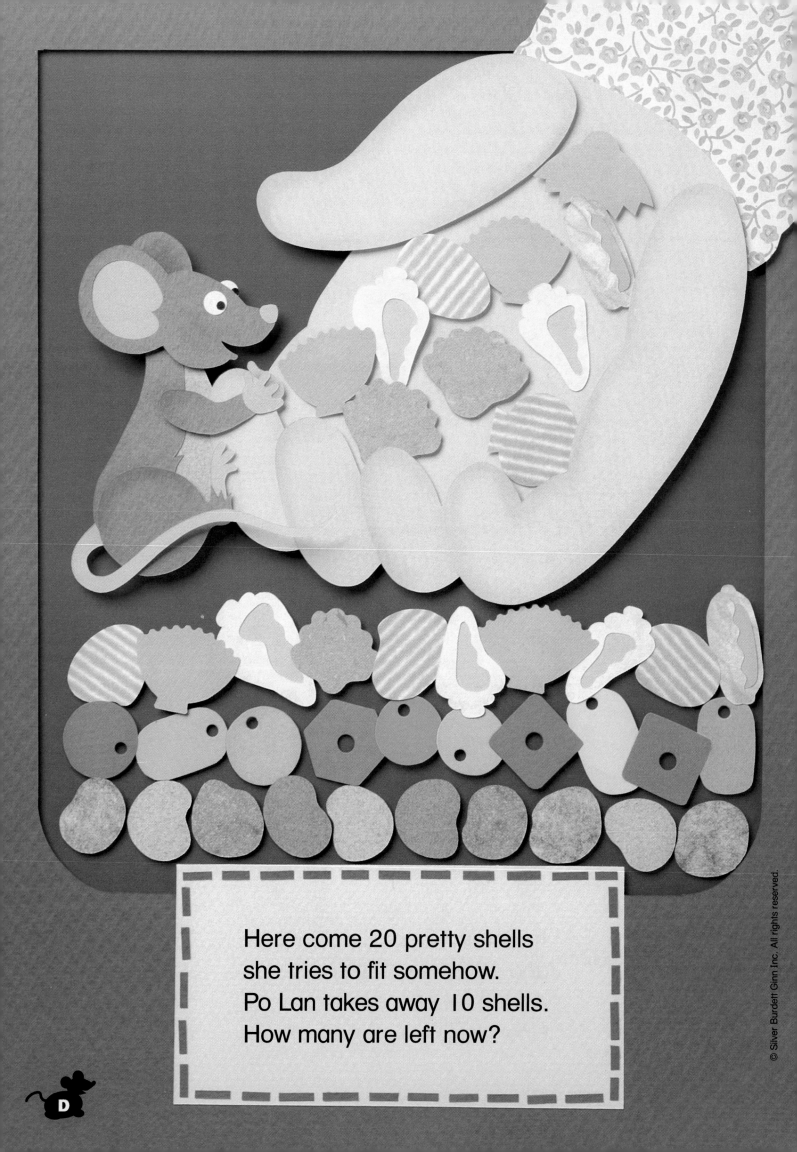

Here come 20 pretty shells
she tries to fit somehow.
Po Lan takes away 10 shells.
How many are left now?

Here come 10 brown acorns.
She drops them and they fall.
She drops 10 seeds on top of them.
How many things are there in all?

Here come 2 new jacks.
And 3 leaves from a tree.
But the best thing Po Lan finds
is something just for me!

Draw some things that you like.
Then count up what you see.
If you had 10 more of them,
how many would there be?

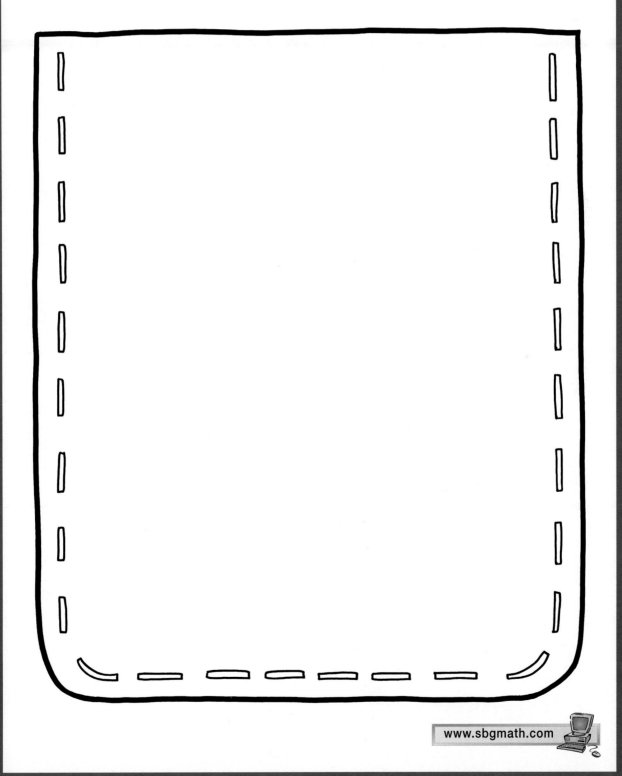

A Note to the Family

**Here are some learning ideas
you can share with your child.**

Enjoy *Po Lan's Pocket* Together

• Read the story with your child. Ask your child to find the total number of items in Po Lan's pocket. Then talk about how to find how many there are if more are added or if some are taken away.

• Encourage your child to show you what he or she drew in the pocket on the last page of the story. Ask your child to make up addition and subtraction stories about things that might be found in their pockets.

At-Home Activity

• Show your child a group of common household items such as pasta, buttons, pennies, paper clips, or dry cereal. Add some to the group and ask your child to tell how many there are in all. Repeat the activity, removing some from the group and asking your child to find how many are left.

Read More About It!

To read more stories about addition and subtraction with your child, look for these books in your local library.

• *Hold Tight, Bear!* by Ron Maris (Harcourt Brace, 1993)

• *Sea Sums* by Joy N. Hulme (Hyperion Books for Children, 1996)

• *Yellow Ball* by Molly Bang (Puffin Books, 1993)

Visit Our Web Site!

www.sbgmath.com

H

Name_____ **Adding Tens**

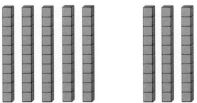

Adding tens is like adding ones.

__5__ ones + __3__ ones   __5__ tens + __3__ tens

__5__ + __3__ = __8__   __50__ + __30__ = __80__

Write the numbers. Add.

Use models and Workmat 5 if you like.

1.

____ tens + ____ ten

____ + ____ = ____

2.

____ tens + ____ tens

____ + ____ = ____

3.

____ tens + ____ tens

____ + ____ = ____

4.

____ tens + ____ tens

____ + ____ = ____

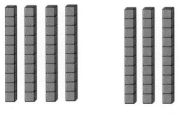 **Home Connection** Your child is learning to use basic facts to add tens. Ask him or her to add numbers that are multiples of ten.

Write the numbers. Add.
Use models if you like.

1.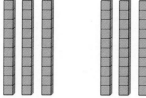

$\underline{3}$ tens + $\underline{3}$ tens

$\underline{30} + \underline{30} = \underline{60}$

2.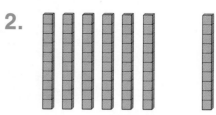

_____ tens + _____ ten

_____ + _____ = _____

3.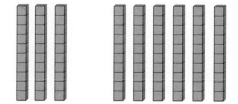

_____ tens + _____ tens

_____ + _____ = _____

4.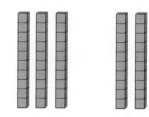

_____ tens + _____ tens

_____ + _____ = _____

 Critical Thinking Corner

Number Sense

5. Find each sum. Look for a pattern.

4 tens + 4 tens = _____ tens   40 + 40 = _____

5 tens + 5 tens = _____ tens   50 + 50 = _____

6 tens + 6 tens = _____ tens   60 + 60 = _____

You can count on to add.

Start with 32.
Count on 3 ones.
32, 33, 34, 35

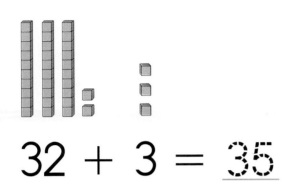

32 + 3 = 35

Use models and Workmat 5.
Count on to add.
Write how many in all.

	Number	Add	Number in all
1.	16	2	18
2.	42	3	
3.	30	3	
4.	55	1	
5.	22	2	
6.	61	3	
7.	27	2	
8.	36	3	

Home Connection Counting on 1, 2, or 3 can help
your child learn to add. Choose a two-digit number.
Then ask your child to add 1, 2, or 3 to that number.

three hundred forty-three **343**

Write each number.
Circle the greater number.
Count on to add.

1.

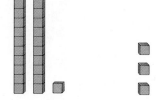

$\left(\widehat{21}\right) + 3 = 24$

2.

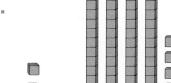

_____ + _____ = _____

3.

_____ + _____ = _____

4.

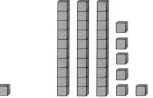

_____ + _____ = _____

 Problem Solving

Count on with pennies.
How much money will there be
in each pocket?

5.

24¢

_____ ¢

6.

41¢

_____ ¢

344   three hundred forty-four

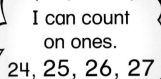

I can count on ones.
24, 25, 26, 27

I can count on tens.
35, 45, 55

$24 + 3 = 27$

$35 + 20 = 55$

Add. Count on ones or tens.

1.

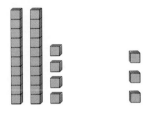

$32 + 3 = \rule{1cm}{0.5pt}$

2.

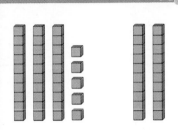

$26 + 30 = \rule{1cm}{0.5pt}$

3.

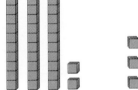

$56 + 10 = \rule{1cm}{0.5pt}$

4.

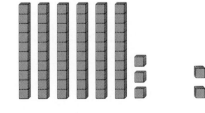

$63 + 2 = \rule{1cm}{0.5pt}$

Home Connection Your child is learning to add ones or tens to a two-digit number. Ask your child to tell you whether he or she counted on by ones or tens for each exercise on this page.

three hundred forty-five **345**

Add. Count on ones or tens.
Start with the greater number.
Use models if you like.

1.   36
   + 2
   ─────
    38   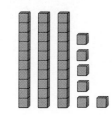 | 25
                                     +30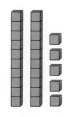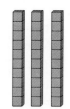

2.   43   51   38   10   69   30
   + 2   +20   +10   + 3   +10   +30

3.   35   66   26   32   11   53
   + 3   + 1   +20   + 3   + 2   + 2

4.   42   17   80   76   64   10
   +20   + 2   + 1   + 2   + 2   +78

Problem Solving

Solve.

5. Randy has 15 shells.
   He finds 2 more.
   How many shells does
   he have now?

   _____ shells

6. Nina has 20 shells.
   She finds 10 more.
   How many shells does
   she have now?

   _____ shells

How many seeds are there in all?

11

32

1 First add the ones.

Tens	Ones
3	2
+ 1	1
	3

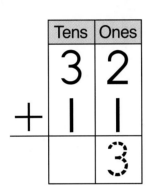

2 Then add the tens.

Tens	Ones
3	2
+ 1	1
4	3

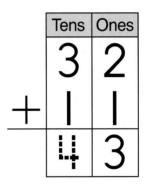

Use models and Workmat 5.
Find each sum.

1.

Tens	Ones
3	5
+ 4	2
7	7

Tens	Ones
5	1
+ 2	3

Tens	Ones
4	3
+	6

Tens	Ones
2	2
+ 6	0

2.

Tens	Ones
3	4
+ 2	2

Tens	Ones
4	9
+ 2	0

Tens	Ones
3	6
+	2

Tens	Ones
2	7
+ 7	2

Home Connection Your child is learning to add two-digit numbers. Ask your child to tell how she or he found each sum on this page.

three hundred forty-seven   **347**

Find each sum.

1.

Tens	Ones
2	4
+ 3	0
5	4

2.

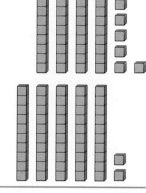

Tens	Ones
4	6
+ 5	2

3.

Tens	Ones
3	2
+	5

4.

Tens	Ones
1	4
+ 6	3

5.

Tens	Ones
2	4
+ 4	2

6.

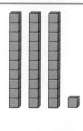

Tens	Ones
3	1
+	5

7.

Tens	Ones
3	0
+ 1	5

8.

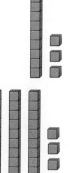

Tens	Ones
1	3
+ 3	4

Name_____

Add. Look for a pattern in each row.
Write the missing numbers.

1.

23	23	23	23	23
+ 0	+ 1	+ 2	+ 3	+ [4]
23	*24*			

2.

40	40	40	40	40
+10	+20	+30	+40	+ [ ]

3.

62	62	62	62	62
+ 5	+ 4	+ 3	+ 2	+ [ ]

4.

34	34	34	34	34
+10	+20	+30	+40	+ [ ]

5.

10	20	30	40	[ ]
+ 5	+ 5	+ 5	+ 5	+ 5

Home Connection Your child is learning to identify a pattern. Ask your child to tell you about each pattern on this page, and have him or her tell you what would come next.

three hundred forty-nine   **349**

Add. Continue the pattern.

1.

```
  14          14          14          14          □
+10         +20         +30         +40        + □
 24
```

2. Write your own addition pattern.

Make Your Own

```
  □          □          □          □          □
+ □        + □        + □        + □        + □
```

Add. Count on ones or tens.

1.
```
  25          48          72          69          55          33
+20         +10         + 3         +20         + 2         +30
```

Find each sum.

2.

Tens	Ones
3	6
+ 3	0

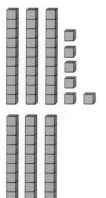

3.

Tens	Ones
2	5
+ 3	2

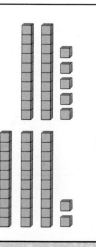

Subtracting tens is like subtracting ones.

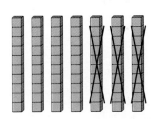

__7__ ones — __3__ ones   __7__ tens — __3__ tens

__7__ — __3__ = __4__   __70__ — __30__ = __40__

Write the numbers. Subtract.
Use models if you like.

1.

____ tens — ____ ten

____ — ____ = ____

2.

____ tens — ____ tens

____ — ____ = ____

3.

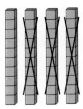

____ tens — ____ tens

____ — ____ = ____

4.

____ tens — ____ tens

____ — ____ = ____

Write the numbers. Subtract.
Use models if you like.

1.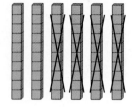

___6___ tens − ___4___ tens

$60 - 40 = 20$

2.

_____ tens − _____ tens

_____ − _____ = _____

3.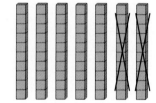

_____ tens − _____ tens

_____ − _____ = _____

4.

_____ tens − _____ ten

_____ − _____ = _____

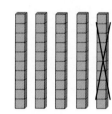

Critical Thinking Corner

Number Sense

5. Look for a pattern. Subtract.
Tell how you found each
difference.

$8 - 4 = $ _____

$80 - 40 = $ _____

$800 - 400 = $ _____

You can count back to subtract ones.

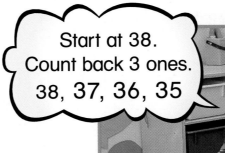

Start at 38.
Count back 3 ones.
38, 37, 36, 35

$$38 - 3 = 35$$

Use models and Workmat 5.
Count back to subtract.
Write how many are left.

	Number	Subtract	Difference
1.	48	2	46
2.	66	1	
3.	49	2	
4.	17	3	
5.	25	1	
6.	38	3	
7.	74	2	
8.	57	1	

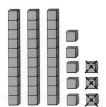

Home Connection Your child is learning to subtract 1, 2, or 3 from a two-digit number by counting back. Choose a number like 27 or 39. Ask your child to subtract 1, 2, or 3.

Count back to subtract.

1.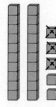

$$25 - 3 = \underline{22}$$

2.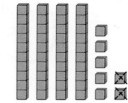

$$47 - 2 = \underline{}$$

3.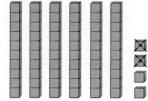

$$64 - 2 = \underline{}$$

4.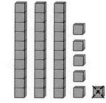

$$36 - 1 = \underline{}$$

5.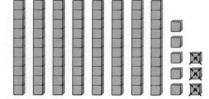

$$88 - 3 = \underline{}$$

6.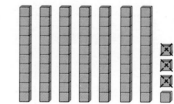

$$74 - 3 = \underline{}$$

Problem Solving

Find each rule.
Use models if you like.

7. Subtract __2__

59	57
58	56
57	55

8. Subtract ____

34	33
33	32
32	31

9. Subtract ____

77	74
76	73
75	72

You can count back ones or tens.

45, 44, 43

$$45 - 2 = 43$$

32, 22, 12

$$32 - 20 = 12$$

Count back ones or tens to subtract.

1.

$$58 - 3 = \underline{}$$

2.

$$83 - 10 = \underline{}$$

3.

$$44 - 30 = \underline{}$$

4.

$$39 - 3 = \underline{}$$

 **Home Connection** Your child is counting back tens or ones to subtract. Ask your child to tell you how he or she counted back in each exercise on this page.

Subtract. Count back ones or tens.
Use models if you like.

1. $\begin{array}{r} 47 \\ -\ 2 \\ \hline 45 \end{array}$ 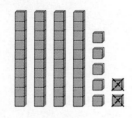 $\begin{array}{r} 88 \\ -20 \\ \hline \end{array}$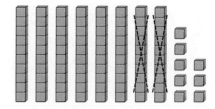

2. $\begin{array}{r} 43 \\ -\ 2 \\ \hline \end{array}$ $\begin{array}{r} 51 \\ -20 \\ \hline \end{array}$ $\begin{array}{r} 98 \\ -10 \\ \hline \end{array}$ $\begin{array}{r} 13 \\ -\ 3 \\ \hline \end{array}$ $\begin{array}{r} 69 \\ -30 \\ \hline \end{array}$ $\begin{array}{r} 20 \\ -20 \\ \hline \end{array}$

3. $\begin{array}{r} 36 \\ -\ 1 \\ \hline \end{array}$ $\begin{array}{r} 66 \\ -\ 3 \\ \hline \end{array}$ $\begin{array}{r} 76 \\ -30 \\ \hline \end{array}$ $\begin{array}{r} 55 \\ -\ 2 \\ \hline \end{array}$ $\begin{array}{r} 24 \\ -10 \\ \hline \end{array}$ $\begin{array}{r} 37 \\ -\ 3 \\ \hline \end{array}$

4. $\begin{array}{r} 28 \\ -\ 3 \\ \hline \end{array}$ $\begin{array}{r} 85 \\ -20 \\ \hline \end{array}$ $\begin{array}{r} 45 \\ -\ 1 \\ \hline \end{array}$ $\begin{array}{r} 16 \\ -10 \\ \hline \end{array}$ $\begin{array}{r} 36 \\ -20 \\ \hline \end{array}$ $\begin{array}{r} 29 \\ -\ 2 \\ \hline \end{array}$

 ## Critical Thinking Corner

Mental Math

 Using Algebra

Do you subtract 2 or 20?

Write the correct number in each shape.

 Journal Idea

5. $62 - \triangle = 42$

6. $78 - \square = 76$

7. $45 - \bigcirc = 43$

8. $95 - \hexagon = 75$

Name _____ **Subtracting Two-Digit Numbers**

59 Rosie

24 Nathan

How many more shells does Rosie have?

1 First subtract the ones.

Tens	Ones
5	9
− 2	4
	5

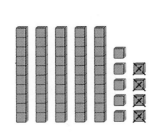

2 Then subtract the tens.

Tens	Ones
5	9
− 2	4
3	5

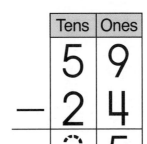
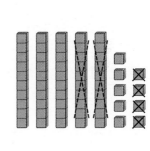

Use models and Workmat 5.
Find each difference.

1.

Tens	Ones
6	9
− 3	5
3	4

Tens	Ones
5	8
− 2	1

Tens	Ones
9	6
− 3	2

Tens	Ones
7	5
− 5	3

2.

Tens	Ones
3	4
− 2	0

Tens	Ones
4	9
− 2	4

Tens	Ones
6	7
−	4

Tens	Ones
3	9
− 1	2

Home Connection Ask your child to tell how he or she found each difference on this page.

Cross out to subtract.

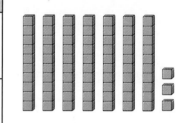

1.

Tens	Ones
6	5
− 2	3
4	2

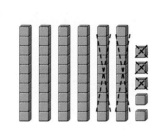

2.

Tens	Ones
7	3
− 4	0

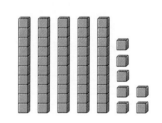

3.

Tens	Ones
5	9
−	4

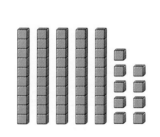

4.

Tens	Ones
5	7
− 1	2

5.

Tens	Ones
4	8
− 2	3

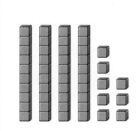

6.

Tens	Ones
3	7
−	2

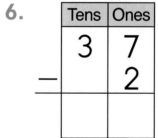

Problem Solving

Solve.

7. Ben has 27 feathers.
He finds 10 more.
Then he loses 3.
How many feathers does he have now? _____ feathers

360   three hundred sixty

Name_____

There are many ways to subtract.

You can count back ones.
47, 46, 45, 44

You can count back tens.
58, 48, 38

You can use models.

$$\begin{array}{r} 47 \\ -\ 3 \\ \hline 44 \end{array}$$

$$\begin{array}{r} 58 \\ -20 \\ \hline 38 \end{array}$$

$$\begin{array}{r} 36 \\ -12 \\ \hline 24 \end{array}$$

How do you like to subtract?
Can you think of another way?

Subtract.
Tell how you found each difference.
Use models when you like.

1.
$$\begin{array}{r} 89 \\ -71 \\ \hline \end{array}$$
$$\begin{array}{r} 73 \\ -50 \\ \hline \end{array}$$
$$\begin{array}{r} 66 \\ -\ 3 \\ \hline \end{array}$$
$$\begin{array}{r} 38 \\ -12 \\ \hline \end{array}$$
$$\begin{array}{r} 67 \\ -23 \\ \hline \end{array}$$
$$\begin{array}{r} 56 \\ -\ 2 \\ \hline \end{array}$$

2.
$$\begin{array}{r} 77 \\ -31 \\ \hline \end{array}$$
$$\begin{array}{r} 28 \\ -\ 7 \\ \hline \end{array}$$
$$\begin{array}{r} 91 \\ -40 \\ \hline \end{array}$$
$$\begin{array}{r} 58 \\ -\ 1 \\ \hline \end{array}$$
$$\begin{array}{r} 38 \\ -24 \\ \hline \end{array}$$
$$\begin{array}{r} 64 \\ -30 \\ \hline \end{array}$$

3.
$$\begin{array}{r} 43 \\ -10 \\ \hline \end{array}$$
$$\begin{array}{r} 65 \\ -\ 2 \\ \hline \end{array}$$
$$\begin{array}{r} 76 \\ -51 \\ \hline \end{array}$$
$$\begin{array}{r} 64 \\ -42 \\ \hline \end{array}$$
$$\begin{array}{r} 75 \\ -34 \\ \hline \end{array}$$
$$\begin{array}{r} 29 \\ -\ 2 \\ \hline \end{array}$$

Home Connection Ask your child to tell you how he or she found each difference on this page. Discuss when to use each strategy.

three hundred sixty-one   **361**

Add or subtract.
Tell how you found
each sum or difference.

1.
90	56	71	30	66	43
−30	−32	−11	−30	−33	−31
60					

2.
67	34	52	38	64	89
− 6	−22	−41	−10	−12	−66

3.
67	41	28	53	74	21
+ 2	+30	+10	+ 3	+ 2	+30

4.   60 − 20 = ___   75 − 2 = ___

5.   20 + 40 = ___   50 + 3 = ___

What Do You Think?

I think sometimes one way to
subtract is better than another.
What do you think?

Journal Idea

Use the picture.
Add or subtract to solve.

1. Jesse has 56¢.
   He buys a bag of marbles.
   How much money does he have now?

$$
\begin{array}{r}
56¢ \\
-\ 35¢ \\
\hline
21¢
\end{array}
$$

2. Alice buys a trading card.
   Then she buys a book.
   How much money did she spend?

   _____ ¢
   _____ ¢
   _____ ¢

3. Paco buys a box of shells.
   He also buys a car.
   How much money did he spend?

   _____ ¢
   _____ ¢
   _____ ¢

4. Beth has 98¢.
   She buys an airplane.
   How much money does she have now?

   _____ ¢
   _____ ¢
   _____ ¢

Home Connection Your child is using money to practice adding and subtracting. Put price tags with amounts less than 50 cents on several toys and "go shopping" together.

Use the picture. Add or subtract to solve.

1. Luis has 69¢.
   He buys a pencil.
   How much money does he have now?

   _____ ¢
   _____ ¢
   _____ ¢

2. Molly buys a notebook.
   She also buys a ruler.
   How much does she spend?

   _____ ¢
   _____ ¢
   _____ ¢

3. Tal has 77¢.
   He buys a pad.
   How much money does he have now?

   _____ ¢
   _____ ¢
   _____ ¢

4. Choose 2 things to buy. Then solve.

   Make Your Own

   I buy a _____.

   Then I buy a _____.

   How much do I spend?

   _____ ¢
   _____ ¢
   _____ ¢

Name_____

Subtract. Count back ones or tens.

1. $\begin{array}{r} 37 \\ -\ 2 \\ \hline \end{array}$ $\begin{array}{r} 58 \\ -10 \\ \hline \end{array}$ $\begin{array}{r} 74 \\ -\ 1 \\ \hline \end{array}$ $\begin{array}{r} 59 \\ -20 \\ \hline \end{array}$ $\begin{array}{r} 45 \\ -\ 3 \\ \hline \end{array}$ $\begin{array}{r} 63 \\ -30 \\ \hline \end{array}$

2. $\begin{array}{r} 75 \\ -30 \\ \hline \end{array}$ $\begin{array}{r} 18 \\ -\ 2 \\ \hline \end{array}$ $\begin{array}{r} 32 \\ -10 \\ \hline \end{array}$ $\begin{array}{r} 66 \\ -20 \\ \hline \end{array}$ $\begin{array}{r} 36 \\ -\ 1 \\ \hline \end{array}$ $\begin{array}{r} 39 \\ -\ 3 \\ \hline \end{array}$

Cross out to subtract.

3.

Tens	Ones
6	4
− 2	1

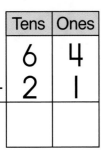

4.

Tens	Ones
4	7
− 2	0

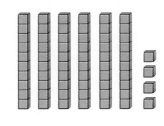

Use the pictures to solve.

5. Sal buys 2 shells.
   How much does he spend?

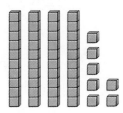

shells
12¢ each

_____ ¢
_____ ¢
_____ ¢

6. Lynne has 66¢.
   She buys a rock.
   How much does she
   have now?

rocks
23¢ each

_____ ¢
_____ ¢
_____ ¢

Name_____

Add or subtract.

Color each sum or difference.   greater than 50 (blue)

less than 50 (red)

equal to 50 (yellow) .

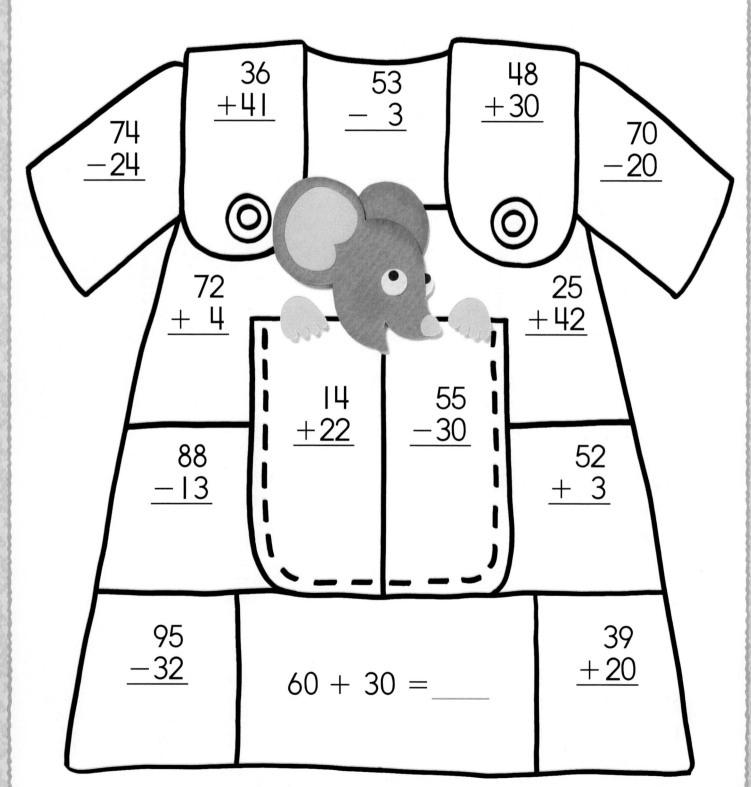

$$74 - 24$$

$$36 + 41$$

$$53 - 3$$

$$48 + 30$$

$$70 - 20$$

$$72 + 4$$

$$25 + 42$$

$$14 + 22$$

$$55 - 30$$

$$88 - 13$$

$$52 + 3$$

$$95 - 32$$

$$60 + 30 = \underline{\hspace{1cm}}$$

$$39 + 20$$

Add or subtract.

Count on or count back.

1.
$$\begin{array}{r} 30 \\ +20 \\ \hline \end{array}$$
$$\begin{array}{r} 51 \\ +20 \\ \hline \end{array}$$
$$\begin{array}{r} 77 \\ +10 \\ \hline \end{array}$$
$$\begin{array}{r} 96 \\ +1 \\ \hline \end{array}$$
$$\begin{array}{r} 66 \\ +3 \\ \hline \end{array}$$
$$\begin{array}{r} 23 \\ +30 \\ \hline \end{array}$$

2.
$$\begin{array}{r} 50 \\ -20 \\ \hline \end{array}$$
$$\begin{array}{r} 37 \\ -1 \\ \hline \end{array}$$
$$\begin{array}{r} 74 \\ -30 \\ \hline \end{array}$$
$$\begin{array}{r} 56 \\ -3 \\ \hline \end{array}$$
$$\begin{array}{r} 36 \\ -10 \\ \hline \end{array}$$
$$\begin{array}{r} 59 \\ -2 \\ \hline \end{array}$$

Find each sum or difference.

3.

Tens	Ones
2	4
+ 1	5

4.

Tens	Ones
5	8
− 3	3

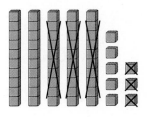

Add. Continue the pattern.

5.
$$\begin{array}{r} 21 \\ +10 \\ \hline \end{array}$$
$$\begin{array}{r} 21 \\ +20 \\ \hline \end{array}$$
$$\begin{array}{r} 21 \\ +30 \\ \hline \end{array}$$
$$\begin{array}{r} 21 \\ +40 \\ \hline \end{array}$$
$$+ \boxed{}$$

$$\boxed{}$$

Solve.

6. Liz has 78¢.

   She buys a game for 51¢.

   How much money does she have now?

¢
___¢
¢

Name_____ **Performance Assessment**

What You Need

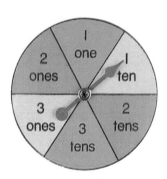

spinner

---

① Spin the spinner. Record.
   Add or subtract.

② Write the number sentence. Solve.

		Add or Subtract	**Number Sentence**
1.	46 +	1 ten	46 ⊕ 10 = 56
2.	68 −		___ ◯ ___ = ___
3.	34 +		___ ◯ ___ = ___
4.	57 −		___ ◯ ___ = ___
5.	45 +		___ ◯ ___ = ___
6.	86 −		___ ◯ ___ = ___

Circle the answer that makes sense.
Tell why.

1. Bill has 22 baseball cards.
   He has 30 football cards.
   About how many cards
   does he have in all?

   about 10 cards
   (about 50 cards)
   about 100 cards

___

2. Cora has 69 shells.
   She gives 20 to a friend.
   About how many shells
   does she have now?

   about 20 shells
   about 10 shells
   about 50 shells

___

3. Doug has 40 marbles.
   He wins 17 marbles.
   About how many marbles
   does he have now?

   about 60 marbles
   about 10 marbles
   about 40 marbles

___

4. Patty plants 11 seeds.
   Then she plants 32 seeds.
   About how many seeds
   does she plant?

   about 10 seeds
   about 40 seeds
   about 100 seeds

___

5. Chris has 49 rocks.
   He gives 18 rocks to Kelly.
   About how many rocks
   does he have now?

   about 30 rocks
   about 70 rocks
   about 100 rocks

Use a to add or subtract.

Write the keys you used.

Write the sum or difference.

Remember to press
ON/C each time.

1. 36 + 12

| 3 | 6 | + | 1 | 2 | = | 48 |

2. 56 − 24

3. 78 − 40

4. 39 + 50

5. 42 + 27

Name_____

Fill in the ◯ for the correct answer.

What are the missing numbers?

1. ____, 7, 8

◯   ◯   ◯   ◯
9   5   6   4

2. 42, ____, 44

◯   ◯   ◯   ◯
43   41   53   45

Add or subtract.

3.
$$\begin{array}{r} 5 \\ +\ 2 \\ \hline \end{array}$$
◯ 6
◯ 8
◯ 9
◯ 7

4.
$$\begin{array}{r} 11 \\ -\ 8 \\ \hline \end{array}$$
◯ 5
◯ 3
◯ 4
◯ 2

5.
$$\begin{array}{r} 8 \\ +\ 7 \\ \hline \end{array}$$
◯ 15
◯ 14
◯ 16
◯ 17

6.
$$\begin{array}{r} 7 \\ +\ 9 \\ \hline \end{array}$$
◯ 13
◯ 14
◯ 16
◯ 17

7.
$$\begin{array}{r} 8 \\ -\ 5 \\ \hline \end{array}$$
◯ 2
◯ 4
◯ 5
◯ 3

8.
$$\begin{array}{r} 13 \\ -\ 7 \\ \hline \end{array}$$
◯ 6
◯ 7
◯ 9
◯ 5

9.
$$\begin{array}{r} 8 \\ 5 \\ +\ 5 \\ \hline \end{array}$$
◯ 13
◯ 10
◯ 18
◯ 17

10.
$$\begin{array}{r} 26 \\ -\ 2 \\ \hline \end{array}$$
◯ 28
◯ 21
◯ 22
◯ 24

11.
$$\begin{array}{r} 30 \\ +40 \\ \hline \end{array}$$
◯ 70
◯ 60
◯ 80
◯ 10

12. How much money is there?

◯ 56¢
◯ 43¢
◯ 42¢
◯ 52¢

13. Which one can you buy?

40¢   27¢   31¢

◯   ◯   ◯

---

14. How many equal parts are there?

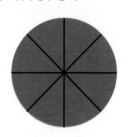

◯ 6
◯ 9
◯ 8
◯ 4

15. What fraction is orange?

◯   ◯   ◯

$\frac{1}{4}$ $\frac{1}{3}$ $\frac{1}{2}$

---

16. How many are there?

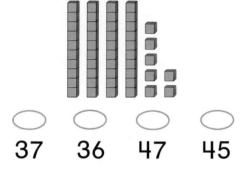

◯   ◯   ◯   ◯

37   36   47   45

17. What time is it?

◯ 2:30
◯ 6:00
◯ 2:00
◯ 3:30

---

18. Does this weigh **more** or **less** than 1 pound?

◯ less
◯ more

19. About how long is this?

◯ about 1 inch
◯ about 5 inches
◯ about 10 inches

---

20. Choose the correct number sentence.

14 deer eat.
6 run away.
How many are there now?

◯ $6 + 8 = 14$
◯ $14 - 8 = 6$
◯ $14 - 6 = 8$
◯ $10 - 6 = 4$

add

$$2 + 3 = 5$$

between

$$6, 7, 8$$

7 is between 6 and 8.

addition sentence

$$4 + 2 = 6$$

calendar

June						
S	M	T	W	T	F	S
			1	2	3	4
5	6	7	8	9	10	11
12	13	14	15	16	17	18
19	20	21	22	23	24	25
26	27	28	29	30		

after

$$7, 8$$

8 is after 7.

centimeter

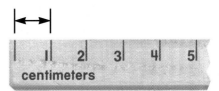

altogether

3   and   1

4 altogether

circle

before

$$5, 6$$

5 is before 6.

closed figure

Picture Glossary

cone 	**cup**
corner 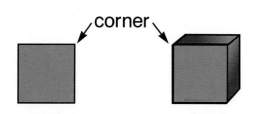	**curves** 
count back 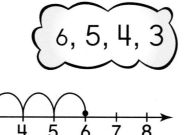	**cylinder** 
count on 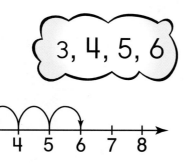	**decimeter** 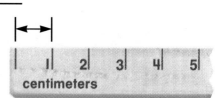 10 centimeters = 1 decimeter
cube 	**difference** $5 - 2 = 3$ $\begin{array}{r} 5 \\ -\,2 \\ \hline 3 \end{array}$ difference

dime

 or

10¢   10 cents

fact family

$4 + 2 = 6$ $6 - 2 = 4$

$2 + 4 = 6$ $6 - 4 = 2$

double

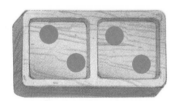

$2 + 2 = 4$

fewer

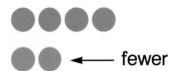 ← fewer

equal parts

2 equal parts

foot

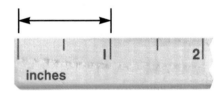
inches

12 inches $= 1$ foot

equals

↓

$3 + 2 = 5$

graph

Favorite Foods

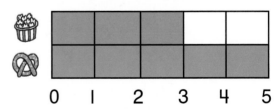

0   1   2   3   4   5

face

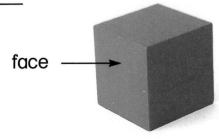

face →

greater

4 is greater than $2.$

Picture Glossary

heavier

heavier→

kilogram

5 peaches weigh about 1 kilogram.

hour

It takes about an hour.

left

5 minus 2

3 left

hour hand

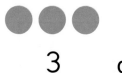

hour hand→

less

2 is less than 4.

in all

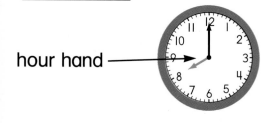

3   and   2

5 in all

lighter

←lighter

inch

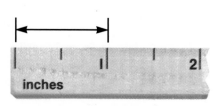

inches

liter

longer

 ←— longer

nickel

    or

5¢   5 cents

minus

$$9 - 7 = 2$$

↑
minus

number line

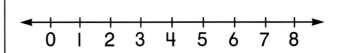

0 1 2 3 4 5 6 7 8

minute

I can count to 60.

It takes about a minute.

o'clock

   9:00

9 o'clock

minute hand

minute hand —→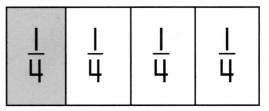

one fourth

| $\frac{1}{4}$ | $\frac{1}{4}$ | $\frac{1}{4}$ | $\frac{1}{4}$ |

more

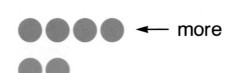 ←— more

one half

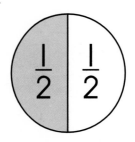

$\frac{1}{2}$ $\frac{1}{2}$

Picture Glossary

ones

4 ones

one third

open figure

pattern

penny

 or

1¢   1 cent

pint

plus

$$5 + 4 = 9$$

↑
plus

pound

3 apples weigh about 1 pound.

quart

quarter

 or

25¢   25 cents

rectangle

shorter

← shorter

rectangular prism

sides

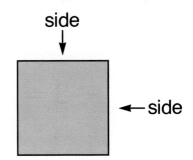

side

→ side

regroup

10 ones = 1 ten

skip count

2   4   6   8

related facts

4 + 3 = 7

7 − 3 = 4

sphere

same

same number

square

subtract

$$4 - 3 = 1$$

taller

taller →

subtraction sentence

$$7 - 3 = 4$$

tally

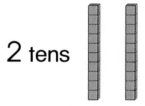

sum

$$4 + 4 = 8$$

$$\begin{array}{r} 4 \\ + 4 \\ \hline 8 \end{array}$$

sum

tens

2 tens

take away

3 take away 1

triangle

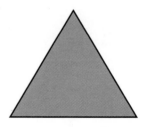

Credits